HUNTING A PSYCHOPATH

The
East Area Rapist /
Original Night Stalker Investigation

The Original Investigator Speaks Out

Richard Shelby

Published by BookLocker.com, Inc., Bradenton, Florida.

Printed in the United States of America on acid-free paper.

BookLocker.com, Inc.
2015

First Edition

A Note of Thanks

I especially want to thank my wife, Ann, and our sons, Brian and Tom, for the patience they've shown over the years that this investigation has been a presence in our lives. My wife deserves a special thanks and recognition for her strength of character in remaining home alone with two small children on those many, many nights I was called to duty.

A special note of appreciation and thank you to Valerie Wood is most definitely owed here. Without her assistance this book would never have been written. A published author herself, it was her unselfishly shared expertise that made this possible.

Also very necessary to this manuscript was the assistance of Margie Smith, retired 8th grade Language Arts teacher in Tulare, CA. Not only did she assist in the editing but she has been heavily involved in the investigation.

Many of my personal experiences with the investigation described in this book were shared with my partner Carol Daly. Thanks to her for our more recent conversations that helped many of those memories resurface. A big thanks to her husband, Ted, as well. Ted contributed some valuable details of which I had been unaware.

Two other people I would like to extend a special thanks to are Investigator Larry Pool and Investigator Larry Montgomery, both of whom have devoted many long hours investigating the Original Night Stalker homicides. Their expertise was always there when a need to discuss specifics of the investigation arose.

Special thanks to Sacramento Sheriff's homicide investigator Ken Clark, his two partners, and their supervisor, Sergeant Burns. Through their efforts alone, several persons of interest, from the original investigations, have now been eliminated by DNA.

Everyone interested in this investigation should give thanks to Russ Oase, a retired Federal Special Investigator, and KC, the expert in research. They have each expended thousands of their dollars and hours doing their part to bring this investigation to a successful conclusion.

Lastly, I would like to violate the norm by including a note of apology with these acknowledgements of appreciation. That apology goes to all those involved in this investigation and especially to the victims and their families. The apology is not for dredging up painful memories but for providing the "as yet" unidentified suspect another moment of public attention. Hopefully, this attention will be his undoing.

Table of Contents

Preface ix

What This Book Is About xi

Prologue xvii

Chapter 1: As It Began to Unfold 1

Chapter 2: The Old Era Fades 8

Chapter 3: Detective Division −1976 11

Chapter 4: A Life-Changing Event 15

Chapter 5: Researching by Gossip 25

Chapter 6: The Sexual Assault 28

Chapter 7: Score Two for Gossip 33

Chapter 8: The Dots are Connected 44

Chapter 9: The First One 45

Chapter 10: The Second One 57

Chapter 11: BOLO 62

Chapter 12: Rape Crisis Clinic and Our Prime Suspect 66

Chapter 13: The Psychic's Turn 69

Chapter 14: A Stroll Down the Ditch 72

Chapter 15: The Night Walker 82

Chapter 16: Nine and Counting 87

Chapter 17: The First Assault 90

Chapter 18: The Second Assault 95

Chapter 19: The Heat is on−Us 100

Chapter 20: Creation of a Task Force 106

Chapter 21: Search for Victim Similarities....................112

Chapter 22: Still Innocent...114

Chapter 23: Sacramento Police Join the Hunt.................117

Chapter 24: Determined Ignorance.............................121

Chapter 25: Early Bird Rapist vs. East Area Rapist..........124

Chapter 26: AD HOC TASK FORCE 138

Chapter 27: Helping the Suspect................................140

Chapter 28: Helping A Stalker...................................145

Chapter 29: Other Law Enforcement Agencies Help 147

Chapter 30: The Visalia Question...............................149

Chapter 31: Victim Draws First Blood 153

Chapter 32: Pursued Shoots Pursuer...........................165

Chapter 33: Revered Suspect....................................167

Chapter 34: Suspect's Stash Found.............................169

Chapter 35: East Area Rapist Ups the Ante...................188

Chapter 36: East Area Rapist or Not the East Area Rapist? 197

Chapter 37: Fingerprinting the Human Torso................209

Chapter 38: Second Stash Found 212

Chapter 39: EAR Gets Careless.................................228

Chapter 40: Wife of a Mafia Lord 238

Chapter 41: Two Bicyclists and One Car.....................246

Chapter 42: Bicyclist in Rancho Cordova....................248

Chapter 43: Exactly Who is Chasing Whom?................251

Chapter 44: East Area Rapist in the Crosshairs 259

Chapter 45: Color Me Gone..265

Chapter 46: Color the EAR Gone..267

Chapter 47: An Accomplice?...274

Chapter 48: Missed Opportunity..296

Chapter 49: An Official Analysis..300

Chapter 50: Rapist to Murderer..312

Chapter 51: The "New" Composite...317

Chapter 52: Dog Therapist..323

Chapter 53: Security Officer's Badge.....................................340

Chapter 54: Catch and Release..379

Chapter 55: The EAR Moves South..386

Chapter 56: Murdered - Dr. Robert Offerman & Dr. Debri
   Manning...393

Chapter 57: Murdered - Lyman and Charlene Smith..........................402

Chapter 58: Murdered - Keith & Patrice Harrington........................406

Chapter 59: Murdered - Manuela Witthuhn..................................409

Chapter 60: Murdered - Greg Sanchez and Cheryl Smith-
   Dominguez...411

Chapter 61: Murdered - Janelle Cruz......................................413

Chapter 62: The Visalia Ransacker Revisited..............................417

Chapter 63: How The EAR Chose His Victims................................426

Chapter 64: Days of the Week...427

Chapter 65: Medical..428

Chapter 66: Education..429

Chapter 67: Military...430

Chapter 68: Real Estate..431

Chapter 69: Security Guard..432

Conclusion – Clusters..433

Epilogue...435

Anecdotal...437

Suspicious Circumstances...439

Carlos...445

Composites...451

Appendix 1...457

Preface

On October 5, 1976, as an inspector with the Sacramento Sheriff's Department, I responded to a report of a home invasion that had just occurred. A young mother and her three-year-old son had been blindfolded, gagged, and their hands tied The young mother had been sexually assaulted. By the end of that day I had come to believe this was the work of a serial rapist. It was not long before this theory was confirmed. Ultimately, this suspect became known as the East Area Rapist. It was when he spread his brand of horror to Southern California that he became known as the Original Night Stalker. There are some who strongly believe he actually began his crime spree in 1974, in Visalia, California, where he was called the Visalia Ransacker. There is no solid evidence to corroborate this. In all, however, he is known to have assaulted at least fifty-three women and murdered twelve people.

Three books have been written about this "as yet" unsolved series of rapes and murders. The first one was written by Sergeant Crompton, formerly of the Contra Costa County Sheriff's Department. Using a mixture of fact and fiction, he wrote *Sudden Terror*. With some fiction used as a back drop, he laid out details of the sexual assaults and a great deal of the actual investigation. The second book was written by someone who apparently had read about this investigation, but was never actively involved, as Sergeant Crompton had been. The third book is the one you are reading at this moment. It adds details missing in Crompton's book and revisits old ones. A fourth book titled *Golden State Killer*, which focuses primarily on the ONS, is now being thoroughly researched and written by Michelle McNamara, an investigative journalist for *Los Angeles Magazine.*

The longer a mystery remains a mystery the more attention it attracts. It is no different with this investigation. In seeking information many have gravitated to forums such as internet blogs. Sometimes the information shared is incorrect which only leads to more misinformation and ultimately confusion. It is my hope of eliminating some of that misinformation that has convinced me to make this manuscript public.

Having decided to turn what had been originally intended as a short informative essay for a few informed individuals into a book, I needed a platform. To that end I determined to relate the investigation as I experienced it. If done right, the reader will be able to grasp how investigations were conducted at the time and under what conditions. They would get a fairly clear picture of just what was going on, at all levels of the investigation.

By relying on my own experiences, notes, reports, conversations with other investigators, and more recent investigative efforts of which I've been involved, I relate what I know of this investigation of the East Area Rapist/Original Night Stalker and the Visalia Ransacker. There is no fiction in this narrative, and all opinions are mine and mine alone. They in no way reflect those of any agency, group, or person.

What This Book Is About

This is a true crime story which took place in California, from 1974 through 1986. There are those who will tell you it is about one, two, or even three separate crime stories. The crimes committed were sexual assaults and murders – most taking place inside the victims' homes. No one has yet been held accountable.

The sole purpose of this book is to help identify those responsible and not to entertain. Anyone expecting to find a book of crafted suspense and drama will be disappointed.

This book chronicles the investigation of the East Area Rapist in Central California, and the Original Night Stalker in Southern California, with references to the Ransacker of Visalia, California. Relying on memory, notes, police reports, sundry documents, and conversations with other investigators, it is as factual as I could make it. I try to make it clear when the information came from sources other than my own. It is, in essence, a report.

One crime story, or perhaps the first chapter of all three, may have begun in 1974, in Visalia. There a prowler, known locally as the Visalia Ransacker, terrorized the community for two years by breaking into homes and peeking in windows. The crime wave graduated from nuisance crimes to an aborted kidnapping and the murder of the kidnap victim's father. The crime series allegedly culminated in December, 1975, with the shooting of a police officer who confronted the suspect when he caught him prowling.

The second chapter (or what some believe to be the first chapter of the second crime story) began in June, 1976, in Sacramento County.

That suspect, like the VR, prowled extensively—except he was thought to be reconnoitering as much as peeping into windows. Eventually this suspect expanded his crimes to sexual assaults against women in their homes. Known as the East Area Rapist or EAR, he changed his method of operation slightly in the spring of 1977. Now he would strike when both a man and a woman were present. Late in that same year, he began to take his reign of terror to jurisdictions outside of Sacramento. In all, there were fifty-two known sexual assaults and two homicides attributed to the East Area Rapist when the series stopped in 1979.

But he only stopped in Central California. That was in July, 1979, after very nearly being caught in the town of Danville. In October of that same year the suspect re-surfaced in the small town of Goleta, California.

Sticking to his rigid modus operandi (method of operation), the East Area Rapist broke into a home in Goleta where he attempted an assault. This couple managed to escape without any physical injury. Twice losing control of his intended victims, and twice being very nearly caught, he would no longer take any chances. From that moment forward he murdered his victims by shooting or bludgeoning.

The EAR had moved his activities to Santa Barbara, Orange, and Ventura Counties in Southern California. Law Enforcement in Southern California dubbed him the Original Night Stalker, or the ONS. The ONS seemingly ended his spree of senseless murders in 1981, but returned in 1984 to kill one more time.

Only after DNA proved the EAR and ONS were the same person did these multiple investigations coalesce into one. The investigation of the Visalia Ransacker is not being viewed as connected to the EAR/ONS crimes by most law enforcement. It is, however, unavoidable not to brush up against that investigation in this review as there are far too many similarities to ignore.

This book begins with a description of the Sacramento Sheriff's Department as I knew it in the 1960's. A description of departmental policies and available equipment in that era sets the stage for just how the East Area Rapist was first investigated by Sacramento Law Enforcement. To keep it authentic, I am as candid as possible. Politically correct curtains are pulled off some matters normally left covered, a fact few appreciate.

Where I begin is not with the first sexual assault. It is with my assignment to the fifth assault in a series of which we were then unaware. Striving for the order in which I learned of these crimes, I take the reader with me as I work backward searching for similar assaults. Only then do I move forward, briefly examining each assault in the sequence in which it occurred.

Describing fifty-three assaults, with an almost identical method of operation, could drive the reader to distraction. It would not be unthinkable to just lump the assaults together, compressing the material. That said, it is important to remember that each of these assaults violated a real person's privacy, sense of safety, even their sense of self, and therefore should not be treated casually.

Common factors between the victims are explored for possible avenues of investigation. Some persons of interest, and the investigations of them, are described. Events resulting from one of these recent investigations will definitely pique the interest of the serious reader. Exactly which investigation may have brought about those events, we are not sure of – yet.

Throughout this narrative every reasonable effort has been made to protect the identities of the rape victims, their families, and others coincidentally involved, no matter how slightly. Names have been changed and care taken to avoid identifying information. The identities of the homicide victims is another matter as their names and family histories were long ago made public by the media.

Included in this bubble-wrap principle are those who were, and may be considered, persons of interest. I did not change the names of the police officers involved. They were all very real people who dedicated long, hard hours trying to bring a successful conclusion to this series of horrors. Although not ultimately successful, they kept the suspect on the run and deserve to be proud of their contributions.

All opinions are mine and mine alone. They are certainly not representative of any law enforcement agency or organization of any type.

I would end this preamble with a word of caution. Anyone wanting to conduct their own investigation should absolutely

keep in mind the rights and privacy of others. Any probing or researching should be limited to the internet or public records. Should any viable appearing results be discovered, contact@truecrimediary.com is an avenue that will ensure the information goes straight to a law enforcement investigator.

> "Not at all surprising he is a loner. If from a larger family then he will most likely be the youngest member. In his daily life, he is almost compulsively attentive to the minutest details and very methodical in his approach to anything he does."

> "There he also has a strong leaning towards the ritualistic. Emotionally he will be immature and insecure. No relationship with a woman is comfortable unless it is a non-sexual one. In fact, always nervous and fidgety, he has no normal relationship. Most likely he has had some homosexual relationships."

> "Adding to the element of risk just ups the ante for him which would include the element of capture."

> "In his ordinary daily life those who come into contact with him would see him as meek and mild. For sexual release he will masturbate a lot and frequent massage parlors and porn shops."

This psychiatrist's description of a criminal profile was taken from a Visalia police report of their investigation into a local prowler-turned-murderer, during the years 1974 - 1975. It is about a sociopath, but since a sociopath inclined towards senseless violence is more likely to be considered a psychopath, I have included it. Psychopath is, as many of us think, an apt description for a rapist/murderer known as the East Area Rapist/Original Night Stalker. Let the professionals dicker over the finer points.

Prologue

In the spring of 2000, twenty years after this investigation had been delegated to the cold case files, I answered the phone to be greeted by a voice from my working past. "Hi, Dick. Do you want to work the EAR investigation again?"

The voice on the other end of the phone belonged to Undersheriff John McGinness of the Sacramento Sheriff's Department, from which I had retired. We had not spoken with each other since before my retirement in March, 1993.

John went on to explain that a comparison of DNA samples taken from the East Area Rapist (EAR) and the Original Night Stalker (ONS) confirmed they were from one and the same donor. This was news to me and several other investigators, only in that it was now a scientifically proven fact. We had believed all along the EAR and the ONS were one and the same person.

At that particular moment in time, the Sacramento County Sheriff's Department was in the process of assigning another (albeit small) group of investigators to be tasked with determining how far they could go with this new information. Would I like to join them? I was willing, but no longer being an on-call reserve officer, the option to participate was simply not there.

A few more years passed. Then, late in 2009, I received another phone call. This time it was from Russ Oase, a retired West Coast District Chief of Special Investigations for the federal government. Russ was living in the Sacramento area when the East Area Rapist had been active. Although Russ's duties took him literally to every state in the Union, he remained keenly aware of that crime wave. Now retired, his attention turned to this investigation. In a word, this investigation was to be his retirement. It was certainly not in my retirement plans.

As Russ became wrapped up in the investigation, he made the acquaintance of KC. KC is from out of state, and as it turned out, an outstanding researcher of public records. They formed a partnership and have both spent thousands of their own dollars and hours pursuing this investigation.

Since it was apparent I was never to be rid of this investigation, I agreed to talk with them both. Born of those conversations was a request that I write down what I might recall of the investigation. It was that request which eventually led to the task of recording what has now morphed into book form. In the meantime, while jotting this stuff down, I have once again found myself involved.

Chapter 1:
As It Began to Unfold

Not many of us have ever seen a free-flowing electron, but those with normal hearing have heard them. All cops rely on them. With no place to call home, the electrons are what we hear when a radio station is improperly tuned, or someone has keyed a police microphone preparatory to speaking. That sound is what you may know as static. That brief sputter of freedom-seeking electrons is how a police officer knows information is forthcoming. It is that expectation of the radio sputter which keeps them mentally on their toes. They do this without even realizing they are eternally on the alert for that static; it is the precursor to their knowing. Officers depend on their radios for necessary information as well as their own security.

It was well into a swing shift, sometime in late spring, 1974, when those escaping electrons grated against my nerves, grabbing my attention. I was the patrol sergeant assigned to Rancho Cordova at the time. A suburb east of Sacramento, it did not officially exist until 1955, when it became populated enough to justify the establishment of a post office.

Rancho Cordova began as a Mexican land grant of 5,000 acres which was used for farming. Then the gold dredges came through leaving behind huge piles of river rock. Later, the untouched parts became a vineyard. Today, the original streets bear evidence of their past by the names they carry as they twist and turn like grapevines through town; names like Gold Run, Coloma, and Zinfandel.

With the American River and its naturally occurring greenbelt areas next door, along with those twisting streets, Rancho Cordova was a prowler's paradise.

The shift had been unusually quiet on this one particular night. Hunkered down in my squad car, green dash lights dimmed way down, I had been driving around posing as a beat officer, waiting for something to happen. In a word, I was bored.

The dimmed dash lights were not by accident either, but rather a habit formed just two or three years earlier. There had been a group from the bay area of California who named themselves Zebras. The so-called Zebras were a group of African-Americans (I am Welsh-American) who declared war on the white man, and in particular the white cop. Initiation rites for new members required the killing of a white man, preferably a cop, although an Asian would do just as well. There was even a movie starring Ernest Borgnine focusing on what was then becoming a favorite American past-time–sniping at cops in a squad car. The Sacramento Police Department lost Dick Bennett in this fashion.

For a while, most patrol officers kept their dash lights dimmed to avoid making themselves better targets. By 1974, the so-called Zebras had crawled back into whatever swamp they had slithered out of, but the habit of caution remained for some. I discovered the dimmer dash lights made it much easier to pick up on details outside the car. It is for that very reason the habit remains with me today.

The call heralded by those escaping electrons, on this one night, was a typical request for assistance. A citizen wanted to report suspicious circumstances at his neighbor's house. He was hoping someone would investigate. Although not at the top of the list, this is the sort of call for which most patrol officers live. To paraphrase author Joseph Wambaugh, "It is the unexpected that keeps cops being cops. If cops already knew the outcome of every call they responded to, they might as well be bakers or bankers." So being both a cop – and bored – I exercised my supervisory powers and notified radio dispatch that I would also be attending the evening's event.

The complainants lived in the house at the corner of Dolcetto and Dawes. It was their neighbor's house on Dolcetto that had their attention. I was only seconds behind the other two squad cars as we all arrived. Before I even stopped my squad car, I could see two people standing in an open side door to the house. Lighted from behind by the interior lights, they were nothing more than two unidentifiable silhouettes, motioning for us to come to them.

The officer, who was actually assigned to this call, spoke to them just long enough to learn why we had been called. They had heard suspicious noises coming from the backyard of their neighbor's house, a house where no one was supposed to be home. The reporting officer and I entered the rather long and empty backyard, while the third officer took a position near the front corner of the neighbor's house. Finding nothing amiss, we all three returned to the side door for the rest of the story.

Apparently, their neighbors were out of town for a few days and had asked our complainants to keep an eye on their property. Hearing noises from next door, the complainants called the Sheriff's Department. The three of us again checked the exterior of the house and the yards for any signs of trespass. Finding none, we said our goodbyes and departed, expecting to return to the boredom of routine.

I doubt if I was more than three blocks away when that brief static enlivened my life once more. The complainants had just called to say the prowler was still there. So back I went. It was no more than a couple of minutes before I was on the scene again. This time, as I pulled up, I spotted the neighbor's garage door rolled up as tight as a rubber band. It had been closed when we left.

Before checking the interior of the house, I made contact with one of the complainants. He told me that right after we drove off, he heard a couple of thumps and looked out to see a white male, about 5 ft. 9 inches tall, with blond hair,16 - 18 years old, and dressed in military fatigues, jump off the roof of his house. Landing upright on both feet, the man ran straight for the back fence, which he vaulted with ease. I notified dispatch to cancel the other officers as the suspect was GOA, or gone on arrival.

Armed with this new information, I walked to the back fence and peered over the side. Immediately behind the fence was a large shallow cement-lined canal. Void of water, travel in either direction would offer literally dozens upon dozens of places for a quick exit. On the opposite side of that ditch was a small area with a lot of tall trees. Bordering that area was Dawes Street. To follow Dawes would quickly lead to the Rancho Cordova High School. Behind the school were large orchards and a nature area that was pretty much then as it was a century ago. Miwok Indians from that era would have felt right at home. For all I knew, there were still a few of them in there.

There was no sense in giving foot chase, so I returned to the open garage door. The first thing I spotted was a piece of firewood, about eighteen inches in length, lying in the open doorway. It was covered in blood– like a lot of thick blood.

I determined not to notify the dispatcher or call for backup. As the sergeant on duty, I would have climbed all over any officer who failed to notify the dispatcher or call for backup. But I knew that if I did, the dispatcher would get excited and clear the air for emergency traffic only. Once that was done, bunches of squad cars would have materialized as if from thin air. You see, cops have every bit the tendency to rubberneck, as does any passing motorist, looking for blood at the scene of a car accident. So I entered the house alone…with a little trepidation, perhaps, but with a regular heartbeat nonetheless.

At the back of the garage were a couple of small steps that took me into the unlighted house. Over the course of my career, I have entered many houses where no one was home. There is always a feeling of empty that weighs heavily in the air. I think this feeling of empty is also recognized by burglars even from outside the house. I have watched a burglar intent on choosing a home to break into, suddenly stop his car, then, without hesitation, walk right up and break in. Somehow they seem to "know" when a house is empty.

But in this instance there was more than a feeling of emptiness.

There is a silence that becomes the size of an NFL lineman when death—any death—is present. That night I felt that NFL silence. Once experienced, you never forget it. Enough so that I almost stopped to request back up.

From somewhere there was enough ambient light to see by, so for safety reasons I kept my flashlight mostly off, using it only sparingly and when absolutely necessary. My thought was to make as little noise as possible while keeping my eyes adjusted to the semi-darkness. If there was anything in a dark corner, I was more likely to spot it with my flashlight off, but my handgun was in my hand, ready for immediate use.

As quietly as I could, I went from room to room searching for what I knew I would find; the source of blood on that piece of firewood. Every room was immaculate. Had anything been out of place, it would have shouted for attention. But the only thing shouting was that unseen NFL lineman.

The master bedroom was the last one I entered. It, as well as the rest of the house, was the epitome of perfect housekeeping; nothing was out of place. That is, right up until I peered at the floor between a night stand and the headboard. There, with its head partially under the bed, lay the family dog. Its intestines were spilling out of its side and onto the floor. It lay right where it had sought escape from evil. That pup had been struck so hard it was disemboweled.

Apparently, I had located the source of blood on that piece of firewood.

I had no inkling, at the time, that I may have just been introduced to the work of a psychopathic personality who would one day be known as the East Area Rapist. Nor did I have any hint that the killer of the dog was going to be a big part of my future. He and I would cross paths again and again.

Chapter 2:
The Old Era Fades

The East Area Rapist started at a time when the Sacramento Sheriff's Department was in the midst of a departmental evolution. Both the structure and department mentality were undergoing a change that had begun sometime in the late 1950s. Organizational structure and attitude of the department, in the early 1960s, was reminiscent of a sheriff's department from the 1920's–1930s; not a mid-20th century law enforcement agency.

Organized gambling and prostitution had once been the order of the day in the Sacramento Delta. An area where deputies were not allowed to venture unless accompanied by the Sheriff, now it had deputies routinely assigned to patrol. By the early 1960s, that era had become a part of the Sacramento Sheriff Department's past.

In 1970 a new sheriff took office and led the Sacramento Sheriff's Department the remainder of the way into the 20th century. He had a hard task ahead of him. Existing equipment consisted of little more than squad cars with red lights and sirens. One squad car boasted of a small gooseneck lamp and a clipboard affixed to the dash. That was the primo car sought after when going on duty. If a patrol officer wanted a spotlight, he had to provide his own. The department armory still boasted of two Thompson submachine guns–no doubt left over from the 1920's.

Using a textbook by O.W. Wilson as a model, the department was quickly given a new internal structure. Immediate cancellation of rotating shifts, plus the introduction of new equipment were giant leaps forward. Equipment like computers, cell phones, even fax machines were still close to the realm of science fiction for many. Today, technology that was the stuff of science fiction then are fact or becoming fact. By comparison we were still perfecting the wheel!

Such massive changes take time, and so it was, in 1976, that some departmental practices remained more or less unchanged; and that is when the East Area Rapist began his depredations.

What was in short supply, if not totally lacking among many law enforcement agencies, were schools in specialty investigations. Training to investigate major crimes, like homicides or sexual assaults, was primarily by OJT, or on-the-job training. POST, a department created by the State of California for the purpose of turning cops into professionals, began its existence sometime in the early-to-mid 1960s.

Prior to 1970, when a major crime such as a rape or armed robbery was reported, the supervisor looked for someone with hands-on experience to assign to the investigation. If the experienced were not available, then he looked for someone holding the short straw—in other words, the nearest investigator. In 1976 this practice still, more or less, existed when it came to the crime of sexual assaults.

Inadequate organization was not the only problem haunting many law enforcement agencies at the time. Poor internal communication was another. What I am alluding to is a lack of division-wide communication, between the detectives, about major crime investigations. Without official guidelines to navigate by, the investigators lived with the departmental habits that had evolved over the decades. There was no provision for investigators to discuss their investigation. People did what they had always done. They gossiped.

That old adage, "Every cloud has a silver lining," was applicable here. The establishment of a sexual assaults investigative bureau, in the Sacramento Sheriff's Department, came about largely as a result of the investigation of the East Area Rapist.

There were two such bureaus created. One was to handle sexual assaults against adults and the other against children. Along with this specialization came improved communications between all the investigative units.

So on October 5, 1976, finding myself once again in the detective division, after my reassignment from patrol the previous February, I was fair game for whatever came up.

Chapter 3:
Detective Division −1976

My newly assigned office in the detective division, about the size of a broom closet or perhaps a hobbit's hole, was midway down the center of the detective division. With walls my only other choice of view, I tended to occasionally watch the detective world as it passed by my door. Actually, there was one other view. Jutting out of the wall, across and down from my office, was a conundrum of sorts.

The first time I glanced in that direction I saw a typewriter, keys flying under the direction of disembodied fingers with a hint of shapely limbs beneath the table supporting that typewriter. It looked like a typewriter imbued with partial leg and finger attachments. It was late in February before I met the owner of those attachments.

Sitting quietly in my cubbyhole office, I spotted an attractive young woman detective headed straight for my office−therefore me. The scary part was she had her arms wrapped around a very large stack of files. What crossed my mind was that a wounded bear would shy away from someone who had the look she had on her face!

Armed with an air of deadly purpose, she came marching in with what was a large number of sexual assault reports. Without fanfare, she dumped them onto my desk. By way of saying both hello and goodbye, while announcing her imminent departure, she said, "The Captain said give these to you. Have fun." At that time I only knew Carol Daly from a distance. We had never even said hello to each other. Come to think of it, we still haven't.

That stack of reports was my introduction to the more notable of the sexual assaults I would investigate in the beginning months of 1976. The reports were records of forty-one victims of a serial rapist known locally as the Early Bird Rapist. He had been active from 1972 to February 4, 1976. The reason I recall the exact ending date is because I was promoted to inspector and transferred back to detectives on February 6, 1976.

Virtually everyone assigned to the detective division, during those four years, had at one time or another investigated this particular series of sexual assaults. I was the last. By standing on the shoulders of the others, I was able to conclude their efforts by April, 1976. Not only did we identify the Early Bird Rapist, but a copy cat, referred to as the Early Morning Rapist, as well.

The suspect in the Early Bird serial rapes had already been identified by patrol officer Ron Smith and his partner. It was Carol Daly and her partner, Sergeant Habaker, who were conducting the followup investigation. Not to take away from Sgt. Habaker, but Carol was an excellent choice for the investigation.

Carol began her law enforcement career with the Sacramento Sheriff's Department in 1968. After routine training, she was assigned to the detective division where she remained until promoted to Sergeant in 1984. Moving steadily up the ranks, she retired as Undersheriff for Sacramento County. When she retired, Gray Davis, then Governor of California, appointed her to the Board of Prison Terms as Commissioner. Six months later he elevated her to Board Chairperson.

Along her climb up the rungs to top management, Carol gained valuable experience investigating homicides and sexual assaults. This experience, plus her gender, made her a perfect choice to work closely with rape victims.

It was Carol, with characteristic compassion and understanding, who undertook to arrange group counseling for all victims of rape, and in particular, the victims of the East Area Rapist. She even arranged to include the husbands, for they, too, were victims.

Not being able to admit they had not been able to protect "theirs," many of the men chose not to attend the counseling sessions. A number of divorces followed these attacks. How many of the divorces are directly attributed to the sexual assaults can only be known by the victims themselves.

To this day Carol remains friends with some of the women assaulted by the EAR. Note the word "victim" is not used here, for over the years most of these women have moved on with their lives. The "as yet" unidentified psychopath no longer controls them.

In a recent conversation with Carol, she commented about the strain that resulted from one investigative responsibility she, and she alone, shouldered.

"I remember when I was so burnt-out on working EAR, supporting victims, etc. The powers-to-be thought going back to homicide would just be more trauma for me. I told them I could handle death, but continuous support of the victims, with no answers for them, was draining."

It would be another nine months, from the time we met, before Carol and I were to work as partners. In the meantime I would, on occasion, join Sgt. John Irwin in investigating sexual assaults. Together we investigated the kidnapping of a woman from a shopping mall. She had been accosted at gun point in the busy parking lot at mid-day. After being terrorized and raped, she was abandoned, nude, by the side of a road. Both suspects eventually received life sentences.

Sgt. Irwin, new to the detective division, was very eager to learn. Blond and standing well over six feet tall, he was intelligent, a quick thinker, and an equally fast talker. Irwin was a unique character who quickly became known for something he created: the aerobic interview.

Always bursting with energy, Irwin would interview people with apparent enthusiasm. Standing in front of them while talking, he would literally bounce up and down. His knees bending to the extent he appeared to be doing aerobics.

This over-flowing energy was oft times cause for some distraction. I am not sure the people he interviewed were more than a little afraid he might explode, leaving them up close and personal to some really messy results. I know I always stood well to the side when he was talking. I stood aside one day, watching as he interviewed a sheriff's detective from Yolo County. The detective's head kept pace with Irwin's body as it moved up, then down, only to move up again–all in a perfect, steady rhythm.

Chapter 4:
A Life-Changing Event

October 5, 1976
Woodpark Way
Citrus Height, California

October 5, 1976, was a life-changing event for a family then living in Citrus Heights, a Sacramento suburb. The event may actually have been put into motion a week or so earlier when Jan Cooper, an registered nurse student and an Air Force reserve lieutenant stationed at Travis Air Force Base, along with her husband, an Air Force Captain, stationed at McClellan Air Force Base, upon returning home one evening, made a discovery. What they discovered were pieces of junk jewelry in their house that they knew did not belong to anyone in their family.

Responding officers soon learned those pieces of junk jewelry belonged to a neighbor who lived at the other end of Woodpark Way. Ultimately it was determined that someone had broken into several houses, taking jewelry from one home only to leave it behind in another.

After the Sheriff officers left, Jan and her husband conducted their own investigation. Beginning at the apparent point of entry, which was their three year-old son's bedroom window, they back-tracked across a field behind their house. In the middle of that field they found one of her husband's socks which were presumably used as a glove by the suspect.

There had been crank phone calls where the person calling did not speak. The last such call was a week or so earlier. That time the unidentified male voice said he was going to "kill her husband."

At 6:33, on the morning of October 5th, the life-changing event continued to unfold. What was about to happen to Jan would be repeated at least fifty-one times over the next three years.

After seeing her husband off to work, Jan climbed back into bed. There her three year-old son joined her as he often did. They had been lying there giggling and talking to each other for about ten minutes when Jan heard a light switch being flipped on, then quickly off. Thinking her husband had returned, she called out, "John, did you forget something?" The response was not what she expected.

Her heart must have skipped a few beats at what she saw. Rushing down the hallway towards her was something out of a horror movie. That the intruder's head was entirely covered in a gray/green mask had barely registered in her mind as he exploded into her room. In the very next instant the masked intruder was beside her bed saying, "Shut up. All I want is your money. I won't hurt you. Shut up and stay there. Cooperate and you won't get hurt. I have a knife." To show he was serious, he lay a cold knife blade against her body.

Rigid with fear, her baby son pressing against her, Jan told the hooded man, "Take my money and go. Please go. Please go."

He didn't go, as she so fervently wished. Instead, using shoe laces he brought with him, he tied her hands behind her back, then blindfolded and gagged her with towels he had torn into strips. Once he was sure Jan could not defend herself, he switched from, "All I want is your money and I won't hurt you," to blatant threats. "Shut up or I'll use this knife. I swear I'll use this knife." Those were his most common threats. Jan was later to say if he said "Shut up" once, he said it fifty times. Even when she tried to answer a question put to her by the assailant, his response was, "Shut up."

Lying in bed and fearing the worst, Jan could hear him opening and closing every closet and drawer in the house, including the kitchen.

Even though her house was not large, her assailant returned to her bedroom every few minutes ensuring that she and her son were still tied. At times he would slide a small knife blade along her body, and at other times he would quietly stand beside her. When this happened, Jan would mumble a question, around her gag, just to determine if he was still around. Each time she did this, she would be greeted by, "Shut up," followed by yet another threat to use the knife on her.

Eventually, the assailant got down to his real purpose for being in the Cooper household. Entering the bedroom for the umpteenth time, he stood beside Jan and said, "Play with my penis." Lying on her stomach, Jan's response was to ask him not to touch her. That elicited the same response as before, "Shut up and do what I say or I'll use this knife." Then she felt her assailant straddle her back and place his penis into her hands, again saying, "Play with it." She noticed that his penis felt very small and slippery, and then she remembered a few minutes earlier she had heard what must have been the assailant applying lotion to himself.

After a few moments, Jan felt him untie her feet, and with the thought, "Oh no, not this," she realized what was about to happen. She could tell he was getting aroused, but he never climaxed. During the actual rape, her assailant said, "Do it like you do with the captain. You looked good at the Officers' Club." Earlier, he had made the statement he had seen her at a dance with the captain at the McClellan Air Force Base Officers' Club.

After sexually assaulting Jan, her assailant announced he was going into the kitchen to prepare something to eat. If he heard any movement in her bed, he would come back and kill her. Jan thought to herself, "Really, just how weird is this guy?" It was when she heard him at the slider door that she knew he was leaving. After what seemed an interminable amount of time, she decided to take the chance and make a break for it.

When Jan managed to remove her gag and blindfold, she saw that the suspect had tied her three year-old son's hands and feet with towels as well. Telling him to stay in bed, she made her way to the back sliding door and after some effort got it open. With hands still tied behind her, she hobbled around the back corner of the house and over to the gate. With the gate open Jan was able to elicit the help of some neighborhood children.

The request for detective assistance came when the early arrivals to work were still clustered around the coffee pot, preparing for the days events.

Captain Stamm, armed with a strong voice and personality to match, could take control of a crowded room at will. With his voice booming (at low volume), he announced to the coffee klatch that a woman had just been found; bound, gagged, and raped inside her home. Patrol Officer Irwin Hatfield was already at the scene and was requesting detective assistance. Apparently, Captain Stamm already had in mind just who those detectives were to be.

It was a few minutes after eight that morning when Sgt. Irwin, Carol, and I found ourselves in front of a single-story white house on Woodpark Way, a middle-class neighborhood in the east area of Sacramento County.

Woodpark Way is a short street connecting on the east end with Dewey Boulevard. At the north end of Dewey is Greenback Lane and at the opposite end, Madison Avenue. Both are main thoroughfares which parallel Woodpark Way. A cement-lined drainage ditch lies between Woodpark Way and Greenback Lane.

Pulling up to the curb we were greeted by a somewhat excited woman. She was there to take us to the victim. We first laid eyes on Jan in the house of the woman who had rescued her.

Jan, who was sitting just to the right of the front door, was being attended by her rescuer when we entered. What I saw was an attractive, intelligent looking woman with long dark hair. Sitting, rubbing first one wrist, then the other, she had a look of tenseness about her face. She looked totally vulnerable. To be sure, she was angry, but in control. When I asked about her wrists, she held them out where I could see the red marks.

The marks were red, with clearly visible, deep indentations. Jan said the shoestrings used to bind her had been tied so tightly her hands turned black by the time she was freed. With that, she handed me a single length of black shoestring. It was apparent there had been two shoelaces. They had been tied together, then cut to free her, as they now came as one unit. The knot used was one I was not familiar with. Later one of the identification technicians (Crime Scene Investigators), after some research, identified the knot as a diamond knot, which is also known as a lanyard knot. Considered a nautical knot, it is also used when working with horses as well as in interior decorating, such as macramé.

After the customary introductions and a few preliminary questions, Sgt. Irwin and I left for the crime scene across the street. Carol remained behind, explaining to the victim the procedures in a sexual assault investigation, while gathering pertinent information. She also had to arrange for a medical examination, to be conducted later, at the county medical center. For those who don't know, the purpose of the medical examination is twofold. First, it ensures the physical well being of the victim. Next, it is a way to collect and preserve any physical evidence. Every victim of a rape goes through this process.

The suspect's description, as provided by Jan, was that of a young white male, 30 to 40, 5 ft. 9 in., medium weight. He spoke in a quiet, soft, yet normal voice.

A week or so after this initial conversation, Jan was watching her husband who was standing about where she first saw the suspect in the hallway. Mentally comparing his height with that of the suspect, she confirmed in her own mind he was probably 5 ft. 9 inches tall.

When Jan was describing her ordeal, she pointed to a minor wound on her left shoulder. In her opinion this was an "accident" that happened when he placed the knife against her shoulder. Somehow we had come to the conclusion the knife had a serrated edge. Since the wound was an abrasion, and not a single laceration, then it was probably caused by a serrated blade.

I thought then, and now, that he wanted to hurt her and hurt her badly. In my opinion, he was probably controlling a strong urge to do some real harm to his victim. But this was only my opinion and was not based on any kind of solid facts. Many of his later victims would also suffer minor "accidental" injuries such as this one.

When describing her ordeal to us, Jan's voice had lowered a bit while she reiterated that it seemed to her he did not have a very large penis. In fact, she said, he was very small in that department. Jan noticed that at no time did he allow his full weight to rest on her, nor did he ever allow his face to come close to hers.

Jan's comment, about the suspect having a very small penis, caught us a bit off guard. I doubt if any of us had ever given a passing thought to the size of a rapist's penis. It was probably because her comment came right out of left field that it stuck with us. What possible relevance could that information have? As it turns out, it well might have.

After interviewing Jan, and conducting our own crime scene investigation, we waited for the identification technicians to arrive. Meanwhile, I requested the dispatcher to contact an individual who owned a bloodhound that had been trained to track people.

This would be my first time to use a bloodhound in any kind of investigation. The idea came to me because Detective Pat O'Neal used this same dog in a homicide investigation a few years earlier. A canine unit officer commented to someone that the Sacramento Sheriff's Department started using canine units because of my use of that bloodhound. I have no idea if there is any truth to that statement, but if so, the credit should go to Pat O'Neal; I was just emulating him.

The bloodhound led us from the child's bedroom window to the fence. Considering the age and size of both the dog and his handler, we circumvented the fence by going around to the end of the block then back to the fence where the scent was picked up once again. From the fence, the dog led us straight across a field to where the trail ended at the curb. The distance was approximately 200 feet.

The field was "L" shaped, and with the exception of a trailer house located at the bottom (west side) of the "L," was overgrown with weeds. It was bordered by Dewey Boulevard on the east side and a one block long street named Shadow Brook Way on the west.

There were only two houses on the west side of Shadow Brook Way. The bloodhound lost the scent at the curb, across from those two houses.

Mrs. Jackson, occupant of one house, left for work between 7:15 and 7:20 that morning. Her husband stepped outside right after she left and did not see any car parked by that curb.

Mr. Williams, who occupied the other house, routinely took his garbage out at 7:00 A.M. For some reason, on this day, he took it a few minutes earlier. As he was setting the can down, he noticed a dark colored car parked across the street. Later, I spoke to him by phone and he described the car as 1952 green Chevy coupe. When he left for work at 7:00 A.M., the car was gone.

Four or five days ealier, the woman living on the south east corner of Shadow Brook Way, saw a stranger standing next to her car parked in her driveway. They stood and stared at each other for a couple of minutes, at which time he calmly walked across the street, got into a dark green car, and drove off.

She described him as a white male adult, 30-35, 5 ft. 9 inches, 170 pounds, with thick, dark hair. This description turns up a few more times in the investigation. However, the description of the East Area Rapist was generally of someone younger, more fit, with light-brown hair worn collar length.

What I took from these early steps in the investigation: The suspect was very well acquainted with the neighborhood and had been in several of the houses before this fateful day.

How did he select his victim? There was no indication other than possibly he had seen her or a photo of her, while in her home.

Someone had made a number of phone calls to several people living in that neighborhood. Each time the phone was answered, the caller would hang up without speaking. There were crank calls to Jan as well. The last one was a week before the assault when he threatened to kill her husband.

The probability of this being a crime of opportunity was unrealistic. The timing was too punctual to have been a coincidence. This rapist had come with a detailed plan. I was sure we would hear from him again.

The usual steps were followed in this type of investigation. Delivery people were contacted. Parole and probation officers were contacted in the hope they had some likely "persons of interest" in their case files. Registered sex offenders' files were also checked, but nothing relevant turned up.

Chapter 5:
Researching by Gossip

It had been less than five months since I had investigated a serial rapist–actually two serial rapists. Neither rapist had devoted more than a day or two of planning before taking action. It was more likely they never spent more than two or three hours in preparation. This latest sexual assault appeared to be vastly different. It had the appearance of having been meticulously planned with every detail covered. It probably took several days, if not weeks, to accomplish the plan before it was put into action.

Sacramento had been a magnet for sociopaths, psychopaths and other assorted perverts. Lurid, media-created nicknames such as "Vampire Killer" and "Thrill Killer" would seem to support this statement. Now it seemed we might have yet another rapist at work in Sacramento.

On the chance this was true then it had to be confirmed or disproven and quickly. I felt the first step was to look for other sexual assault reports with a similar method of operation. Wanting fast results I relied on a personal observation. That being the average person will talk mostly about people, things and what recently happened in their own lives. They gossip.

This was how I quickly learned Detective Wally Koozin was investigating a report of two sisters sexually assaulted in their home in July 1976.

I located Detective Koozin in the Sacramento east area where he was doing investigator things. After I called him for a 940 (cop talk for meet me) he gave me a location for a rendezvous. As we sat with our cars parked about 10 inches apart facing in opposite directions he told me of a sexual assault on two sisters. But first he told me of another assault he was investigating. This was a physical assault occurring in the same area a few days prior to that sexual assault.

In this seemingly unrelated incident, a man about fifty years old, stepped from his house into his garage. As he took those few steps into the garage, he was probably as surprised as the man he found rummaging through his tool boxes and cabinets. When confronted, the intruder, swinging an odd looking club, came straight for him. Fearing for his life, the man sought safety by crawling beneath his car parked in the garage. He ended the night by going to ER for treatment.

The club was described to officer Koozin as a short stick with some sort of a white pad on one end. A small revolver added to the suspect's armament.

Hearing Detective Koozin describe that club, my first thought, after wondering why he would use a padded stick as a weapon, was a pugil stick. Never having seen one, I had seen photos of them. They are sticks padded on both ends and used by the military in basic training. Ultimately, the club was identified as a training baton used by the military police in their basic training, prior to 1975.

At the time, there were five military installations, an hour's drive or less, from Sacramento. Mather Air Force Base alone had 7600 personnel. Add to that number the personnel at

Travis, McClellan and Beale AFB's, plus the Army Depot, and you had one extremely large pool of people from which to draw suspects. This meant working closely with the Air Force Office of Special Investigations (OSI), as well as all the other branches affiliated with those bases.

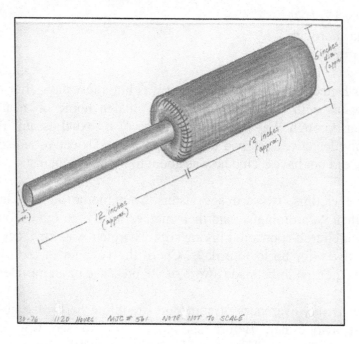

The pre-1975 military police training baton

Chapter 6:
The Sexual Assault

July 17, 1976
Marlborough Way
Carmichael

As Detective Koozin had said, it was but a few days after the assault with the "padded weapon" that a home on nearby Marlborough Way became the scene of a sexual assault. The only detective assigned to investigate was Detective Koozin. He did not have a clue he was about to bump up against.

The victims, two teenage sisters, were home alone. Their father, a cardiologist, and their mother were both out of town on a church-sponsored hiking trip. The plan was for them to be away for up to four days. Cheri, the younger of the two, was the first to be made aware of the presence of an intruder.

It was the awareness of someone straddling her prone body that awoke her. Before she could turn to see who the uninvited guest was, a forced whisper said, "If you make a move, I'm going to stab this right through your neck." The pressure of what felt like a dull knife, being jammed against her neck, while at the same time being thumped on the back of her head with a fist, left no room to doubt the sincerity of his threat.

Immediately, Cheri felt her hands being tied tightly behind her back, then a stocking stuffed into her mouth. Apparently, wanting to be sure the gag remained in place, the intruder wrapped a belt around her head and over the gag. Only then did he leave the room. But not for long.

Several times Cheri heard the intruder leave her room only to return within a couple of minutes. It was during one of these brief absences that Cheri heard a struggle, in the hallway outside her room, and her sister shouting, "Goddamn it, what's this queer doing in here?"

The prelude to this hallway battle came when the suspect quietly slipped into the bedroom of Susan, the older sister, where she too was asleep. Clamping his hand over Susan's mouth, he whispered for her to do what he said. Susan's immediate response was to do just the opposite. She screamed, and in the next instant jumped out of the bed. Landing on both feet, she struck straight up with her fist. Unfortunately, she missed her target striking the intruder on the thigh instead. Realizing she had done little damage, she headed out of the bedroom and into the hallway, her attacker hanging onto her all the way. Not being particularly meek, she continued to struggle while the intruder kept pounding on the back of her head with his fists. Finally, he managed to force her to the floor where he quickly tied her hands behind her back with string he had brought with him.

Dragging her back into the bedroom, he pushed her onto the bed where he tied her feet together. It was then he whispered, "If you move or make this bed twinge, I'll kill you." He then returned to roaming around the house, returning every few minutes to check on each of the girls. When speaking, it was always in a forced whisper through clenched teeth. If he felt like he was not getting his way, he began to breathe heavily through his mouth.

29

He told Susan he had seen her at the junior prom. A photo of her and her prom date sat in plain view on top of her dresser. Junior prom, and the date, were written on the back of the photo. The intruder also asked the sisters where their father kept the drugs. It has to be assumed there were documents lying about that showed their father was a medical doctor.

As in the "yet to happen" sexual assault on Woodpark Way, the suspect applied lotion to his penis. Over the course of the time he was in the house, he placed his penis in the bound hands of Susan three or four times, each time ordering her, "Play with it. Play with it."

About the time both girls felt their assailant was gone, they heard a car engine start then leave. They agreed it sounded like a standard four-speed vehicle.

Their combined description of the suspect painted him as a white male, 17 to 20, 5 ft. 10 inches to 6 ft. tall, with a muscular frame. His clothing consisted of a print shirt and dark-blue corduroy pants. Covering his entire head was some kind of light-brown or flesh-colored mask. His shoes were lace up type boots. No odors, other than baby oil, were detected. Never did he allow his full weight to rest on either sister. One relevant observation by one sister was that even though he raped her four times, he never once climaxed.

Officers investigating the scene found entry had been forced through the rear sliding door. They also found two, empty, Coors beer cans just outside the house and one more inside. None of the beer cans belonged to either of the victims or their parents.

Footprints, about twelve inches long with a wavy, sole pattern, were found beneath the bedroom windows.

One responding patrol officer, Syd Curtis, notified Detective Koozin of a man known for lewd conducting then living on Battlewood Way, Carmichael. As soon as he learned of this Detective Koozin went to the address in question. Parked in front of the house was a cream colored Valiant, California WHZ--. The owner's date of birth was in 1933, so he was out. But they ran his name without the middle initial, and came up with a James Vincent, white male, 5 ft., 130 pounds, brown eyes and brown hair. Robert was a student at the same school was the two sisters. His size alone excluded him from being a person of interest.

The significant elements of this assault were clearly the same as those in the assault on Woodpark Way, the one that I was already investigating. Prowling, binding hands extremely tight, promises of no harm would be done if money was found followed by threats, blindfolding, gagging, ransacking, application of oil on his penis, time spent in the kitchen; these all matched perfectly. Even the repeated whispered demands of "Shut up" and telling his victim he had seen her before, they all matched. There was little doubt in my mind this was the same suspect responsible for the assault on Woodpark Way.

After speaking with Koozin, I felt the probability of another serial rapist on the loose was all but a foregone conclusion. Before I raised the proverbial red flag, I needed solid proof. It would not have been necessary for me to raise that flag had a better system for investigating sexual assaults been in place. The information from this sexual assault was already part of the record when the one on Woodpark Way had taken place. It was just that no one had picked up on the distinctive similarities.

Chapter 7:
Score Two for Gossip

September 4, 1976
Crestview Drive
Carmichael

Again it was office gossip which led me to Sgt. Jim Bevins. It was rumoured he was investigating a sexual assault against a woman in her home.

Sgt. Bevins, with the thick shock of prematurely white hair crowning his 5 ft. 10 inch frame, is one of those people who is immensely popular with just about everybody with whom they come into contact. Possibly because of what at least two women have described as "his big, soft, soulful, brown eyes."

When he was promoted to sergeant Bevins had been transferred to the detective division. Having been promoted to sergeant myself a few months earlier I was then working at the Roger Bauman Maximum Security facility of the Rio Consumnes Correctional Center, or as it is better known ,"Branch Jail". One night as my shift was just beginning I stumbled into what amounted to a major scandal involving one of the Sheriff's long time sergeants. Two days later Sgt. Bevins (who had been a detective for about two days) and I traded places with me going to the detective division and him to the Branch Jail. Needless to say the story of that scandal never saw the light of day.

But all of that was four years in the past. Now I was asking Sgt. Bevins about his investigation of a woman assaulted in her own home. He said he had investigated a rape of a woman in her mother's house on Crestview Drive, in Carmichael, a suburb of East Sacramento.

Listening to Bevins describe that assault, I could not help but feel it was the same guy responsible for those other two sexual assaults. That was an opinion shared by Detective Walt Koozin, but not necessarily by Sgt. Bevins.

When I voiced my opinion, he fixed those large, soft, soulful, brown eyes on me and somewhat forcefully said, "BULLSHIT! The guy was a prowler who saw an opportunity and took it." His opinion was valid, but I was not quite ready to accept it as the only option.

In this latest assault, Christi, a young mother of two, recently separated from her husband, was employed as a clerk for the California Department of Community Colleges on "S" Street in downtown Sacramento. Her husband, who was employed for the Social Sciences Department at Sierra College, lived in Roseville, a small town in a neighboring county.

It was about 6:00 P.M. when Christi arrived at her mother's house on Crestview Drive, Carmichael. Her plan was to use the washer and dryer in the garage, then go home. Because her mother's car was in the garage, she had to park her car in the driveway. As it was cloudless and 6:00 in the evening, she felt there should be no problem with leaving the garage door open. The world was right.

After five hours of laundering clothes, she came face-to-face with pure evil. That was when her life took a sudden leap into hell. As she turned around with a final armload of clean laundry, was when it happened.

Suddenly she felt herself being grabbed from behind. As she was being forcibly spun around, she caught a glimpse of a masked figure. In the same instant she was struck in the nose with his fist. Dazed by what had just transpired in mere seconds, she was barely able to comprehend that her assailant had flashed a small pocket knife in her face. Pushing and pulling, the assailant forced Christi into her mother's backyard.

As they made their way into the backyard, this evil in human-form kept whispering that all he wanted was her car and money so he could get to Bakersfield. He did whisper the added enticement that if she looked at him he would slit her throat.

After tying her hands, he forced Christi into her mother's house. As he pushed/pulled her from room to room he whispered through clenched teeth, "Is anyone expected home soon?" After a quick check of the house, he forced Christi to lie on a bed where he tied her feet then blindfolded and gagged her.

Key here was the fact he asked her who was home and when someone could be expected.

As in the assaults on Woodpark Way and Marlborough Way, the suspect repeatedly left the bedroom where his victim lay helpless,. Apparently wandering from room to room he could be heard rummaging through drawers and closets, returning to check on her every couple of minutes. Here, as in those other two assaults, he was heard in the kitchen–presumably eating. The officers were to find two, empty, Coors beer cans in the kitchen.

In keeping with what we were beginning to understand as his method of operation, her assailant applied lotion to his penis before placing it in her bound hands with instructions, "Do it right or I'll kill you." That was when he cut Christi's clothing off with a knife and began to sexually assault her.

Unlike the assault on Marlborough Way, he reached a climax. For the experienced investigator this is important information. As this series of sexual assaults continued, the sexual performance and interest by the suspect steadily declined. There is, no doubt, a myriad of reasons for this, but our concern was that it might indicate he was slipping into an even more dangerous state of mind.

Twice while tormenting Christi, he commented on what a nice body she had and wanted to know if anybody else had ever told her so. He claimed to have made love to all the girls when he was in the army, and he never met one who did not like it.

When rescued, Christi's hands, like those of the other two victims, had turned black from lack of circulation caused by the tightly knotted shoe strings around them. The deep, red, indentations caused from being bound so tightly lasted for hours. In Christi's case, the shoestrings that caused those marks had been tied with a square knot under a half hitch, which was under an overhead knot. These knots, as others to come, would later be identified in a book describing nautical knots and terms.

Investigators on the scene found the air conditioner had been unplugged and all but one light was off. An escape route had been prepared by leaving the back door open and a chair placed in front of it.

Christi was not able to provide much of a description of the suspect as she had been immediately struck in the face and forcefully turned away from him, and not long after that he blindfolded her.

Once she heard him talking very low as if on the telephone, but she could not be certain. When he did talk to her, it was in a whisper through clenched teeth. There is no record available showing the telephone company was contacted regarding that possible call.

Before escaping in Christi's car, he tied her to a patio post. Her car was found within a couple of blocks of her mother's house.

Christi described her assailant as a white male, 5 ft. 8 inches to 5 ft. 9 inches tall., with a slender build. She never saw his hair, but she did notice his pubic hair was very dark with a lot of lighter hair on his legs.

His mask appeared to be homemade out of gray cotton with holes for the eyes and mouth. A dark green T-shirt, black imitation leather gloves, and a black belt were all she was able to see of his clothing.

It is common after a major crime has occurred for the police to contact each family in the neighborhood, a routine they call a neighborhood canvass. This means the families of every house in the neighborhood are asked predetermined questions. This had been done after the assault on both Woodpark Way and Crestview Lane. There is no record available indicating it was done after the assault on Marlborough Way.

However, the results of this neighborhood canvass revealed numerous reports of prowling and burglaries all up and down Crestview Lane. That is exactly what had occurred on Woodpark Way prior to the assault on Jan.

One week prior to this latest assault, a house on Crestview Lane had been forcibly entered but nothing was taken.

Two doors from where Christi had been attacked, another neighbor had chased a teenager out of his backyard a few weeks earlier. This prowler-chasing neighbor worked for the California State Motor Pool at 10th and "N" Street, near the Capitol Mall, in downtown Sacramento—not all that far from where Christi was employed.

The neighbor, Christi, and the father of the two girls who had been assaulted on Marlborough Way, all worked in downtown Sacramento. Their father's profession, and that of Jan on Woodpark Way, was in medicine. Jan was a nursing student and Christi was employed with the State of California in the Department of Education, while her husband was a teacher at a junior college. There was something there. I could almost smell it.

There was no mention, in the Crestview report, of houses for sale or people receiving an unusual number of hang-up phone calls. The question was probably not even asked as there was no real reason to entertain the idea of a real estate connection, or phone calls being part of the MO. There had been a for sale sign across fom Jan's house on Woodpark Way.

October 9, 1976
El Segundo
Rancho Cordova

Best informed guesses placed the time at 4:30 A.M. when a man climbed through an open window into the bedroom where Margaret lay peacefully sleeping. She was never sure if it was the sound of someone calling her name or the hand roughly clamped over her mouth that woke her up. All she knew was she had been alone and now she was not. In that same moment something sharp was being jammed into her back and a voice was telling her, "Don't scream or I will kill you."

Afraid to even flinch, she lay motionless as her hands were tied behind her back and she was gagged then blindfolded.

As soon as she was defenseless, the intruder pulled her out of her bed then roughly pushed/walked her towards the patio. In between short rapid breaths, as they stumbled along, he whispered loudly in her ear that he had been dreaming of her and wanted to fuck her. Once on the patio he forced her down onto a rug where he bound her feet together.

The intruder was not quite ready to assault Margaret. Lying there, petrified with fear, she heard him go back into the house. After a few moments she could tell by the sounds that he had returned and was now walking around the backyard. He made trips in and out of the house more than once. On one of the return trips to the backyard, he asked where her money was, saying he needed a fix. Still talking in forced, loud whispers he added, "Better have money," in such a way as to imply a threat if she did not.

After his question and comments about needing money, the intruder returned yet again into the house. Then a few moments later he was back, only this time he was right beside her. He was so close to her, in fact, she could feel him as much as hear him. This was when she heard him masturbating, all the while continuing to breathe in short, rapid breaths. It was then he poked her with something sharp and said, "You better let me do this," and with that, he straddled her back placing his penis in her bound hands. After this perverted game, he raped her.

After the third assault on Margaret, she heard him at the far side of the house putting something into a paper bag. It was only minutes later that she felt the rug, on which she was lying, being pulled. When the pulling stopped, she felt herself being tied to a pole. With a warning not to scream (he said he lived just down the street and would hear her and come back and kill her) her assailant left.

Margaret was able to free herself from the pole but not the other bindings. Once free from the patio pole, she hopped into the house to call for help. There she found both phones lines had been cut. So, having no phone and no way to free herself, Margaret lay there helpless. It would be a few more hours before a friend would stop by and rescue her.

Investigating officers found there had been some ransacking but it was not extensive. This time the suspect had cut a clothes-line in Margaret's backyard and used it to rig up a rather unique alarm system.

First, he tied the line on the doorknob of the father's bedroom door, then he ran it over to the brother's bedroom door where he did the same. From there the line went over to Margaret's bedroom door, then into the kitchen, finally ending in the hall bathroom tied to the bathtub faucets. It was done in such a manner the doors could not have been opened, nor could anyone have run down the hall.

Margaret never actually saw the suspect but believed him to be white, 22 - 27 years old. She did see his shoes and described them as black-patent, squared-toed leather. Within minutes, a person of interest would be developed. Someone should have asked Margaret if this POI was wearing similar type shoes.

A viable suspect was developed right there in Margaret's home. A neighbor, who was about the right age and height, introduced himself to the reporting officer telling him his house had been burglarized, or at least he thought so, but there was no sign of forced entry and nothing seemed to have been taken. The neighbor left only to return a short time later, saying he found six rings in his house that he did not think belonged there.

Officer Crowder noticed that this rapidly developing suspect seemed unusually interested in the crime scene and kept trying to look around. Finally, Officer Crowder expelled the curious neighbor from the house. This was how a man named

Dorcas turned himself into a prime suspect in this "as yet" developing investigation.

Later, Officer Crowder found that Dorcas's bedroom was in a direct line across from Margaret's bedroom—a bedroom which was never locked. Margaret assumed a plant, which was in front of her uncovered window, offered privacy. Dorcas would probably have known that Margaret's father was out of town, and Dorcas drove a small, green Vega that matched one seen in the area of the assault on Woodpark Way. As suspects go, Dorcas was the best thing yet for the investigation, and it was he who put himself in that position.

Officer Crowder also learned that Margaret, a nineteen year-old clerk, frequently attended dances at Denker Hall on Mather Air Force Base. In order to gain entry to Denker Hall, a name and address were required.

Neither Carol, Irwin, nor I responded immediately to this call, although Carol did interview Margaret at a later date. One of the pitfalls in not having the same investigators on the same type of crime is not asking questions designed to seek out specific information. In this particular case, Officer Crowder did a really great job of on-the-scene investigating, but he was not aware of what to look for. As a result we do not know if there were homes for sale, under construction, or if any kind of services had recently been done in the homes in the area. Nor were any questions asked about phone calls. However, one year later Sgt. Bevins re-interviewed Margaret who said she did not recall receiving any unusual phone calls during that time period.

A neighborhood canvass was not conducted. I personally did not even know about this assault until days after it occurred. Just another textbook example of information free-floating around the department as apparently were some of the investigative assignments.

Chapter 8:
The Dots are Connected

The somewhat opaque veil of anonymity surrounding this serial rapist and his actions was rapidly dissipating and would be gone by the end of the October 18, 1976. That day, just thirteen days after the assault on Woodpark Way, two more women were assaulted, but in different locations of the county. The method of operation in those two assaults was definitely the same MO now being associated with the other assaults.

Chapter 9:
The First One

October 18, 1976
Kipling Drive
Carmichael

The first of those two assaults occurred in a quiet residential neighborhood on Kipling Drive, Carmichael. This time it was Carol, Irwin, and I who responded to the call.

As in the previous assaults, this one took place in a quiet, albeit slightly more affluent, neighborhood. Like the other's, this victim's house was a well-kept, one-story home. There was a large open area directly behind the house.

The open area was more of an expanse of open ground that was waiting to be developed into a neighborhood. Originally intended to be part of Highway 143, the new Governor, Jerry Brown (also known as Moonbeam) managed to get that project cancelled, and then made the land available to developers. It was probably a thousand or more feet long. At the time it was soggy, with an occasional puddle of water as it had rained the day before.

The original plans were to turn the area into a typical, suburban neighborhood. More than just bare lots were for sale, however. Some established homes on both sides of that strip of bare ground had recently been sold or were on the market. Indeed the victim's house had just been sold by TRW Real Estate Company, whose sign was still in their front yard.

It was about 2:30 A.M. when the family dog, penned up in their 10-year-old son Ted's bedroom, began to bark furiously. Wanting to know why the dog was barking, as much as to shut him up, Ted took him out of the bedroom with the intent of letting him outside.

As Ted was opening the door for the dog, he spotted a man wearing a mask, a blue T-shirt, white underpants, and tennis shoes, busily prying at the sliding door to the patio. Ted did not notice if the man was wearing gloves or not. The quick thinking lad let the dog out another door and watched as the half-dressed man ran to the fence, jumping on top of it. There he sat, watching the barking dog. He must have decided the dog was only a nuisance, so jumping down from the fence, he ran straight to the kitchen window. Apparently he had already opened the window, as it slid open and he easily climbed through.

When Ted saw the pervert heading towards the kitchen window, he went straight to his mother's room to warn her. The first thing Jenny did was grab the telephone and dialed the operator, then a neighbor. Not receiving an answer, she started to dial the sheriff's department. By then the naked intruder was stepping around the door into her bedroom.

Grabbing the telephone out of her hand he whispered, "Don't scream. Do what you're told or both you and your son will die." Still whispering, he asked, "How many people in the house?" Clearly he had not reconnoitered this house before he decided to force his way in. Jenny's very young daughter was in her bedroom asleep. Quietly, the intruder closed the door to the daughter's room.

While this was going on, the family dog was still in the backyard barking furiously.

After hanging up the phone, the suspect whispered to Jenny to bring the dog into the house and to shut him up or he would "butcher them all." Fearing for their lives, Jenny did as he said and locked the dog in a bedroom where he finally quieted down. Before stepping out of the room, the suspect cut the telephone cord.

With the phone inoperable and the dog locked away, the suspect felt he was in control. That was when he ordered Jenny's son, Ted, to go back into his bedroom. After making sure Ted did as ordered, the suspect escorted his victim into the living room where he told her to sit on the couch.

Using cords he cut from her venetian blinds, Jenny's hands and feet were tightly tied behind her back. Then exactly as he did on Woodpark Way, he ripped apart towels and used the strips to gag and blindfold her.

As Ted was sitting on his bed, wondering how he could take on the role of man-of-the-house and protect his mother and baby sister, the pervert walked in.

There he was, the cause of this nightmarish disruption in their lives, standing in the middle of his bedroom. Ted, being unusually calm and collected for a 10-year-old, had all his wits about him. It was here, as the intruder walked about the room, passing back and forth by a lighted lamp, that Ted added to what he had already noticed about the intruder.

Ted said he definitely had dark-blue eyes and heavy, black hair on his arms and legs. He thought he might have seen a tattoo on the suspect's right leg, but he was not sure. He also noticed when the suspect walked into his room that he walked a little differently than most people. When walking, the suspect's posture left the impression he was possibly bowlegged, or walked in a slouched position.

After tying Ted to the headboard, the suspect returned to the living room where Jenny lay incapacitated. That was when her real nightmare began.

Up until Jenny was tied and blindfolded, the intruder kept whispering that he was not going to hurt anyone. All he wanted was some money and he would leave.

Jenny had to endure the same charade as the other victims of whom we were aware. "All I want is your money," was followed by threats of death if it was not forthcoming. The ransacking of the house, eating in the kitchen, verbal abuse, forced masturbation—it was all there. Essientially, this was a carbon copy of the other three assaults.

Later investigators found two, empty beer cans not belonging to the victim or her family. It would appear the suspect brought them with him. The problem with that conclusion is he had not been seen carrying a container of any kind. So where did the beers come from? The fact is, that question has never been answered, and it seems to have been ignored.

What the suspect did after disrobing Jenny was probably unique. With the point of a knife, he drew a line first down one leg then back up, a movement he repeated on the other leg. Still using the knife, he outlined a "Y"up her adomen and across her chest from shoulder to shoulder. What he did was to outline, on her pregnant body, the "Y" incision used in autopsies. He also managed to inflict a minor cut on the bottom of her foot making her another victim of an "accidental" injury

At one point, Jenny tried to psych the suspect out by telling him he was good. He did not buy her ploy for a moment. Instead he played along and told her people laughed at him because he was so small. That statement was probably true, but I doubted it when he said that his face had been badly scarred.

When the suspect, left he took several rings with him. Among them were Jenny's wedding rings. In spite of her pleading with him not to, he worked at getting her wedding rings off. The more difficulty he had in trying to get them off her finger, the more upset and emotional he became. Jenny, fearing this whacko might just cut her fingers off, told him to use soap. Because of the gag in her mouth, she had to tell him three times. In the end he untied her just long enough to allow her to get the rings off, after which he retied her, only this time to the dining-room table.

Shortly after the suspect had gone, Jenny heard what she took to be a large American car engine start. The sound seemed to come from somewhere to the east, in the large open area behind her house. To what extent her knowledge was about car engines I have no idea, but she was probably correct.

By the time Carol, Irwin, and I arrived at the scene, patrol officers responding to the call, as well as a number of well-meaning neighbors, were all milling about. Mr. Kurpicki and his tracking dog were still on their way.

Fortunately for Jenny and Ted, one of their neighbors was a doctor. By the time Carol, Irwin and I arrived, he had already set about making sure both Jenny and Ted were cared for as much as possible, under the given circumstances. Jenny had suffered two minor cuts to her ankle and knee.

One of the first things we spoke to Jenny and Ted about was the physical description of the suspect. Jenny told us the only light she could see by was the ambient light from her backyard lights. As that was the only light available, she was unable to see the suspect clearly. She did notice the hair on his arms was dark. Later in the discussion, Jenny told us the suspect was under-endowed in the male parts department.

Again, a rape victim had volunteered a description of the suspect's penis. Again, it was being described as small. We were beginning to wonder if maybe this pervert had a genetic problem that could lead to his identity.

She gave his height as no more than 5 ft. 7 inches, a medium, solid build with no body fat or belly. The suspect's clothing consisted of a mask with a round top, dark-blue T-shirt, white jockey shorts, and black tennis shoes. His gloves were confusingly described as dark, but maybe black and white. Every time he spoke, it was a whisper through clenched teeth. There was an added attraction; he sometimes stuttered.

His weapon was a knife which, having a blade of three to four inches, may have been a pocket knife. It was well sharpened. When I first heard of this knife, it was described to me as an ice pick. That is the description I gave out to patrol and other law enforcement agencies. Eventually, an ice pick was used in two EAR assaults, and I tend to think it possible we gave the suspect the idea. That, or he had used one in this assault.

Not long after we arrived on the scene, Mr. Kurpecki and his blood hound arrived. Almost immediately the dog picked up on the suspect's trail. Starting inside the victim's house, the dog showed us the convoluted route the suspect had followed to get to the home of his victims.

Based on the dog's nose, the suspect parked his car in the same area where the victim heard a car engine cough to life. It was indeed as she said—some distance east of her house in the middle of that huge expanse of wet dirt. The tire tracks clearly indicated a large car, but because of the damp earth, the tracks mostly resembled racing slicks. One thing we did notice was that a tire track passing through a wet gutter gave us a unique way to measure the distance between tires. As the tire passed through the water, only part of it became wet. Where that wet part next touched the ground, a wet spot remained . Every time the tire turned over, it repeated this process. The distance between those wet spots was exactly eighty-four inches, telling us it was a large and probably an American car.

From where the suspect parked, it was approximately three hundred feet, in a straight line, to the back fence of the victim's next door neighbor. After crossing the fence, he went directly to a window of the neighbor's house.

We were told the man who lived at this house was a medical doctor. This doctor was not connected with the military and was in no way affiliated with Jan, who lived on Woodpark Way. There is no indication he was acquainted with the doctor living on Marlborough Way, whose daughters were assaulted.

Apparently not seeing anyone home, the suspect walked around the doctor's house, then walked through the side gate to a car parked in front. Circling the car once, the tracking dog cut a bee line to the victim's backyard, across their patio, and straight up to the kitchen window, and then to the patio door.

Based on the suspect's trail, as defined by the bloodhound, we all believed it was most likely the suspect had been intent on the victim's neighbor and not the woman attacked. We were informed the neighbors had changed their routine and were out of town that night.

Finding himself dressed for the occasion, the suspect simply went shopping and finding the house next door occupied, he forced entry. The fact that he did not know about Jenny's young daughter indicated he hadn't been in her house before–a fact sure to garner a smile from Sergeant Bevins.

It was after everybody was gone that we three sat on the patio, waiting for the identification technicians to arrive and process the scene for evidence. I was sitting with my back to the pool, Carol on my right, and Irwin, jogging back and forth between us and the patio door.

As we discussed the situation, I told them I was now certain there was yet another serial rapist in Sacramento County. They needed some convincing, so while I was justifying my opinion, I caught a glimpse of Jenny walking by the open, sliding door where entry had been tried earlier. I know she was looking at us as she walked by, but I could not be sure if she overheard us. She may have.

We were later told Jenny and her husband traveled in the same social circles as the editors of both newspapers in Sacramento: *the Sacramento Bee* and *the Sacramento Union*. Someone speculated it was because of her social circles that the local newspapers focused attention on this serial rapist so early into the investigation. It was not because these victims were wealthier than those of the Early Bird Rapist, for many of them were not. We would soon learn of a more likely way the media picked up on this series of sexual assaults.

Even when the three of us were on our way to the crime scene, other officers were carrying out prearranged assignments. Those assignments were to get an " eyes on view " of specific persons of interest.

One of the suspects was Henry White. Two deputies had been assigned to watch his house every night and if he went anywhere to follow him. On this night they found him in bed asleep, so he was finally eliminated as a suspect.

The second "person of interest" was the one who brought himself to the attention of the Sheriff's Department, and that was Dorcas.

There were no officers assigned to watch his house on this particular night. But when the officers found him, he was home taking a shower. Dorcas willingly accompanied those officers back to Kipling. He arrived while the bloodhound was in the actual process of following the suspect's trail. Without a pause, the dog wandered right past Dorcas, not even glancing at him as he snuffled and sniffed his way by.

After all the hours and money expended investigating Dorcas, he was eliminated in an instant by a dog. No one thanked the dog, not even Dorcas.

Not really being able to rely on a dog's nose as proof-positive, Dorcas was kept under observation by two-man surveillance teams. Later he was eliminated by officers watching his house when yet another assault occurred. Knowing he was inside settled any question about his guilt or innocence. But the fact is, those investigating him had already reached this conclusion before the assault on Kipling.

Out of the four sexual assaults of which we were aware, three of them involved people associated with the medical profession. In the 1970's the ratio of medical doctors per 1,000 population was somewhere around 1.5/1000. We had just had four families involved in a series of sexual assaults. Of those four families, there was one doctor, one RN, and one pregnant victim. No member of the four families worked together, or as far as we could determine were even acquainted with each other. If the doctor living next door to Jenny had been a target, the four became five.

By now it should have been no surprise to learn Jenny's neighborhood had prowlers and other suspicious circumstances.One neighbor saw car lights in the field behind her house about 9:00 P.M. Another heard dogs barking at 2:30 in the morning. Yet another neighbor heard what they thought was a four cylinder engine start up in the middle of the night. Someone else heard a car engine, in the field behind their house, start up at 5:00 A.M. sharp. It warmed up for a few minutes, then drove off.

One neighbor said someone opened the gate to their backyard between 10:00 P.M. and 2:30 A.M. The blood hound did not lead us to this person's yard.

Living next door to Jenny, a woman was awakened in the middle of the night by a woman's screams and a dog barking. She looked outside for about five minutes, but seeing nothing unusual, she went back to bed.

As part of the investigative routine, an officer contacted the newspaper delivery boy. He was a substitute and had been driven along the route by his mother. His mother said it was about 6:30 A.M. when she saw a Lincoln Continental parked at the end of Jacob Lane, a dead-end street near the victim's house. The car was again there on the morning of the attack. As she approached, the car pulled away. It was driven by a white male in his 20's – possibly as old as 30. His hair was straight and unkempt.

The license was CAT –- possibly "505." No tire was mounted on the trunk, which may have been white in color. Sergeant Irwin ran all possible combinations of numbers and got what a fighter pilot would call "No Joy." None of them came back with a matching car.

Later, Irwin spoke with narcotic investigators who told him the car belonged to a known doper who did a regular business on Keane Drive, which is right off Jacob Lane.

After returning to our office that morning, I informed the Executive Officer, Lieutenant Ray Root, of my opinion another serial rapist was at work. He asked me for my reasons, and to his credit did not dispute my conclusion. Instead, he began focusing on preparations for what was sure to be more sexual assault reports forth-coming, and come they would.

While cleaning her house the day after the assault, Jenny found a spoon beneath the couch where she had been assaulted. It was a common dinnerware spoon with the handle bent almost double. There were no marks, such as burn marks or scratches visible. She immediately turned the spoon over to Carol Daly, who in turn passed it on to me. Over the coming months much effort was put into tracing this spoon, but it was just too common a spoon to be positively identified.

Soon after this assault, Jenny and her family completed an already planned move to Danville, California. Not long after, the EAR attacks began to occur in that area. In 1991 or 1992, Jenny received a phone call where the caller whispered to her, "You know who this is." She was positive…it was him!

Of all the fingerprints lifted at the crime scene, only the one designated as "12b" remains unidentified. 12b was one of two latent prints lifted off a closet door, on the west side of the southern-most hallway.

Chapter 10:
The Second One

October 18, 1976
Los Palos
Rancho Cordova

Had there actually been any lingering doubt that another psychopath-turned serial rapist was active in the Sacramento area, it would have been fully erased less than twenty four hours after the attack on Kipling. This time the victim was a nineteen-year-old woman returning home from the Sacramento Army Depot, where she worked as a receptionist.

It was about 11:00 P.M. when Carla stopped her car in her driveway. As she turned the motor off, three things happened. A man wearing a mask whispered, "Don't move or I'll kill you." He reached through her open car window, clamped a hand over her mouth, and grabbed her head while trying to pull her from the car. Carla was a little less than enthusiastic about being part of his plan.

Carla's struggling stopped when the suspect held a knife to her throat and whispered through clenched teeth that all he wanted was her car and for her to stop fighting. If she didn't, he said he was going to cut her up. In the car with Carla was her small dog, and, as most small dogs are prone to do, it did nothing.

As soon as Carla stopped resisting, he pulled her out of the car, then he half dragged-half pushed her into her own backyard, nearer to a fence where there was a dark, shadowy area. After he made her lie down in the deep shadow, he tied her hands and feet with a cord. Later she would learn this cord was from the clothes-line in her own backyard. As a result of her struggle, Carla suffered a minor 1 ½ inch laceration on her elbow.

As he was moving Carla towards the darkened area, he kept whispering through clenched teeth that all he wanted was her car and money. Finding no money in her purse, he forced her out of the yard, around the corner, and into her neighbor's backyard. As she stepped into her neighbor's yard, she spotted rags uniformly laid out, as in preparation.

These rags were used to blindfold and gag Carla, who was again forced to lie down on the ground. Over the next few minutes the suspect continued to threaten Carla verbally while poking her with a knife. After a few minutes of this nonsense, he went back into her purse and pulled out her keys.

It was about then he whispered to her that if she moved, "Blam, Blam, Blam." She never saw a gun nor felt one on him, so she did not believe he had one. He also said if she moved he would slit her throat and cut her guts out. This she believed.

Then all was quiet until she heard her car engine start up and the car backing out of the driveway. The last she heard of her car, it was moving away down the street.

It only took a few moments and Carla had herself untied and headed for home to call the Sheriff's Department. For whatever reason, the suspect did not tie her bindings so tight the circulation was completely cut off. There were other differences between this assault and the other four, but not many.

There are two interesting points about this incident that jump right out; under ordinary circumstances, the woman who lived around the corner would have been home. However, on this particular night, she was away. Was this an example of the suspect not finding who he was looking for, and simply took the next target to come along?

The second point of interest is that Carla was accosted at the only time she is alone. She lived with both her parents and brother. Typically, they all arrive home within minutes of each other. This reliable schedule leaves Carla home alone from 11:00 P.M. to about 11:30 P.M. – thirty minutes at home alone, the absolute most. The suspect left. Carla tied up in the backyard at 11:30 P.M., just before the rest of her family came home for the evening. Was he just tormenting her? You can bet he knew her schedule.

Neither Carol nor I were dispatched to this scene, which was probably because there had not been a sexual assault. However, Irwin got wind of it and assigned himself to the immediate follow-up, which was a good idea. It was Sgt. Irwin who located Carla's car with her dog locked in the trunk. It was parked just a few blocks away from where it had been taken.

Carla described the suspect as about 6 feet tall. She came to this estimation by comparing the suspect's height with her boyfriend, who was 5 ft. 7 inches tall, and with Sgt. Irwin's height, about 6 ft. 3 inches tall. She was positive he was close to 6 feet tall. Jan, however, the victim from Woodpark Way, was positive he was 5 feet 9 inches tall. Each of them reached the estimation of his height by comparing the suspect's height with that of the man in their life.

She put his weight at about 170. She described his clothing as a ¾-length, heavy, gray jacket with buttons and gloves of brown wool. For a mask, he wore a man's brownish-gray sock with holes cut out for the eyes. She noted he was wearing brown, desert or ski boots. As before, he spoke only in a whisper through clenched teeth.

The assault on Carla marked the sixth assault in this new series of which we had recently been alerted. Or better to say, I recognized it as the sixth one. It would turn out to be the eighth, but that knowledge was yet to come. Of the six, I knew a lot about two of them, and a little about two others. But from my limited involvement, I had already reached my own conclusions about the method of operation of this pervert.

It was clear to me the suspect prowled extensively in selected neighborhoods. Reconnoitering would be a better term. As a result, he knew a lot about the schedules and routines of one or more families in a given neighborhood. In the case of Jan on Woodpark Way, it seemed he knew the schedule of more than just the victim and her family. To know this much meant he probably spent days if not weeks studying neighborhoods in both day and night.

I also considered he might be using the telephone as a means of learning the times and days people would be home. He could do this simply by calling them and then hanging up when someone answered. In Carla's case, the question of hang-up calls, or whether there were homes for sale in the neighborhood, was never put to her, or at least is not in the report. So, that is just one more unknown.

The question of how this suspect came to have those phone numbers was one that has never been conclusively answered. Answers forthcoming from Pacific Bell Telephone company left me to believe he got them the only way he could; by breaking into houses or tapping phone lines where they connect to the house in question. There was, of course, the possibility he was an employee for the phone company and got the phone numbers while working at the top of a telephone pole or perhaps while sitting at a desk somewhere, deep in the bowels of the company apparatus.

Chapter 11:
BOLO

When police broadcast a BOLO (be on the lookout) alert, followed by a description, it is hoped someone will stumble across the object of that BOLO and that the information will find its way back to the police.

It was after the assault on Kipling that I posted a BOLO with the suspect's description. Two days later an alert Sacramento police officer, responding to a radio dispatched call, spotted a man closely matching the description.

The officer arrested a man on an unrelated charge who was identified as Art Pinkton, 5 ft. 9 in., with black hair, blue eyes. He carried a knife in a leather pouch. It got even better when a records check revealed he had been arrested in the 1960s for a series of rapes in Sacramento and was then classified as a mentally- disoriented sex offender. It was just too good to be true.

When booking him into the Sacramento County Jail, a conscientious deputy, Lee Reros, inventoried the following items belonging to Pinkton:

1. Leather pouch, Craftsman brand, with name Eric Paren written in ink
2. Three screwdrivers
3. One round file
4. Metal punch
5. One serrated steak knife

6. Silver colored spoon with the handle bent double
7. Two car toggle switches
8. Business card for Raymond Reland, psychiatric social worker, State Department of Health
9. One pocket knife; style Buck
10. Two rocks

Items used by the suspect in the assault on Kipling seemed to match some of the items found in the possession of Pinkton. Of particular interest was the silver spoon and the serrated steak knife. There were no marks of any kind on the spoon.

I don't recall where I first spoke with Pinkton, but it was the same day I learned of his existence. When we did meet, I noticed he had a quiet demeanor. He seemed willing to cooperate with law enforcement. As anticipated, he denied any involvement in the recent assaults.

As I looked into Pinkton's life, I learned his mother once worked for the Sacramento Sheriff's Department, but never within the sworn personnel departments. Scattered about Sacramento and its suburbs were a number of his siblings.

One of his siblings, a sister and her husband, contacted me with an offer to help with the investigation. Art had his personal tool box stored in their garage. Being sure in their own minds that he was the rapist for whom we were searching, they invited me to search the tool box. I searched, in hopes of finding some little something belonging to one of the victims. However, I found nothing in the tool box but rusty mechanic's tools.

From this sister I learned some of their family believed Pinkton once planned on assaulting yet another woman, only it was not rape he had in mind—it was murder. His plan called for shooting her just to see what committing a murder would feel like. He had gone so far as to obtain a rifle and lie in wait. For whatever reason, the woman did not walk by that day. Whoever that woman was, she probably has no idea just how lucky she was.

Art Pinkton told me (but it was never officially confirmed) that after his return from Viet Nam, he was diagnosed as mentally disturbed. He also told me it was because of this "officially designated status" as a mentally-disordered sex offender, that he had been declared incapable of holding a job. This was how the State of California justified paying him, Pinkton, a convicted rapist, $1,040.00 a month. He was making more than we were, and his income was tax free!

Although Pinkton was never connected to any of the assaults under investigation, I was able to place him within two blocks of two rapes at the time they occurred in San Diego. One victim was in her 70's and the other her 50's. They were bound and blindfolded with torn towels. The San Diego Police Department was unable to factually connect him with either of those rapes.

In 2008, I was contacted by a homicide detective who told me Art Pinkton had been arrested at Lake of the Pines in Nevada County, California, for the murder of one of his brothers. The deed was done with an arrow through the neck. After his arrest, DNA was collected, tested, and then compared to the East Area Rapist. Obviously, it did not match, or there would be no need for this book.

There has been enough time spent and information gathered on Pinkton for an entire book to be written about him and this investigation. In my opinion one sentence is more space than he is worth. Like a bad odor, Pinkton just never seems to go away.

Chapter 12:
Rape Crisis Clinic and Our Prime Suspect

It was around the time I met with Pinkton's sister that I learned Pinkton had a relative who was instrumental in the then developing rape crisis clinic. I never bothered to confirm this, but for awhile I had to wonder if it was true.

As the rape crisis clinic was being formed, we had no idea what to expect. But, a visit to their office by Detective Carol Daly and Alix Magness, another woman detective, gave us a hint. The two detectives, giggling and sputtering as they returned from a visit to the rape crisis clinic, was our clue that a tale was in the offing.

As they opened the front door to the clinic, they were stopped in their tracks. There, plastered on the wall in full view of anyone stepping through the door, was a life size picture of a woman, sitting with her legs spread wide, without the cover of underclothes. For the woman in that picture, there were no longer any secrets to her lower anatomy.

One quick look at that revealing photo and the two detectives, saying their polite hellos—followed by very quick goodbyes, fled back to the detective division and the sanctuary of their respective offices.

From what I was able to determine at the time, what that rape crisis center seemingly accomplished was a great deal of interference with sexual assault investigations. I make this statement based on conversations with some of the rape victims, along with one rumor that I personally chased down. To be very clear; it is my understanding that clinic later became a valuable, and highly regarded resource, for victims of sexual assault.

Here is an example of why I was not so impressed with the clinic in the beginning. I received a phone call one evening from a woman who had several questions about the procedures used by police when investigating a rape. In particular, she wanted to know about the relationship between the police and the victim. After I answered her questions, a male voice came onto the line. It was apparent he had been listening in on the conversation and was very upset. He wanted to know why the women at the rape crisis clinic made it clear to the two of them that the police totally disregard a rape victim's personal feelings, as all they wanted was another arrest statistic. The people at the clinic left no doubt what their message was; that being, any rape victim would be worse off if they reported the rape to the police. Their advice to a rape victim was call them first, then the doctor. and to stay away from the police.

I tried to get the woman who called to report that she had been assaulted, but she would not. Over the years I have spoken to a number of rape victims, and I am here to tell you, I know that she was sincere. Whether or not she was assaulted by the EAR we will never know.

Later after I had returne to patrol, some of our detectives arrested a man for burglarizing a woman's house. Some months later, after a particularly hard foot chase, this same man was arrested in Utah. The Utah officers said he was very fast, leaping tall fences in a single bound. Naturally the description caught the attention of Sergeant Bevins and a deputy district attorney. The two of them met up with this suspect in Utah, for the purpose of interrogating him about the sexual assaults in Sacramento.

This individual freely admitted he had been lying in wait for the Sacramento woman to come home with the intention of raping her. His plan was to make it look like the East Area Rapist was responsible. To do that he was going to cut her nipples off. Somewhere he had heard this was part of the EAR's MO. The only thing that stopped him was being arrested by the Sacramento Sheriff's Department.

I personally traced the source of this nipple-cutting rumor back to the wife of a deputy in a nearby county who was then affiliated with the rape crisis clinic of Sacramento. Everybody should be thankful that clinic grew and matured into a force for the better.

Chapter 13:
The Psychic's Turn

With his head hanging down as it was, that shock of white hair preceded the rest of his body through the doorway into the detective division. Passing through the door and all the way to his office at the back of the detective division, Sergeant Bevins could be heard muttering to himself, "After today, nobody better ever tell me I haven't earned my retirement."

Sgt. Bevins had just returned from an assignment to interview a self-proclaimed psychic. He did not want to go, but had been ordered to go. Before an interview could be done, it was necessary for the psychic to enter into a trance, she told the now more-apprehensive-than-curious Bevins. To enter into that trance, she had to sit cross-legged on the floor while eating a quantity of raw hamburger. This then followed by some required chanting. Only then would she be ready to come up with a message. Probably other than possible parasites, nothing ever came of that session. Sergeant Bevins never elaborated.

It was also about this time Detective Sergeant Bob Dinkins wandered into my office with a request. He wanted to take the bent spoon, found at the assault scene on Kipling, to a local psychic.

By now, we had self-proclaimed psychics appearing from around every corner. It would not have surprised me to open a closet door to find one. They all meant well and were volunteering their services, so, why not? Sergeant Dinkins took the spoon to a woman known as Kate, a professed psychic who also taught the subject at a local junior college. The tape he made of her comments was interesting.

On the tape, Ms. Kate spoke of seeing a very scared young man, hiding beneath a bridge, in a canal, as the police drove above searching for him. She then saw him getting into a large car and driving away. As she related the story, it was apparently a long drive home for she saw him driving past a Safeway supermarket, and then a bowling alley (or maybe the reverse of that). He continued on until he was in a rural setting. There she described an old house. Not far from the house was an old car. The wheels to the car where nearby. Not far away was an old shed.

This shed was kept locked because this was where he stored his personal property, which included what he stole from his victims. He felt it was safe there because no one else would access the shed.

Ms. Kate "saw" the suspect walk up some wooden steps at the back of the house. As he entered the house, he looked over at an older woman asleep in a chair. Looking at her, as she slept slouched over, he had a very strong urge to walk over and bash her head in.

The age, rage, and desire to really hurt women are three points upon which the psychic, Kate, and I agreed.

We received calls from other psychics as well. One in particular telephoned me every few weeks. She claimed that just before an assault she felt vibrations on the top of her head. Later, after I was transferred, she began to call other detectives. They quickly dubbed her "Veronica Vibrations" and hung up on her.

Chapter 14:
A Stroll Down the Ditch

November 10, 1976
Greenleaf Drive
Citrus Heights

If someone had looked. Simply looked. They would have seen two people rapidly striding down the middle of a drainage ditch. That same ditch paralleled Woodpark Way. That same ditch was, undoubtedly, already explored by the prowler and rapist who had been active on Woodpark Way a few weeks earlier. Maybe they would have noticed the girl was walking, head bowed, hands behind her back, her companion holding onto her arm. Maybe they would also have noticed that the man holding onto her wore dark clothing with a hood over his head. But even with the ample ambient light, they would not have seen the knife in his left hand, nor the slits in the hood over his head which were cut out for his eyes and mouth.

With the number of homes and barking dogs lining both sides, it is a wonder no one saw them. Or perhaps they did but thought nothing of it. Just two people in a hurry to get somewhere.

It was probably about 1:30 A.M. when I answered the phone to hear that distinctive low boom of Captain Stamm telling me there had been yet another assault. This time it was about three blocks from the assault on Woodpark Way, on Greenleaf Drive, a distance of less than three blocks.

It was 2:00 A.M. before I found my way to Greenleaf Drive. Once there I found the victim, 16-year-old Marcy, sitting across the street from her home. Her parents, and the neighbor who cut her free, were with her. Like the victims before, her wrists bore deep, red marks from where the shoestrings, used to tie her wrists, had cut in. It would be seven hours before feeling fully returned to her wrists.

Earlier that day, Marcy's parents visited their son in a hospital. It would be 8:30 P.M. before they would return home. Marcy would be gone, but they would think she was on a date with her boyfriend. Besides, it would not yet be her curfew time, so they would not be concerned.

With her parents visiting her brother in the hospital, 16-year-old Marcy was left at home alone. With nothing to do but homework, she was watching TV in the den. Her focus was interrupted by a loud noise in the living room. The poodle in her lap acted nervous, but that seemed normal for the dog, so she ignored him. For whatever reason she also ignored the loud noise; a decision she would regret.

Sitting comfortably in front of the TV, Marcy was shocked when someone wearing a leather hood suddenly jumped at her from behind and pointed a knife at her. Her immediate instinct was to scream. As she did, the hooded man whispered through clenched teeth, "Shut up or I'll stab you. All I want is your money." During these introductory moments, the family dog did what most family dogs do, and that was to show the guest what great noise-makers they are. The knife-wielding, hooded figure kicked the dog, then whispered, "Shut the dog up or I will stab it. All I want is your money. " When she said there was no money and that her parents had their money with them, he muttered, "Damn, no money. Ah man, no money."

But, shocked as she had been, Marcy was not so shocked she did not notice that he was wearing what appeared to be military fatigues, a coat, and a leather hood. The hood had small slits for the eyes and a slit for the mouth. She would observe more later.

Afer she quieted the poodle, Marcy's assailant tied her hands behind her back then quickly escorted her outside and into their backyard. Stepping out the door, Marci glanced at her bicycle which was at the opposite end of the yard. Shoestrings were neatly hanging off the handle bars. It was these that he used to bind her ankles.

Now, not able to stand–much less walk, Marcy watched as her assailant replaced the screen to the window where he had made entry into her home. Once he had hidden his point of entry, he went back inside the house. We later figured out he was eliminating all indications that he had been there by turning the heater and lights on, and the TV off. He even locked the door as he left. To further prevent anyone from stumbling onto the scene, he took Marcy over a low split rail fence into the neighbor's backyard. From there, it was just a few steps until they were into the cement drainage ditch, the same ditch described in the assault on Woodpark Way.

The only evidence found at the scene, that might have indicated an intruder, was a small, round hole in the screen near the window lock. To get into the house from that window it was necessary to step on the window sill then onto the couch. It was probably this couch, slapping back against the wall, that made the noise Marcy heard.

With Marcy leading, her father and I retraced the steps she and her assailant had taken earlier in the evening. Along the way, I noted the ditch was about twenty feet wide at the top, and never very deep. In places the sides sloped gently, and in other spots they were steep.

At the time, there was water running down the middle, but it was never more than an inch deep and never covered the entire bottom. We did see shoe prints pointed west, which appeared to be about the same length as those found at the other assault scenes. Marcy had been barefoot, but since she did not leave any prints, she most likely walked in the water. With the water moving as it was, her prints would have been washed away. We did not see any prints headed in the opposite direction.

As the two of them walked, Mary tried to ask questions, but each question elicited the same response, "Shut up. If you're not quiet, you'll be silent forever, and I will be gone in the dark."

No psychologist am I, but my response to that one statement was; here's a nut living in an illusory world, stuffed with images of melodrama. An international spy, maybe? That one statement told me that each and every action and statement he made in these assaults was probably well-planned and well-rehearsed.

Marcy noticed, as they moved down the ditch, that her assailant was holding a small flashlight. It was so small that it completely disappeared in his hand. When switched on, the beam was about six inches in diameter.

While describing the flashlight, she recalled some details about his shirt. She thought he might have been wearing a zipped-up sweatshirt with front pockets and a hood.

Marcy led us to an ancient, willow tree that was growing just above the north side of the ditch. That gnarled old tree had, no doubt, witnessed many happenings in that canal, but that night must have been a whole new chapter for it.

A hundred feet behind that tree on top of a small rise sat a house. Marcy said the lights in that house were on at the time, as they were still on when we got there some hours later. It was probably the only house along the ditch without a barking dog.

Fifty feet beyond the willow tree, and just above the ditch, was an old tree stump sticking out of some weeds. Pointing to it Marcy said,"That's where he made me sit down." On the ground near the stump were cut up shoestrings, a pair of cut and ripped Levi's, and green panties.

It was not until they reached the tree that Marcy was blindfolded. Fortunately, the blindfold slipped a little and was loose over her left eye. It was during his pacing back and forth, and once when he bent to pull up his sock, that Marcy was able to get at least a partial description of her assailant.

She described him as a white male between 18 and 23 years old, about 5 ft. 10 in., and 165 lbs. He had brown hair with a very pale complexion. His hood, with small slits for his eyes and mouth, extended down and under his shirt. All she could say about his coat was that it was heavy. Her first impression had been a military fatigue jacket in which the "heavy' would certainly fit. Soft, tan, leather gloves adorned his hands, and under the heavy jacket, he was wearing military fatigues. His leg hair was brown and his eyes were dark. His shoes were black and square-toed.

Using his right hand he cut her hands free. However, he held the knife in his left hand the rest of the time. When her feet were free, he cut one leg off her Levi's then tried to rip the other one off. When he had trouble, he whispered, "This isn't working right." He eventually managed to get all her clothes off. As she sat there nude, he placed his hands on her thighs and leaning into her face whispered, "Don't I know you from somewhere?" This was when Marcy noticed a very foul odor coming from the suspect. She thought that it was possibly his breath.

When asked what her name was, Marcy replied with a phony one to which her assailant did not respond. Then he asked if she was a student at American River College. When she answered, "No," he held a knife to her throat and accused her of lying. When she told him she was a high school student, he stood up and paced back and forth for awhile.

It is worth noting that Marcy had a neighbor to whom she bore a strong physical resemblance. That neighbor had once been a student at American River Junior College. The information that night was she had recently moved. Without access to the reports it is not known who later spoke with her, or what information might have developed.

While he was pacing, Marcy heard him whisper something about waiting for his parents to leave so he could go home and then something about leaving in his car. She was not sure if he was whispering to himself or her. In either case she did not believe what he said.

Apparently preparing to depart, he escorted Marcy back to the old willow tree where he made her sit on the ground. As he was leaving, he said to her, "Within twenty minutes, make one move and you'll be silent forever and I'll be gone in the dark of the night." Here again, the practiced phrase.

Not until she was sure he was gone did she make an effort to free herself. She managed the bindings on her feet but not her hands. Feeling caution was the best policy, Marcy waited for what she felt was an hour before running back home. When she came out of the ditch she spotted her neighbor across the street and ran screaming to him. It was this neighbor who cut her free then called her parents who were, by then, home.

From the point where Marcy had been tied and assaulted to the nearest road (Woodhills Way), there was a vacant lot on the north side of the ditch. Crossing that lot was a well-worn trail. In the ditch, near the road and pointing east, more footprints were found in the mud.

The next day Sergeant Irwin and Detective Sandy Carlson re-interviewed Marcy. Once again Marcy relived her nightmare by traveling down the ditch to the spot where she had been assaulted.

As they walked, Carlson paid attention to Marcy as Irwin tried to match his stride to that of the suspect. To do so, he had to walk at a fast pace. The resulting stride measured over a yard. Marcy said that was about the rate the suspect had walked. Sergeant Irwin said he, himself, measured 6 ft. 1 in. My rookie mug shot shows me at 6 ft. 3 inches, which means 6 ft. 1/4 inches barefoot. Irwin is, in fact, taller than I am.

Marcy told all of us that she had not been raped. She told Detective Carlson that she was menstruating at the time which is why she was not raped. That never stopped him in the future, but there would be other times he did not rape his victims.

The knife used to threaten Marcy may have come from Marcy's kitchen. Later, when her mother checked, they found there was a paring knife with a serrated edge missing from the kitchen. Overall, that knife was about six inches long.

The victim's home was like all the others being targeted by this suspect at the time; one-story, middle-class home, second from the corner. The doors all had double locks, and the windows were of the slider type.

Traci and her family had been receiving the crank phone calls, the last one being a week or two prior to when she was assaulted. The same type of information came from the neighbors.

The leather hood, described by Marcy, sounded like one of those hoods worn beneath a helmet worn when using an arc welder. In an attempt to learn who might have recently bought one, I contacted the manufacturer of the hoods, TAO Production, Inc. The owner said that type of hood was a seldom sought after item, only one was sold in 1976, and that was to someone in Michigan. He agreed that one of those hoods, if turned around, could be used as a mask if slits were made for the eyes and mouth.

I also contacted a number of local welding suppliers in an effort to determine if that mask was an older welder's mask, and if so where it might have come from.

It was generally agreed by all the salesmen I spoke with that it could have been a type of hood worn by an arc welder. One such was sold two weeks prior to the assault. The salesman was to contact me later. He did not contact me, but I located him. There was nothing he could tell me about the sale.

The man from National Oxygen stated he special-ordered such a hood for a customer, but then the customer went out of business. He was wondering what to do with the hood when a man walked in off the street and bought it.

He described the man as a WMA, 6 ft., 175 lbs., with dark hair. He was not sure if the man paid by check or not. I told him our department would provide all the help necessary to go through his records. He declined the offer.

On the 11th of November, a salesman for Moores Brothers Welding Supplies contacted me. Mr. Echols remembered selling the same kind of hood to a white man in his late twenties, about 6 ft. to 6 ft. 2 inches, with a medium build and dark short hair. The man who bought it was an employee of Frederickson Tank Lines in West Sacramento. The sale was charged to them, and the man who picked it up signed his initials RMP or PMP. This piece of equipment was ordered for that company.

Contacting welding equipment suppliers was not the only avenue I followed in tracking down that hood. Besides the usual contact with parole and probation officers, and searching through the records of known sex offenders, I went after the S & M crowd. That was an enlightening experience

I began with the so-called intelligence division of the Sheriff's Department. They functioned more like a vice-squad, really. If anybody in the department had their finger on the pulse of that part of the world (S & M), it was those people.

With a little effort, I was able to get my hands on the subscribers' lists for a couple of S & M magazines. I was surprised to find the largest majority of the subscribers were Asian females. They were almost all locals, living either in Sacramento or across the Sacramento River in West Sacramento which is in another county.

I contacted the people on the subscribers' lists, but I did so delicately − probably out of fear, as I had no idea how their minds worked. There were no possible suspects developed from this avenue of investigation. Personally, I think they all thought my real goal was to arrest them. While the investigation of the kidnap and assault on Marcy was not dropped, it did take a back seat to the next assault.

Chapter 15:
The Night Walker

November Evening - 1976

Even before the official recognition of this latest psychopath, my days and nights had been very, very busy. The same could just as easily be said about most of the other investigators. While the rapist was preparing for his next victim, we were putting together a request for a search warrant for where ever Art Pinkton was then living which, as it turned out, was with his mother.

One night, about a week after the sexual assault on Marcy, we were going to serve that search warrant. The plan was for Sgt. Irwin to accompany a deputy district attorney to a judge's home and get it signed. Once the signed warrant was in hand, they would contact us by radio and we would meet with them to serve the warrant.

In the meantime "we" consisted of Sandy Carlson who would ride shotgun with me. Sandy, a former radio dispatcher from Sacramento Police Department, was a new arrival to the Sheriff's detective division. Her height matched the length of her hair, as in short. Thick and curly, it was the kind that if caught in a rain storm would quickly sprout into a mass of uncontrollable curls. She had a personality to match in that she was quick on the uptake, would go to battle in an instant, and did not worry much about with whom.

To keep busy while we waited for Sgt. Irwin, we drove to Dewey Boulevard where it intersects with Woodpark Way and Greenleaf Drive. It was just about 10 P.M. as we passed Woodpark Way when we spotted a man walking north-bound on the west side of Dewey Boulevard. He was passing the empty field, mentioned in the assault report on Woodpark Way, as we came even with him. I got a clear look at him in our headlights.

Years of driving a patrol car taught me to look closely at anyone who appeared out of place, no matter how slightly. Other than the recent history of that area and the time of night, there was no reason to bother with this guy. However, this was different. The internal cop alarm was already beginning to sound. As soon as we passed him, I made a cop-type U-turn and doubled back.

That took about ten seconds and already he was out of sight. He did not cut across the field, for it was open and too large for him to just disappear, nor could he have entered a house without our noticing. So, glancing down the street to the intersection with Greenleaf Drive first and seeing nothing, we turned onto Woodpark Way. Still no sign of him. I knew he had to be somewhere close-by, for he could not have disappeared that quickly unless he was trying to avoid us. If that internal alarm in my head had been audible, people would have thought there was a four alarm fire nearby.

What did catch my eye, as we turned down Woodpark Way, were the lights inside the house on the SW corner of Woodpark Way and Dewey Boulevard, for they went out just as we turned the corner. The people inside might have seen or heard someone in their yard and turned their lights off to better see outside. After all, the recent assault on Woodpark Way and Greenleaf Drive had occurred no more than a block away, which no doubt meant the entire neighborhood was on the alert.

By this stage of the investigation I probably knew that neighborhood as well as the rapist or any of the residents, for that matter. After making a normal U-turn on Woodpark Way, we accelerated south on Dewey Boulevard as if we were leaving. A couple of blocks later we doubled around and back onto Shadow Brook, the short street bordering the vacant field used by the rapist in the Woodpark Way attack.

Driving over the curb then straight across that field we stopped next to Dewey Boulevard. There he was, very purposefully walking back in the direction from which he had been coming when we first spotted him. He was just staring straight ahead as if he was unaware of a car driving across an empty field at night—a sign any cop would spot as, "Who, me?"

Just about every cop instinct I possessed was shouting. I was sitting there working out just how to go about it, figuring in little things like my partner's lack of experience, when Sgt. Irwin came on the air announcing he had the search warrant in hand and to meet at Pinkton's mother's house. To this day I regret not taking the time to call Sgt. Irwin as backup and checking this guy out. Knowing what I now know, he would probably have taken off at a dead run or pulled a gun. That would have been perfectly okay as I would not have approached him empty-handed, and unlike his victims, I would have had a fighting chance.

There is no way I can say positively this guy was our suspect, but any experienced street cop will understand exactly what I am talking about. In my defense I can only say, at that time, I was certain Pinkton was the rapist.

The image of the guy we saw walking that night remains with me, and even now, if I saw a photo of him from that time-period, I would recognize him. A name I will forget in an absolute instant, but a face or voice stays with me for a very long time.

He was about 5 ft. 9 in. tall, 160 or 170 lb., late teens or early 20's. His hair was light brown and appeared to be styled, or at least freshly cut. He was wearing a brown, 3/4 length jacket. The jacket may have been leather, but I could not be sure. It may have been corduroy. He walked with head up, eyes forward, and his back ramrod straight. In a word, he was well-dressed, groomed, and with a military bearing.

I have been told it was about a year or so later, and long after the EAR had moved into other areas of the state, that a woman living in San Ramon saw a man jump over her fence and into her backyard. He walked towards her back door where he was met by her dog. Apparently her dog, which was still indoors, took offense at this stranger and did its best to remove the door so he could explain his disapproval up close and personal. She described him as 5 ft. 9 in. tall, with blond hair, and someone who obviously frequented a gym. He was well-dressed and groomed. When she told him to haul ass, he responded with, "I'm just passing through." The attitude and description of this trespasser seemed very close to the man we saw walking that November night.

As planned, we met with Sergeant Irwin and the DA at Pinkton's mother's house in North Sacramento. When we entered, we found Pinkton visiting with his mother and her lady-friend in the living room. He did not seem surprised to see us, and in fact was instrumental in talking his rather embarrassed mother into just sitting back while "they do their job." Nice of him I thought. Needless to say, we found nothing. It was right about then I realized just how badly I had screwed up, just a half an hour earlier, by not stopping that guy on Dewey Boulevard.

And just a note here. In 1978, right after I was transferred back to the patrol division, a convicted sex offender was being developed into a highly viable suspect. The individual lived on Clement Way, just a few blocks away from where we saw the walker and which also connects directly with Dewey Boulevard.

This new suspect had been eliminated as a suspect by Detective Bettenhausen at the time. In 2011 the investigation into the possibility of this guy being the EAR was reopened and a District Attorney's investigator assigned. He has since been cleared by means of DNA. But their MOs were so close, it is wondered if it was possible the EAR had a mentor.

Chapter 16:
Nine and Counting

There had never any doubt in my mind, but by the time the report of the assault on Marcy was finished, there was not even a shred of doubt in anyone's mind, a serial rapist was on the loose. What was not yet clear to any of us was just how totally focused this psychopath was on rape. He was treating it like a military mission. He gathered intelligence then went after his target.

His total dedication to what he was doing made him unlike any other serial rapist ever experienced in Sacramento County and probably anywhere else. For me that meant few, if any, of his assaults were crimes of opportunity.

I was now actively investigating three sexual assaults and knew of four others. With those statistics firing me up, I dedicated my time to going through report logs, looking for additional reports with similar circumstances, instead of just asking around the office. Not surprisingly, there were a few.

The first report I found was of a rape that took place in November or December, 1975. The only detail recalled about that assault was the victim said the suspect may not have had any pubic hair. Shy any evidence or circumstances to attribute this assault to the current serial rapist, I classified as "not likely."

There was one earlier reported sexual assault considered by some the work of the East Area Rapist. It occurred in late October, 1975, on Dawes in Rancho Cordova.

There a mother, as well as her eighteen and seven- year-old daughters, were all three sexually assaulted in their home. The suspect was described as black. It had also been dismissed as not being the work of this current rapist. A year later, other investigators arranged a hypnosis session for these three victims. That session resulted in a change of the suspect's description, as well as other details. However, the investigators still dismissed this assault as being part of this sexual assault series.

What is believed by all to have been the first sexual assault by this serial rapist, happened on June 18, 1976, on Paseo Drive, Rancho Cordova. This was followed by another one on August 19, 1976, on Malaga Way, Rancho Cordova.

This is how the EAR's track record stood on November 10, 1976:

1. June 18, on Paseo Drive, Rancho Cordova
2. July 17, on Marlborough Way, Carmichael
3. August 29, on Malaga Way, Rancho Cordova
4. September 4, Crestview Drive, Carmichael
5. October 5, Woodpark Way, Citrus Heights
6. October 9, El Segundo Way, Rancho Cordova
7. October 18, Kipling Drive, Carmichael
8. October 18, Los Palos Drive, Rancho Cordova
9. November 11, Greenleaf Drive, Citrus Heights

As far as I could determine, there had been nine known sexual assaults over a six month period and all apparently by the same suspect. Yet no one had seemed aware they were by the same person. But now everybody was aware, and Lieutenant Root was deep into preparations for an intensive investigation. He knew what was coming. He had "been there—done that" more than once, and usually with a successful conclusion. Who better to be in charge?

What follows are the two additional assaults I learned of in November, 1976

Chapter 17:
The First Assault

June 18, 1976
Paseo Drive
Rancho Cordova.

What was probably the first assault by this one suspect happened on June 18, 1976. That was when he sexually assaulted a 23-year-old woman in her bedroom on Paseo Drive, Rancho Cordova. This young lady shared a house with her father, who at the time of the assault was vacationing on the East Coast. She was employed as an insurance rater for Pacific Bell Telephone, and her father was retired from the Air Force. His last duty assignment prior to retirement was at Mather Air Force Base, which for all practical purposes was in Rancho Cordova.

It was maybe 4 A.M. when the sound of someone calling her name penetrated her deep slumber. In an instant she was on full alert and was well-aware of who was saying name. There, standing in the doorway of her bedroom, stood a man wearing a ski mask, but not much more. Groggy, after being jerked from a deep sleep, she immediately understood his intent. Wearing only a shirt and mask, without any pants, his erection was obvious.

Waving the tapered point of a three or four inch knife through the air, he whispered, "If you make one move or sound, I'll stick this knife in you." Showing a flair for stating the obvious, he then whispered, "I want to fuck you."

Using twine he brought with him, the ski-masked psychopath bound Gladys's hands behind her back, but not before having her completely disrobe. Using a cloth belt which he found in her closet, he tied it over the twine. What was to become one of his trademarks was how tight those bindings were; tight enough to cut off circulation, causing her hands to turn black and for her to lose all feeling in her hands.

In this assault, as he wandered about the house, the sounds of a paper bag being opened and closed were heard. There was the sexual assault but only one type; the missionary position. He fondled her breasts, very briefly and only once, and that without removing his gloves.

There was a moment when he was in the living room she thought she might have heard someone else speak. Then she heard the suspect whisper somewhat loudly, "I told you to shut up," followed by what she thought might have been another person. She still thought, however, that he was the only other person in the house. This was to become another trade mark; his being overheard talking to someone else.

Using a square knot and loop, he tied her feet together, after he assaulted her. Only then did he gag her with her slip. That was also when he asked her if she had any money. "You better have money in the house." Another developing trade mark. When the suspect left, he took ten dollars in paper money, plus three or four silver dollars, along with several packs of Winston cigarettes.

Later it was figured out, by both Gladys and the investigators, the suspect had lubricated himself with Johnson's Baby Oil prior to the rape. That was one more trademark of this developing rapist.

Investigators found a bird bath in the backyard that had been placed on top of a block of wood. It was generally agreed this was done in an attempt to reach the outside telephone lines in order to cut them. The suspect only managed to cut the insulation, leaving the telephone in operating condition.

Gladys was menstruating at the time but that did not deter the suspect. He had her remove the tampon and toss it on the floor beside the bed.

She described her assailant as a white male adult, between twenty and twenty-five, somewhat broad shouldered with a moderately muscular build–definitely not the rippling kind of muscles. He was no more than 5 ft. 9 in., weighing about 165 or 170 lbs. He had a lot of dark hair on his arms and legs. She added that he seemed to be under-endowed. In her words, "Not well-endowed." Again, a description to be often repeated.

He wore a mask made of a coarse-knitted material with a seam down the middle, the only opening for the eyes. He wore a dark navy-blue T-shirt with short sleeves and a pocket over the left breast. His gloves were like the mask, a coarse material but with elastic bands at the wrist–similar to the gloves a landscaper or gardener might wear.

Gladys suffered a small scratch next to her right breast. She also had a small scratch above her right eye of which she was unaware until the officers pointed it out. This apparently happened when the suspect held his knife next to her eye as he threatened her. Again, another developing trademark for this sociopath was to hold the knife close to his victim and somehow manage to inflict a minor injury.

Prior to this assault, Gladys had received two phone calls where the caller simply hung up when she answered the phone. Then, over a two week period after the assault, she received five or six more hang-up calls.

As it turned out, this did not happen with most of his victims. He generally stopped calling them a week or two before the assault. It was only after he left the Sacramento area that he began to call his victims after assaulting them.

Gladys had the feeling that of late she was being watched. It was nothing she could put her finger on, but still it was there. She did see a man in a green car around the area whom she had not seen before.

Months later, while being re-interviewed, she remembered the suspect held the knife in his left hand, and in her opinion was left-handed

One other point of interest came out of this hunt through the reports for other victims. Gladys, who lived on Paseo Drive, recently had contact with the military hospital at Mather Air Force Base. As it was told to me by another investigator, her mother died in that hospital. Since her father was retired military, it was entirely plausible Gladys's mother would have been admitted there for treatment.

While I was aware of a possible connection between the East Area Rapist and the medical field, I had not yet considered a possible connection between people just visiting a hospital or those who worked in them. For the time being that tidbit of knowledge was mentally tagged and stored.

For the record, the Mather base hospital was not a large one, nor did it have a large staff. While investigating the murder of a twelve year-old babysitter in 1972, I had reason to visit the facility. It consisted of a long corridor with something like three or four rooms on each side. At most, the entire hospital staff numbered no more than three or four people on duty at any time. When a member of the hospital staff became a suspect in the murder of the young girl, insisted he was working the night of the homicide, it was absurdly easy to shatter his alibi.

Chapter 18:
The Second Assault

August 29, 1976
Malaga Way
Rancho Cordova

About 3 A.M., the younger of two sisters awoke to the musical sound of the chimes hanging from the curtain rod in her bedroom. What she saw got her instant attention. There, at her bedroom window, was the silhouette of a man prying at the window with his left hand. A strong smell of after shave lotion reached her through the still closed window. Her physical response was immediate and definite; she went directly to her mother's room and woke her up.

With the mother now awake, the two of them tried to wake up the fifteen year-old sister. Refusing to get excited, the older sister chose to remain in bed, leaving it to her mother to call the Sheriff's Department.

Instead of making an emergency call, the mother and her youngest daughter returned to the window where the silhouette had been seen. As they walked into the room they saw a figure run across the backyard towards the fence. Thinking the prowler was probably gone, they went into the kitchen to call the Sheriff's Department. Wanting to keep as low a profile as they could, they sat on the floor to use the phone. Before they could dial a single number, they heard those singing chimes as they hit the floor. Almost immediately a half-dressed figure lunged around the corner into the kitchen and straight at them.

Whispering, "Freeze," through clenched teeth, while pointing a gun in their direction, the half-dressed figure commanded them to hang up the phone. That was when Mrs. Roberts grabbed the wrist of his gun hand, turning it away from her and her daughter. The gun-bearing intruder responded by beating her over the head with the gun and a short, twelve inch, yellow, wooden club that he holding in his left hand.

As Mrs. Roberts succumbed to the brutal beating, he whispered, "Don't worry, all I want is your money. You won't be hurt if you cooperate."

After a moment, when Mrs. Roberts ceased to struggle, he got the two of them to sit on the couch. Once they were sitting, he began tying their hands behind their backs. Mrs. Roberts, still not very fond of this plan, began fighting her way towards the front door. As they struggled across the room and out the door, the half-naked assailant continued beating her on the head. Ultimately, both intended victims made their way out the front door to their next-door neighbor's home, who let them inside.

Hearing the struggle raging, and her mother telling someone they should accept God, the older sister made a quick exit out the bedroom window. She also made her way to the neighbor's house where the three of them were reunited.

Later, during the neighborhood canvass, a woman who lived across the street reported hearing the commotion. When she looked outside, she saw Mrs. Roberts and her youngest daughter running, screaming to a neighbor's house. She last saw them as they disappeared inside the house.

As she watched this drama unfolding in front of her, she saw a man in white shorts hide in some bushes. It was not until Mrs. Roberts and her daughter were safely inside the neighbor's house that he stood up and calmly walked down the street. She couldn't help but notice that he walked upright, with the bearing of a military person or police officer. The interviewing officer told her the man was not wearing white shorts but was nude, which took her by surprise.

There was a sheriff patrol car two blocks away at the time of the assault. By the time the call for help had been placed, a unit assigned, and it actually arrived on the scene, ten minutes had passed. By then the suspect had "disappeared in the dark of the night." He probably just walked two blocks and was home.

Mrs. Roberts described the suspect as a white male, between eighteen and thirty years old, light-complected and slim. His legs were well-tanned, without much hair on them. He was not very heavy or very strong. She felt that in a fair fight she could take him, a sentiment to be shared by others. His estimated weight and height was 165 lbs., 5 ft. 9 inches.

He wore a stocking type mask, but it was not nylon or knit material. His shirt was a light-brown T-shirt. Around his waist he wore a wide, brown, lineman-type utility belt. His gloves were black. On his feet were ankle high, dark-brown shoes with laces.

The youngest sister, who had been the first to see him, described him as about the same height, slim, and with a light complexion that tends to go with people who have blond hair. His legs were well-tanned, but his butt was not. Obviously there was enough of a contrast that the woman from across the street thought he was wearing white shorts.

Mrs. Roberts described the suspect's speech as a forced whisper, which she took as an attempt to make his voice sound much deeper than it actually was. She thought his voice was normally high pitched. When he began to get nervous, his voice sounded shaky.

Two days later, at 3:30 A.M., the neighbor who saw him hide in the bushes had an intruder inside her house. Nothing was taken, nor was she confronted.

Mrs. Robert's husband was a dispatcher for SMUD, a Sacramento utility company. This may have been why she felt described the belt that the suspect wore as a lineman's utility belt.

The club described by the two victims was almost certainly the kind considered part of standard police equipment, up until about 1970. The gun also sounds like what might have been used as an off-duty weapon. The description of the belt sounded like the standard Sam Browne belt, except it was brown as was the suspect's clothing. Considering the color of the clothing and the description of the equipment, there is a very good chance there was a connection with the Army, Marines, or possibly a private security company. It would not have been part of Air Force issue, however.

No questions were asked of the victims about homes for sale, hang-up phone calls, or burglaries in the neighborhood, until one year later when they were re-interviewed by Sergeant Bevins. He was told there had been no homes for sale, nor any hang-up calls, nor burglaries. I am willing to bet a canvass of the people living in that neighborhood, at the time of the assault, would have revealed a different story.

Chapter 19:
The Heat is on—Us

As public awareness of this latest serial rapist grew, our telephones rang almost incessantly. As often as not, the calls were from that den-of-inequity, also known as "the 4th floor." That floor was where all the top brass hung their hats. Thanks to the growing media attention, they were beginning to receive pressure for a quick resolution to this series of rapes, now officially dubbed the East Area Rapist.

This was about the time that Carol and I became partners, sometimes riding together and other times going in opposite directions. We always conferred at the end of the day, putting together our gathered information and working up directions for what to do next. This was a professional relationship that was to last for the next eight or nine months. To this day, we remain the best of friends.

It was Captain Stamm who figured out how the title "East Area Rapist" probably came into existence. Captain Stamm also figured out the person who alerted the public to the existence of this latest serial rapist. The credit for that most likely falls on the shoulders of one journalist. As a reporter for the *Sacramento Bee*, Warren Holloway's beat was the police beat. Of all the journalists I've ever known or heard of, he was the only one that cops trusted—at least minimally.

Having some trust meant Warren had free run of the detective division. It may have been, when wandering around the detective division, he spotted the one page bulletin I had patched together, alerting detectives that a serial rapist was on the loose in the east area of Sacramento. The next step was an easy one. The title "East Area Rapist" quickly took hold, and endures to this day.

With all the growing publicity over these crimes, Chief Deputy Fred, from the fourth floor (who was my personal nemesis), along with the Sheriff, began to take a personal interest in how the investigation was progressing. It was early one morning that Captain Stamm came into my office to say the Sheriff wanted us both in his office; so off we went. It was pretty apparent when we entered his office he was already two sheets to the wind. I say "already" as it was well before noon. Bottom line, the Sheriff wanted an update on the investigation and exactly what was being done about it from my end. As we were walking out the door, I told the Sheriff it was entirely possible we had not only one serial rapist on the loose, but three. The Early Bird and Early Morning rapists, although identified, had not been arrested. So, they still had to be counted.

That apparently was a mistake. For that reason, and two others of which I am aware, I suddenly attained a lofty position on the Sheriff's septic list, which meant the entire fourth floor as well. This also meant Chief Deputy Fred was no longer my only detractor in that part of the kingdom.

In spite of Fred, my relationship with the fourth floor had been fine until that morning. From then until the Sheriff was unelected and Fred retired, my relationship with higher management became less than sterling. To say that this happens only in the Sacramento Sheriff's Department is nonsense. This kind of political BS happens in just about every place where there is a command hierarchy. A couple of years later, when a new Sheriff was sworn in, I was invited into his office for a friendly visit.

Years after both the former Sheriff and I retired, he invited me to his house for a visit. I think it possible that after he left the public arena and got away from the ego-building atmosphere, he slowly descended back down to earth. I never did stop by for that visit. I lacked both trust and respect for top management to establish any kind of relationship, no matter how inconsequential or fleeting the relationship might be.

Born of this sudden public awareness of the East Area Rapist, brought on by the local news-media frenzy, was a demand for a public forum. People wanted to know what was going on. It was decided Carol and I would attend the meetings at the Del Dayo Country Club. We were to provide an explanation to the general public and answer their questions as best we might.

It had only been nine months since the last rape by the Early Bird serial rapist (for whom there had been little media attention). Now, suddenly the media had the public stirred to near hysteria. They apparently had no idea this was a totally different guy. The media never once made any attempt to claim the EAR and the Early Bird suspect were one and the same. It was always the members of the two local law enforcement agencies who insisted they were the same. Still, the pressure led to the public forums. We even made a private presentation to the local FBI, in their office.

Carol and I spoke at two public forums. Probably because I outranked her, she agreed to do the presentations. She was clearly nervous, but being chivalrous by nature, I felt better her than me. Carol was doing really great, but when she seemed to be getting into trouble over some minor details, I joined her. I was better able to answer some of the questions because I was the one who had been micro-analyzing the collected information. Together we answered all the questions presented to us that night and the following night.

Near the end of the second night of our assignment, a man stood up and berated the Sheriff's Department for not having already arrested the suspect. Strutting up and down the aisle, he loudly proclaimed that in Italy, where he was from, this kind of thing would not be tolerated and would be dealt with quickly. After a few minutes of this nuisance, I asked him what he was worried about, that he was not going to be raped. He made a caustic comment, then shut up and left. Although there were two more forums conducted by the Sacramento Sheriff's Department, this was the last one I had to attend.

Seven months later the strutter and his wife were targeted by the EAR; note I said seven months, and not the next day, as many seem to think was the case. Personally, I do not believe they were selected because he shot his mouth off at the meeting. They may have been selected for that reason, but there was another possibility that we would not be aware of until after the next assault.

While we were inside, regaling the public with our ignorance, Sergeant Irwin was tasked to wander around the parking lot on foot, watching for anything that might strike his interest. This is a tactic investigators often use when investigating a homicide. Someone will be assigned to attend the funeral, or any other place where people will gather in response to someone's death or a major injury. They typically film the event as well.

Officer Barbara Tahara-Skay, who was patrolling the area with the same assignment, pulled over a light-colored VW bug as it was leaving the parking lot. It was being driven by WMA with thick curly black hair. He was 5 ft. 9 in., 170 lbs., late 20's. He was employed by the California Department of Justice (DOJ). I collected his personal information, which I followed up on later. Had that guy confessed to the rapes at that moment, our response would have been the same as it would have in 1978 and beyond; arrest, hold for 72 hours, then release—for there was zero evidence. But today, it would be well-worth the effort to investigate him a little further, such as checking his DNA.

In 2008, long after I retired, I contacted Assistant District Attorney Ann Marie asking permission to review the reports of the EAR investigation for the express purpose of looking for some open-ended leads—among them the identity of that DOJ employee. Her immediate response was, "Why? What are you going to do with the information?" I never did get to see those reports. I'm not sure she even had possession of them. Lieutenant Root told me that he was also not allowed access to them either.

The irony in not being allowed access to the reports is this: Before I retired, I was asked to take those reports home, which I did. Unable to store them properly, I turned them over to Lieutenant Cheris. Toss in the fact that not only would those reports not exist but for me, I probably wrote more than a few of them, so you can see why I feel it's ironic. According to the production manager of a TV show that aired a program about the East Area Rapist, the problem of territoriality is basic to all entities he deals with, which includes the agencies charged with this investigation.

I have since learned those reports are now in the custody of the Sacramento Sheriff's homicide division. The captain in charge at that time stated that no one, other than a full-time, sworn, police officer with a valid reason, will be allowed access to those reports.

Chapter 20:
Creation of a Task Force

Early in November, 1976, I was sitting in my cubby hole, interviewing a victim of sexual assault (behind a closed door) when Lieutenant Root blew in, unannounced.

His entry into my pocket-sized office reminded me of a similar entry by another detective executive lieutenant only a few months earlier. Under very similar circumstances, I was in my office interviewing a victim of the Early Bird Rapist, when the office door (which due to the personal nature of the conversation was closed) suddenly burst open with a loud bang. In came all 300+ pounds of said lieutenant. Without uttering a single word, he looked directly into the face of the rape victim, who was sitting just a few feet to his left, belched loudly, then refocusing his glare, went straight to the file cabinet behind my desk. Grabbed something off the top (of which he probably had no interest), turned, and stomped out. Not once did he utter a single word to either of us. This time, Lieutenant Root, who in no way other than rank resembled his predecessor, took the same four or five steps necessary to reach that very popular cabinet, announcing along the way that there was a task force being created, and he was there to collect my reports.

Always the gentleman, Lieutenant Root said, "Hello," when he entered and, "Goodbye," to the sitting lady as he retreated out the door with a handful of papers.

Later on, I was to share an office with Sergeant Bevins and Carol Daly which meant a bigger–as in much bigger–office. This was probably because somebody was worried about me being behind closed doors, unchaperoned, with the occasional rape victim. Or maybe it was that popular cabinet, with the mysterious papers, that they were worried about. Probably they needed a place to store their broom.

The task force, I learned, was to consist of Lieutenant Root commanding, and Sergeant Bevins, the lead investigator. To assist them would be a number of officers pulled from their regular duties in the detective and patrol divisions. Like a lung inflating and then deflating, the size of this task force would be constantly changing. Their sole focus would be the East Area Rapist investigation.

Although not officially part of that task force, Lieutenant Root wanted me to continue as I had been. This meant my assignment was the same as when I first worked for him, as a rookie detective, in 1972. I would begin at the crime scene and work backward. Sgt. Bevins would follow the more traditional role; begin at the crime scene and follow clues to where ever they led.

As Detective Bureau Commander in 1972, Lieutenant Root followed the philosophy that real detectives did not have to be assigned cases to do their job. His thought was to go out into the world and develop sources of information. From those sources learn of crimes committed and the identity of the suspects. His tactic worked perfectly.

Now, I was to follow a similar path with this current investigation. My efforts would be devoted to researching each assault before and after the fact, analyzing the information, follow any clues that I came across while looking for ways to improvise.

To do this, I intended to do what I was already doing. I began with each assault, learned what facts I could leading up to the assault, and monitored all reports of prowlers, burglaries, and suspicious circumstances. I hoped to determine how the suspect selected his victims. My ultimate goal was to predict where and when he would strike next. In short, a crude, pattern analysis. I'm not sure I even knew what pattern analysis was.

This also meant I was free to work the hours I wanted, when I wanted, where I wanted, alone or with a partner– just so long as I focused my efforts on the serial rapist. There is not an investigator out there who would object to those conditions. Not one. I had an enviable assignment.

There was more to this task force than a just lot of detectives assigned to follow leads. Some strategy was to be employed.

"Fight fire with fire" must have been part of the strategy, as five deputies were assigned to prowl on foot all night. Referred to as "X-Ray Units," they were to wear street clothes, wander around backyards, sit in trees, and be present in the areas where the assaults had occurred in Rancho Cordova. Officers in unmarked cars were around as well as a group of volunteers. The volunteers were all CB radio operators and dubbed "EARS" Patrol.

These five X-ray officers were not the only ones who wandered at night in the areas the EAR was known to travel.

I, too, was one of them. But I was in a comfortable car with a borrowed, military, night-scope, and I did not confine my prowling to Rancho Cordova.

At the time the night-scope was called a star scope, and it was not nearly as powerful as they are today. Armed with keys to all the county parks, I spent a lot of time along the American River trails and public parks. Always someone was with me, as backup. I even had people posing as night fishermen on the American River. We did stop a few people of interest, and hopefully we did not release the real suspect.

Sergeant Jon Bowman, of the Sacramento Sheriff's Department, was one who often rode with me on those nights. Once, my nemesis Fred heard Bowman talking about the night surveillance. Talking to Bowman, but looking straight at me with a rather meaningful look, he commented that more officers should be out there doing the same. He had no idea that it was I who was taking Bowman on those expeditions.

Additional eyes, in the form of reserve deputies, were added to the force—all looking for this psychopath. Two, with whom I was personally acquainted, were neuro-surgeons who drove patrol cars at night. Their day job was performing brain surgery while instructing student doctors at the Sacramento Medical Center. Originally owned by Sacramento County, this hospital had been taken over by the University of California, Davis.

This was also when someone decided another good investigative tactic would be to set up a trap house. That is a phony household. To this end, Sergeant Mike Henretty and a female detective took over a house in Rancho Cordova. There they pretended to be Mr. and Mrs. Normal Person. I have no idea how they went about this, and if the two detectives were ever "at home" in the evening. In hindsight, it was a foolish maneuver. Whoever set up the trap house had no concept of just how the suspect went about his self-appointed tasks. Needless to say, there was never any indication of a prowler in or around the house they had rented. That particular project lasted for a few weeks and then was abandoned.

A few days after this task force was implemented, I noticed something in the new process that was slightly amiss. It was something innocuous, like a system for handling the reports. Really no big deal.

That same day, Captain Stamm meandered into my office, chewing on an apple, just to visit. Thinking I was being of some help, I told him what I had noticed. He stood there looking at me, his mandible working like a hungry machine, then turned and walked out the door. I clearly remember his muffled comment as he snapped off another bite of apple, "Sounds like sour grapes to me." I also remember thinking something about, " Ignorant ass, " and grade school.

So I did what any experienced and dedicated cop would do. I called the Sheriff's personal secretary. After explaining to Lois Spencer what I'd noticed, I mentioned the subtle fact that if my name were connected, the brass would just ignore it. Agreeing, she said she would take care of it. Apparently, she did. The next day, the problem, whatever it was, had been corrected. With Lois as my clandestine intermediary, I went to her one more time with the same successful result. People rarely appreciate how invaluable a good secretary is.

In 1993, while in the process of retiring, a reporter from *the Sacramento Bee* interviewed me about this case. She also interviewed Lieutenant Root, who told them I was unhappy with the task force because I wanted to be in charge. Root knew that was an absurd statement. His comment was probably based on Captain Stamm's response to my comment regarding a small problem in his developing task force.

Chapter 21:
Search for Victim Similarities

Destined to become an integral part of the newly-formed task force was Sergeant Mike Henretty. Mike, a tall, soft spoken, dark haired gent, left the Sacramento Sheriff's Department years before, but like many otherts who had followed that path, he was soon to return. Now he found himself responsible for compiling all available data on the victims, along with any concrete results of the investigation.

The closest he came to success was when he found three successive victims who had been to the same pizza parlor in the same month. He was much closer to the answer than anyone suspected.

The Big Top Pizza Parlor, now gone, was located on the west side of Manzanita Avenue, between the two exits leading onto Winding Way. The pizza parlor was almost across the street from the Crestview Bowling Lanes. Those papers, with the information Sgt. Henretty had compiled, were also in my possession when I retired. However, they were beginning to fall apart which was one of the reasons I was prompted to pass them on to someone else.

To assist in that search for similarities, I found myself responsible for creating a questionnaire for the victims. In actuality, several of us participated in this project. The packet totaled about two pages of detailed questions regarding the victims' activities, where they shopped, etc. Carol Daly came right to the victims' defense, saying they would all object, thinking they had already endured as much invasion of privacy as they could stand. The project was approved. Naturally the responsibility for delivering, explaining, and recovering those packets went to Carol .

Years later, when I came across Mike, he told me it was after a show-and-tell, to office brass and visiting investigators, he realized we knew no more than when we started. So, he quit the department again and moved on. But before he quit, he received a phone call about a suspicious subject seen in a woman's backyard. Both Mike and I met with this young woman at her place of employment, and then we visited her house, where she lived alone.

This young woman was a bank teller on Watt and El Camino Avenue, but she lived off Sunrise Boulevard in Citrus Heights. She was home one afternoon when she saw a man enter her backyard from the front gate. He was dressed all in khaki but did not have a clipboard with him. The khaki-clad man wandered around her backyard and never looked at the meter. He wore no identifying name tags or insignia that she could see. She called the local utility company to learn they had no employees in that area that day, nor was her meter due to be read for several more days.

Chapter 22:
Still Innocent

December 18, 1976
Ladera Way
Fair Oaks

While the task force creation intermingled with office politics was going on the EAR was also active. He proved it when he targeted a fifteen-year-old girl. He introduced himself to her just as he did with Marcy. Catching her totally by surprise from behind, he held a knife to her throat. In a forced whisper through clenched teeth he said, "Make a move and I'll kill you. Do you have any money in the house? When are your parents coming back? You better tell me so I will know how much time I have." These statements were just about word for word the ones he whispered to Marcy, except now he whispered them to Alice.

After his self introduction was over, he marched Alice into a utility room. As they walked towards the room he threatened her with, "Get moving. If you say anything or flinch I'll push the knife all the way in and I will be gone in the dark of the night." He really liked that phrase.

What occurred over the next hour or so was a literal repeat of the assault on El Segundo the previous October. He forced her into the backyard where he tied her, then he began ransacking the house. He could be heard putting something into a paper bag. As he was leaving, he tied her to a picnic table.

It was on that table a bloodied Band-Aid was found. It was carefully collected, logged, and transported to the crime lab. The blood stain was found to be group ABO, specifically type A+. Alice had no injuries requiring a Band-Aid, so it was thought to belong to the East Area Rapist.

It is worth noting he did not cut the telephone cord this time as he did in other assaults. Why he did not is anyone's guess.

Alice described her assailant as maybe 6 ft. tall with a regular build. His whisper was loud and she believed intended to sound rough, but she felt his natural voice was probably higher pitched. That was a description we were to hear again and again. He wore a nylon ski-type jacket, with a zipper in front, and a dark ski mask.

By deduction, Sergeant Irwin located the only port of entry into the yard which was past a neighbor's geriatric poodle in the yard directly behind the victim's house. All the other nearby backyards were inhabited by younger, unfriendly canines.

As with the other crime scenes, there was a school nearby and another large drainage ditch. The difference here, as Sergeant Irwin discovered, was part of the drainage ditch was below ground.

Having never experienced sex, Alice had no frame of reference by which to judge the suspect's penis size. But even better than her opinion was the doctor's medical report which stated her hymen was intact. This was after she had been raped three times!

One other thing happened at this scene that stands out. While in the victim's house, doing whatever I did, Captain Stamm arrived on the scene, which was something he rarely did. Asking me to step outside, he handed me a set of car keys. Pointing to a car parked at the curb, he told me it was mine for the duration of my assignment to this investigation. Apparently he and Lieutenant Root felt that since I was putting in so many hours on this case, and responding to all the scenes, I should have a car permanently assigned. I felt like a high-school kid who just got permission to drive the family car. That car remained with me until I was transferred out of the detective division. It was greatly, greatly appreciated.

With the exception of one house that was located around the corner from where the victim was assaulted, there is no record available for what was learned when the neighbors were contacted during the neighborhood canvass.

That one house, on Galewood, had an unwelcome visitor a week or so earlier. Somebody broke in while the woman living there was on the phone. Whoever it was left without harming or even speaking to her.

Chapter 23:
Sacramento Police Join the Hunt

January 18, 1977
Glenville Circle
Sacramento

The first assault in 1977, by the EAR, occurred on Glenville Circle. Broadly speaking, Glendale Circle is located at the southeast corner of Watt Avenue and Highway 50, which puts it within the city limits of Sacramento and smack in the jurisdiction of their police department–a fact that was not at all unappreciated by the staff of the Sheriff's Department. It was this assault that inspired the Sacramento Police Department (SPD) to form their own investigative task-force.

There was no doubt that this attacker was the same one responsible for the other attacks that had occurred over the past few months. Imagine waking up to a bright light shining in your eyes and the feel of a knife against your neck, hearing a muffled whisper forced through clenched teeth, "Be quiet. I won't hurt you. All I want is your money. Just your money, and I'll be gone."

It didn't bother him that this time his chosen victim was five months pregnant. After all, he already had one pregnant victim behind him. As with his other victims, he tied her hands behind her back, but this time with an electrical cord. Already blindfolded with a bandanna, he placed her panties over her head. His MO did not vary, not even a little bit, in

117

this assault. The ransacking, eating in the kitchen, sex acts, applied lotion–it was all there.

The only indication that the suspect had left was when his pregnant victim heard her car being driven out of the garage. Later, the car was found a few blocks away.

The victim in this assault was a secretary in the State Capitol building, in downtown Sacramento. She was not the first, nor would she be the last, EAR victim who worked in that area.

She described her assailant as a white male, about twenty-five years old, 5 ft. 11 in., about 180 lbs. His man organ was maybe six inches long. Compared to the other victims' comments, that was a glowing review.

 He wore all dark clothing. His jacket was light weight, and he wore leather gloves. The ski mask hiding his face was pulled all the way down to his neck. His pants may have been polyester.

Her description of the flashlight matched that of Marcy; it was very short with a bright beam.

The police investigators on the scene made an effort to contact all the residents in the area. They learned a blue sedan, with one occupant, had been seen on Glenville the night before the assault. No one in the neighborhood recognized the car.

One week prior to this assault, a neighbor, who had already experienced being burglarized, saw a man peeking into a window of a neighbor's house about 7:00 P.M. The neighbor coughed, letting the peeping Tom know he had been spotted. Turning, the peeper looked straight at the neighbor. He then immediately walked north on Glenville Circle. He was described as a white male, 6 ft. to 6 ft. 1 inch, twenty-five to thirty years old, with a medium build and dark hair.

About 10:30 P.M., on the 12th of that same month (January), another neighbor stepped outside to see a white male adult walking across her front yard. Spotting her, he immediately took off running. She described him as 5 ft. 7 in. to 5 ft. 8 in., late teens to early twenties, thin build, wearing a beige sweater with some sort of design, and tennis shoes.

The following night this same witness noticed that her porch lightbulb, which had been on the night she saw the trespasser, had been removed from the fixture.

At 8:30 P.M., on the night of the assault, a young mother and her son, whose house faced onto Glenville, watched a man walk from the street into their backyard. Taking a huge chance, she stepped into the garage to be sure the door was locked then quickly back into the house. Peeking out a back window, she saw the same man standing in her backyard, looking at her as she was looking at him. In her words, he took off like a rabbit, going over the fence into her neighbor's backyard.

This trespasser was described as white male adult white male, 5ft. 11 in., 175 lbs., medium build with a small waist and broad shoulders, giving him a very athletic appearance. His facial features were those of a thirty-five or forty-year-old man. He appeared extremely agile and fast. His hair style was a type worn in the 1950's, cut as it was above the ears, combed up in front and back, in a pompadour style. His hair was so neat as to possibly have been done by a hair stylist. It was either salt and pepper or blondish colored. No facial hair was seen. Clothing worn by this suspect consisted of a dark blue, light-weight jacket and dark colored pants.

His appearance struck her as if he belonged in the neighborhood. Had he gone back out the gate he entered, she would have thought no more about the incident.

One month before this January assault, another neighbor saw a man walking out of their backyard. When asked what he was doing the man said he was taking a short cut. He too was white male, twenty-three to twenty-six-years-old with a dark complexion, 5 ft. 8 in. to 5 ft. 10 in., and 165 lbs. His build was muscular and similar to the man whose hairstyle seemed to be out of the 1950's. Out of all the suspicious persons seen in this series of crimes, this was the only one to have a tattoo. It was a blue one on his upper right arm.

There were other reports of prowlers in the immediate area after the ones already described. One was a white male, twenty-three years old, who was seen crouching in the bushes behind 112 Waterglen Circle.

Chapter 24:
Determined Ignorance

By this stage of the investigation it seemed everybody, as in everybody, in both the Sacramento Sheriff's Department and Sacramento Police Department, were convinced; the East Area Rapist and the Early Bird rapist were one and the same person. From where I stood, it looked like this had become a major issue. The result being departmental treasure, in the form of money and hours wasted trying to combine two separate and unrelated investigations into one. No progress was possible.

Carol Daly and I not only knew who the Early Bird suspect was but also the identity of a copy cat known among local investigators as the Early Morning rapist. Had anyone, at any level, at any time, bothered to ask either of us, or even read our reports, they would have received instant enlightenment. There may even have been a clap of thunder or bolt of lightning. A judge, who signed not one but two search warrants submitted for the body hairs and blood of this Early Bird suspect, volunteered both times to sign an arrest warrant if we wanted one.

This argument, about whether or not the rapes by the EAR and the Early Bird were committed by the same suspect, reached a crescendo one morning, at the end of 1976. That morning Captain Stamm again told me there was to be at a meeting in the Sheriff's office, and I was to be there. Again, I asked if I could decline the invitation, and again he told me no, that I had been specifically ordered to attend. So attend I did.

As Captain Stamm and I entered the Sheriff's office, I noticed a lack of the usual chatter that accompanies small meetings. I spotted Undersheriff Phillips sitting in a chair to the right of a small divan, in front of the Sheriff's desk. Seated on the divan, directly across from the Sheriff, was Sergeant Mike Henretty, then Fred, and next to him, Captain Stamm. I took a chair next to Captain Stamm, which was about as far removed from that big hulk behind that desk as I could get.

The presence of Fred confirmed what I had anticipated. He and I had an established working relationship dating back years. To call it mutual contempt would be sugar-coating it. Mike Henretty was there because his duties as analyst gave him a more complete comprehension of the investigation.

During this entire fiasco, the Sheriff, gazing down from his lofty perch at his supplicants seated upon the low-sitting-divan with shortened legs, hammered questions at Sergeant Henretty. In answering, Sergeant. Henretty frequently quoted Sergeant Irwin. I have no idea why, as Irwin knew virtually nothing about the earlier rape series.

All through that meeting, the only two people allowed to speak were Sergeant Henretty and the Sheriff. Being the only person present who had actually studied ALL of the reports in depth, I occasionally tried to interject.

Not once was I allowed to comment. Based solely on Sergeant Henretty's comments, the Sheriff concluded that Sergeant Irwin must be right in his conviction that the same person was responsible for all the rapes that had occurred in Sacramento over the past six or seven years. So why wasn't Sergeant Irwin there instead of me?

I left that gathering, gnashing my teeth while speculating on the probabilities of genetically-inherited lobotomies, and any statistical correlation to those with one long eyebrow. In my opinion, there was some good research material available.

It was only a few weeks later that the Sacramento Police Department detectives apparently figured out there were two separate suspects with which to contend. It was about then that somebody, somewhere in the Sacramento Sheriff's Department must have uttered a quiet, "Oh." The change in the investigative emphasis, by both departments, was so subtle I almost missed it. With that change came a closer cooperation between me and the Sacramento Police Department detectives. Finally, being on the same page, we were able to communicate.

In October, 2004, during a brief stop at a coffee shop in Auburn, I came across Mike Henretty. We visited for a short while. Naturally the conversation passed onto the subject of the long, frustrating investigation. Mike chuckled, saying he remembered that meeting well, and wondered why I was there.

That was the last time I was to see my friend Mike. Mike died later that same month.

Chapter 25:
Early Bird Rapist vs. East Area Rapist

Since there was obvious confusion about whether or not there was one or two rapists, I'll take time to clarify this issue. Even today, there are those who insist they were one and the same.

Late February or early March, 1976, Carol Daly, following Captain Stamm's orders, dropped a stack of sexual assault reports on my desk. That had been my introduction to the Early Bird Rapist. Until then, I only knew of that serial rapist through local news media and the occasional report I might have reviewed as a patrol sergeant. There were more than forty such reports. They were right on par with the yet to happen EAR series. Although it did gain some media attention at the time, it did not begin to gain the same amount of attention as the EAR.

For both the curious and the non-believers, let me lay out a few substantiated facts about these two depraved individuals.

Both were white males. That is undisputed.

The suspect referred to as EAR was believed to be late teens to early 20's, 5 feet 7 inches to 5 feet 9 inches tall, with a thin to medium build, and in athletic condition. He probably had dirty-blond hair worn to just above the collar. He was very light complected yet tanned in the summer. He had either dark blue or brown eyes and light brown hair on his legs. He preferred single story homes that were located second from a corner. His was a very distinct method of operation. This applies to both before and during the sexual assaults.

A tipoff the East Area Rapist was in an area was an increase in the number of illegal entries and prowlers. Crank phone calls and suspicious circumstances only cinched that he was active. His haunts were always near schools and green-belt areas, with main thoroughfares close by. Houses for sale, sold, rented, or just built were close by as well.

His method of confronting a victim, and how he proceeded from there, was rigid. His forced whisper, anger, and the need for tight control were all apparent. When upset his voice tended to rise to a higher pitch. He didn't fondle his victim. He might look at her breasts, but he seldom touched them. The more pain he could cause his victim when assaulting her, the more he seemed to enjoy it. There were some indications he was homosexual—possibly in denial, or angry about it.

In the first two EAR related assaults that I responded to, the victims had volunteered the suspect seemed to have a very small penis. At first we took these comments as just that—comments. As I located other reports of assaults by the EAR, I found other victims had provided the same information. So, we began asking each victim for a description. The descriptions of his penis were so consistent that we actually contacted a medical doctor to learn if the cause for this had a medical name.

So, what to do with that information was the next question. It was (hopefully) a given that none of us were going to physically examine any suspect's private parts. The decision to use this description, as just another physical marker in determining whether or not a sexual assault assailant was the EAR, came about on its own—very much like height and weight estimates are used. For those same reasons, we also hoped to determine whether or not the suspect had been circumcised. Some descriptions were definite; he was circumcised. Others were not so sure.

The EAR's actions and statements could best be characterized as someone who spent the majority of his time fantasizing about sex and his dramatic role in it. Comments like, "I will be gone in the dark of the night," indicated a lot of alone time spent fantasizing. His actions tended to show he held a lot of real anger with most of it directed at women in general.

The Early Bird suspect was 5 ft. 9 inches tall, in his thirties, with a stocky build and a paunch. He preferred to strike in apartment buildings. When assaulting a victim, he would first take time to fondle her, perhaps in hopes of making her more receptive to what he was about to do. He did not prowl beforehand.

None of his victims, nor their neighbors, received the deluge of hang-up calls or indications of prowlers or burglaries which were peculiar to the EAR attacks. Homes for sale were not all that common in the areas where he struck. No comment was ever volunteered about the size of his penis, as was the EAR's. The actual act of sex by this sociopath was restricted to intercourse. He did not force the victims to engage in sodomy, oral sex, or make them masturbate him. He never used lotion on himself. There was no indication he was living in a fantasy world of his own making.

The Early Bird Rapist held a grudge, conceived in the 1960's, against the Sacramento Sheriff's Department and not women in general. His grudge began when two Sacramento Sheriff Department deputies arrested him and an accomplice for possession of stolen property.

Once, when he thought the boyfriend of his victim was a deputy, he sat and waited for him to come home. He fancied himself as pretty tough and assumed he could whip anybody he encountered.

The identity of the man, thought to be the Early Bird Rapist, was developed when his van was seen by a neighbor. Three deputies parked at a field near the scene of an attempted rape. His intended victim, who saw him standing next to a lighted lamp, tentatively identified him by a driver's license photo-lineup conducted by the responding patrol officer, Ron Smith. A lot of circumstantial evidence was to follow that indicated he was, in fact, the Early Bird rapist. I remain convinced to this day. I would bet my life on it. But as anticipated, as soon as word got out why we were investigating him, his friends would circle the wagons and change their stories. That is precisely what happened. Better to let a serial rapist go free than hurt a friend's feelings. May the women, who are in the lives of those "friends," sleep secure in their beds every night.

In April, 1976, this suspect, who lived in a nearby mountain town, suddenly uprooted his family and moved to Montana. He returned for two or three days in early May, then left again. He was lucky and he knew it. His luck got even better when the East Area Rapes began, and in the eyes of his family and friends, proved his innocence. He was innocent of the EAR series of rapes, but not those others. Both he and I know it.

The copycat suspect was a different story, and came as a total surprise, for he was the son of a locally prominent individual. Let's call him Doug. Detective Arnie Petty, the polygraph examiner for the Sacramento Sheriff Department, was the one who administered the polygraph test to Doug.

Arnie rushed into my office right after the test saying, "Dick, he failed the test big time." An observer from the Department of Justice, who was monitoring the polygraph test through a hallway window, commented, "That guy has a major problem." Right after Arnie left, Doug came into my office. There were sweat stains literally from his armpits down to his belt.

There was only one reason this guy even entered my mind as a possible suspect. He had an all-consuming interest in those rapes, which he explained away by claiming he wanted to help with the investigation. His presence around the office was not noticed so much because his father was around a lot of the time himself.

I developed an all-consuming interest in Doug as soon as I became convinced there was a copycat rapist mixed up in this series. There was literally no evidence, physical or circumstantial, and with DNA still in the dream world of scientists, there was nowhere to go. Perhaps a better interrogator could have gotten him to confess. But with polygraph results not admissible, and no evidence of any kind, he walked.

Oddly enough the Early Bird and Early Morning series of rapes stopped just as attention was brought to bear on both of these suspects.

January 24, 1977
Primrose Drive
Citrus Heights

It was their habit, these two boys, to share the walk to Kingswood Elementary School every morning. Their conservations were typically about sports and "What did she really mean when she said...?" So wrapped up in the trials and tribulations of growing into young adults, they never noticed much of what they passed on those treks, for after all, a neighborhood never really changes. Lawns got mowed, people went to work, school had to be endured, and life moved on. Except there had been a minor change in the environment which they did notice but thought little of at the time. It was not until a Sheriff's deputy knocked on their front doors very early one morning did they really give that change any thought.

Over a three or four day period, these two boys, walking to school, passed close by a dark colored American made car parked on Primrose Drive. Each time they passed, the driver looked down and to his right as if looking at something on the seat. His face averted as it was, they never got even a glimpse of his profile.

The school those two boys attended was Kingswood Elementary. Kingswood is situated atop a small rise off the east side of Primrose Drive. Sprouting out of that rise, between the school and the street, is a small stand of conifer trees. As if exiled from the king's woods, a solitary tree stands below those conifers next to the curb. It was beneath this exiled tree that the two youths saw the car parked, facing north on Primrose.

Both boys agreed to undergo a hypnosis session in an effort to recall any details about the driver or the car. They agreed, but then a few days later, when I offered to schedule a time, they had changed their minds.

From the vantage point of the unidentified driver, large block red letters "JB&H Realty FOR SALE" could be seen. The home that was for sale, which was about a block and a half away from the driver, was where the East Ares Rapist struck early in the morning of January 24, 1977.

Earlier, the evening before, a small gathering of friends had been gathered. Some of the guests were, no doubt, from where Gloria worked as an accountant on Capitol Mall in downtown Sacramento. Leaving the party aftermath for a morning cleanup, Gloria, the sole occupant of the home, was in bed by midnight.

It might have been 1:00 A.M., or it might have been 3:00 A.M., Gloria was not sure of the time, but she was sure of what happened. She was jerked from a deep slumber by a pair of hands which grabbed her around the shoulders. Gloria's instinctive response was to scream and struggle against those hands. She was sure her life depended on it.

A low sounding, or hushed voice, whispered a warning; if she screamed again she would be killed. With that threat, she felt a small sharp point pressed against her neck. That was when she stopped trying to escape whoever had invaded the sanctuary of her bedroom.

Once she decided on compliance, Gloria felt herself being turned onto her stomach and her hands tied behind her back. As soon as that was done, she was blindfolded, gagged, and her feet were tied together. Here, as in his other assaults, her hands were bound so tightly it would be hours before full feeling returned to them.

Still, in that terror filled room, unable to see or move, she not only maintained her rationality but her awareness of smell. She could not help but notice the pervert, who had just captured her, had a really, really bad body odor about him. He just plain stank!

Besides his bodily stench, she quickly noticed two things about her assailant; he had a very small penis and it had lotion on it. She described his penis as no more than five inches long and thin.

Besides the forced masturbation, there were the feeble attempts at rape and ransacking of the house. Once she heard him in the kitchen gulping from a can. During these sexual assaults he repeatedly spewed forth vulgarities aimed at her, then ordered her to repeat them, only to tell her to shut up when she tried to comply. She had the impression that he was not interested, not even a little bit, in the act of sex.

He assaulted Gloria twice, removing his gloves the first time but not the second. Finally, when the nightmare began to end, he untied her only to re-tie her, this time with a different material, taking the original bindings with him. This was a new trick for the EAR. He probably wanted the originals as a souvenir.

In this assault, as in the others, an attempt to mislead her, or possibly the police, was made as he called her by name. Most of his victims were never fooled into believing they and the suspect knew each other or had ever met.

The first officers to arrive on the scene were patrol officers Bill Roberts and Mo Bailey, both of whom did an outstanding job of establishing the basic facts and protecting the crime scene. Sandy Carlson and I arrived a short time later. I don't know where Carol was, but she would interview Gloria at a later time as she would ultimately do with every victim.

The very first thing I noticed when I walked through the front door of that house on Primrose was a short breakfast bar. With the kitchen on the left side and the living room on the right, there was a large block of cheese perched on this breakfast bar.

Someone, presumably the suspect, had gnawed on the end of that cheese leaving behind some obvious tooth marks. Detective Vin Sant, who arrived at my invitation, walked through that door with me and wondered aloud, "Would the ID technicians be able to get any useable tooth impressions from it?" Sitting in the kitchen were two, empty Coors beer cans. We later learned these had been drunk by the suspect.

Shortly after we arrived, the blood hound, with Mr. Krupicki hanging onto the other end of the leash, burst in through the front door. Within seconds, the dog was on the suspect's trail. That trail led out the back door, around the corner and down the street, around another corner. There the trail ended at the curb on Guinevere.

Immediate examination of the scene revealed waffle-stomper type prints in a neighbor's backyard but not in the victim's backyard. This neighbor was just around the corner on Farmgate Way. This made about the third time waffle-stomper prints had been found at, or next to, a rape scene attributed to the EAR.

At the time this assault occurred, we had three people of primary interest under twenty-four hour surveillance. As I was being dispatched to this crime scene, I asked to have it confirmed where those persons were. Among them was Art Pinkton. All three were at home, and to all indications had been there all night. Another person of some interest was a janitor at the Sunrise Shopping Mall. Later that night Detective Vin Sant and I confirmed he was, in fact, at work all night. In this case that meant he had been locked inside a department store with fellow employees during the assault. It was probably the best alibi we would ever encounter.

Farmgate Drive and Primrose Drive intersect. It was on Farmgate where a woman reported seeing a suspicious person two days before the assault. About 12:30 A.M., she saw a man walking very quickly and quietly across the front yards of her neighbors' houses while staying close to the shrubbery.

As soon as she saw him, she stepped back behind some bushes. There she felt she could watch him without being seen herself. This man, who was walking across her neighbors' front yards, stopped and looked straight at her. He was standing no more than twenty feet away. No emotion of any kind showed on his face.

Now, a bit more scared than curious, she stepped back to her door calling for her son to come outside. When she looked back the man was gone. Still looking for him, she spotted a man standing in front of a house at the corner of Primrose and Farmgate, however, she could not be sure it was the same man.

Since there was a floodlight shining on the face of the man she saw, she was able to make a composite. A detailed composite was made, photographed, and passed around the entire county.

According to the description provided by this woman, the man she saw was a white male, 30 to 40, weighing about 175 and standing 6 ft. tall. He had a square face and dark curly hair. He wore a hip-length jacket of medium-brown color and dark pants.

A few days later this same woman reported finding a cigarette butt on the decorative bark next to her fireplace. The location was such that it could not be seen at night. The butt was filter type with two thin stripes. She concluded the butt had been deposited there the night of the 27th.

On the day of this assault, at about 12:30 A.M., this same woman's dogs (which she kept in her backyard) went ballistic—to the point the hair on their backs was bristling. She did not investigate, nor did she call the police.

Not long after news of this assault spread around the neighborhood, the same woman, who had watched the prowler, was talking to the newspaper boy when a jogger came by. The newspaper boy commented the jogger did not look like a jogger, which was what this woman was also thinking. Maybe he looked like the guy she had made the composite of? So, she jumped into her car and followed him. She lost him in the nearby Birdcage apartments, then she saw him walking out of an apartment and getting into a vehicle. The registration to that car came back to an oriental male who lived nearby, on Farmgate, and near where she saw the man walking across the lawns.

A couple of weeks after the assault on Primrose, we found ourselves back on Farmgate. Somehow we had learned Art Pinkton had a girlfriend living on Farmgate, just around the corner from the latest victim. Nothing of evidentiary value was found at his girlfriend's house, but once again Pinkton materialized in investigation.

While the investigation was focused mostly on this recent assault on Primrose reports of suspicious circumstances continued to come in from other parts of the county. Here are but two.

January 29th. A woman looked out her back window towards a vacant house on a small rise behind her own home. Standing in the backyard of that house for sale was a white male about 5 ft. 8 inches tall. When she reached for the telephone he took off running.

January 31st. It was between 2:00 A.M. and 2:30 A.M. when a woman pulled up to a stop sign at Oakcrest and Dewey

Drive. Instead of oncoming traffic she saw someone dressed in all black, wearing a ski mask and crawling on his hands and knees towards a front door. She looked to her right then back only to see the crawler knocking hard on her driver's door window.

Immediately and wisely she sped away, turning right onto Dewey Blvd but then slowed down and looked in her rear view mirror for the crawler. What she saw was him pulling a bicycle out of some bushes. Mounting the bike he started pedaling rapidly in the direction of her car. Right about then this woman felt enough already and left as fast as she could.

The idea of placing a phone trap on the victims' phones, should the suspect call them after the assaults, was one I had been working on since early December. It was not until the assault on Primrose that I began making headway on the idea.

A phone trap or trace is the term used when trying to determine where an incoming call originated. In that era, it was up to the person answering the call to keep connection with the caller open for as long as possible, and to jot down the time and day of the call.

It was Captain Stamm who made these traps possible by putting me in contact with the security office for Pacific Bell & Telephone Company. With their help, we managed to place a couple of phone traps on victims' telephones.

As they explained, the problem with tracing a call was with the routing. Each call was directed to a main station. Depending on where the telephone call originated and where it was destined, it might be routed through one or more locations before reaching its destination. The ultimate consequence was that some of them could not be traced; they originated outside the area where the trap was placed, with the trace being broken by the changes in routing.

My real interest in the issue of phone calls was whether it was possible for someone to tap into telephone conversations. As anyone who has ever watched or worked with a telephone installer or repairman knows, it can be done and is done routinely. I was more interested in tapping into the lines from someplace outside of Sacramento. The answer I got from the security office was a flat no, it was not possible.

Just before I retired I repeated this question to different investigators for the Pacific Bell Phone Company and was told yes, it could be done. I was given to understand the answer I had originally been given was to circumvent any chance of bad publicity or civil suits against the phone company.

In the end, it was all a moot issue anyway, for there were no calls from the suspect to his victims of which we were aware. The calls the suspect did make were still in the future.

Chapter 26:
AD HOC TASK FORCE

As might be implied by the presence of Detective Vin Sant at the crime scene on Primrose I already had a working relationship with the Sacramento Police Department (SPD). That relationship became closer once they created their own task force. Among this group were detectives Vin Sant, Sgt. Walker and Sgt. Bakarich. If one of us responded to an EAR related call we would immediately notify the other. In other words we formed our own ad hoc task force. This almost paid off one night when some citizens spotted a prowler in their cul-de-sac.

To get there I had to drive South on some street off American River Drive. The street was L shaped and no more than four or five blocks long. At the end of that street was a weedy field. As I approached this field I had a choice; turn left or drive into the field. I took the left turn then a quick right turn into the cul-de-sac where the prowler had been seen. The house where the prowler call originated backed up against that weedy field.

Again the blood hound was called for. Anybody care to guess where the dog led us? Right across that field and straight to the curb where I had the choice; turn left or go into the field. Then I remembered what had been there as I drove towards that curb but had failed to take note of. An older green Chevrolet coupe.

There were one or two other cars parked near there as well. Naturally that car and the others were gone. But for me not to have taken notice of that car and the surrounding area was inexcusable.

What was noteworthy about this incident was not my missing the car. It was when I arrived the suspect had already fled and the SPD officers were at the scene waiting for me and the tracking dog. The possible suspect car was still parked nearby. It was not until after that bloodhound arrived that the suspect car was gone. It would appear - if in fact that was his car - that he did not always leave the area when spotted or even after the police arrived.

Chapter 27:
Helping the Suspect

It was not long after this incident that the Sacramento Police Department task force troops told me of a change in their departmental policy regarding how their department would conduct this investigation. Once again, superior and forward-thinking of government officials shone forth in all its brilliance.

Orders had come down from the Sacramento City Council to the Police Chief not to call the Sheriff's Department when their officers responded to any call related to the East Area Rapist. They (SPD) would handle the investigation on their own.

This did not put an end, however, to our mutual cooperation. Ignoring that order, we continued to notify each other about EAR related calls and otherwise share in the investigation. Those instructions only showed that our continued cooperation was not shared with those at the top of the food chain.

Soon after the Sacramento Police Department detectives made me aware of this change in policy, a similar incident occurred at the Sheriff's Department. The incident left me very embarrassed and a little surprised with at least one officer, for I expected better of him, but not the other.

It was on February 4, 1977, when this pettiness was going on, that information was developed indicating we had a suspect identified: He might be the one for whom we were all looking.

The suspect was William Paul Boren, twenty-four years old, 5 ft. 9 in., with light brown hair. Boren had forced entry into a young woman's house on Pershing Ave. There he kept her terrorized for three hours while she lay blindfolded with her hands tied. She was not assaulted, nor did he use any lotion on himself. Sacramento Sheriff Department Officer Martin, ID technician, identified Boren from a single fingerprint lifted off a bedroom window.

There were no available deputies at the moment to assist, so I contacted the city task force, with whom I had been working. They were quick to send two of their own to stake out Boren's home. Sacramento Police Department Officer Vin Sant accompanied me back to our detective division, where I would bring the top brass up-to-date.

At the time, there was a conference room with a long table in the center. Detective Vin Sant accompanied me to this room where we were to meet with Fred and others. The memory of what transpired is still with me. Fred was standing just inside and to my left, as I stood in the doorway. At the east end of that long table stood Vin Sant, with two newly arrived computers perched on a counter behind him.

After I explained to the executive officer what I had done with the city troops and why, he walked past me, around the end of that long table, saying as he passed in front of Vin Sant, "I don't want the city involved. We'll do this without their help. Get those city guys out of there and our guys in there." Fred chimed in with, "I agree. I don't either."

I will forever more remember the expression on Detective Vin Sant's face and how his mouth literally fell open, just hanging there, wobbling in the breeze, as he stared after the disgruntled form passing in front of him.

There was not much chance anyone was going to keep any cop, who had worked so hard on that investigation, away–especially when it looked like we had the bad guy. Not even for a moment. In the end, Sergeant Backarich, of the SPD, and I made the arrest. We brought the suspect in through the back door of the Sheriff's Department where salivating reporters were lined up as thick as politicians at a lobbyist sponsored dinner.

No one who was there that day mentioned the subject again. I never spoke to Fred, as in NEVER, so I have no idea if he ever mentioned it.

Make no mistake about it, there was, and I'm sure still is, a strong rivalry between the two departments and I was among its advocates. There is, however, a time for that nonsense and then there is not. For the record the officers of the Sacramento Police Department never failed to provide me with 110% professional support when asked for.

Let me also point out that on the whole, the troops of both departments viewed their jobs as all-encompassing, beyond the neighborhood where they might be standing. They were all dedicated officers.

William Boren became a murder victim in the early 2000s. His DNA was compared to that of the EAR and found not to be a match.

Assault suspect, with head covered, is delivered to sheriff's office Thursday night.

Suspect brought into custody by Inspector Richard Shelby, (standing by car) and Sgt. Bakarich. Photo courtesy of The Sacramento Bee. (February 4, 1977)

Since it had become obvious that the high levels of both departments had neither the desire nor intention to cooperate, a solution was required if the working troops wanted to increase the odds of catching the EAR. That solution was simple; ignore the top brass. But a more appropriate response was crafted by the Sacramento Police Department's task force.

It was only a day after the incident, regarding who was going to arrest Boren, that I received a phone call from the SPD's task force. They wanted to show me an arrest yellow. An arrest yellow is a form filled out when someone has been arrested. It was yellow, in the 1960's, but who knows what color it is now. Anyhow, at the time it was still referred to as an "arrest yellow".

As I walked through their office door, I was greeted by one of them waving an arrest yellow above his head, saying, "We've solved the problem and here's the answer."

These officers had completed an arrest yellow. The spaces for the name of the suspect, his address, and the arresting officer's name were left blank.

The plan was not to notify anybody, above the rank of sergeant, until we were on the scene serving the search warrant. The name of the youngest recruit at the police academy would become the arresting officer. At the time, there were recruits from multiple law enforcement agencies attending the same academy. Imagine a new recruit waking up one morning to learn he had just solved the most notorious crime wave to hit the Sacramento area in years! Unfortunately, we never got to try out this plan. You can bet we would have done it.

Chapter 28:
Helping A Stalker

It was while still investigating the assault on Primrose Drive that Carol and I received a call about an envelope that was full of DMV driver's license photos. We were being asked to contact an employee of the Payless Store, on East Arden Way. As we walked into the store, the manager handed us a white business envelope stuffed with photos. A customer found it on the sidewalk in front of the store. The envelope contained only driver's license photos that had been neatly cut from the licenses. Without exception, they were all of attractive young women of different races. There was no identifying information with them – just photos.

We seriously considered the possibility these had been the work of the suspect responsible for all of the sexual assaults. A large number of people had handled that envelope and its contents, so no prints were developed.

Within a day or two of the envelope event, we received a phone call from a young woman who was being stalked. She lived in a small mountain community east of Sacramento. When commuting to Sacramento, or driving on errands, she would see him in his car following her. She had his car license number for us.

Using that plate number, we located this stalker. Our interview began in his apartment, then as we were leaving, it continued outside on the street. Inside the apartment he was so fascinated by Carol that I was able to wander around the room without his even noticing. It was probably her wigs. Not that she needed them, but she had a red one and a blond one. Most of us preferred the blond wig.

Wigs or not, she kept this guy so focused I was able to poke around without being noticed. I could probably have searched his entire apartment and he would not have even noticed.

It was when talking to this mobile stalker outside his apartment that it became apparent he was distracted by more than Carol's presence. While he was answering questions, I noticed he was standing in the gutter, idly swishing his feet back and forth, as the stream of water flowed freely over his shiny, wing-tipped, leather shoes. So focused on sounding innocent of any wrongdoing, he really had no idea he was standing in a gutter full of water. For her part, Carol looked a little amused.

This stalker admitted he had seen a woman driving her car. He wrote down her license plate number which he took to DMV. There for a small fee, he was able to obtain her name and home address. For him the next logical step was to follow her.

There was really nothing we could do about this gutter crawler, but we could, and did, raise a stink about the practice of selling private information to anyone with a couple of dollars. The practice of selling private information by the Department of Motor Vehicles came to an end a few weeks later.

Chapter 29:
Other Law Enforcement Agencies Help

It was not unusual to answer our home phone at two or three in the morning to the distinctive boom of Captain Stamm's voice assigning a mission. Always it was someplace a rape suspect was being held, awaiting our arrival. The problem was these law enforcement agencies who knew of the current EAR series of rapes were also aware of the Early Bird serial rapist. The people they were holding matched the physical of the EBR and not the EAR.

I almost lost Carol at the Humboldt County Sheriff's Department. We were there to interview a suspect they were holding for us. There were two male deputies and one female clerk at the front counter when we entered the building.

After interviewing the person they were holding, we headed back the way we came in. Only this time there were six or seven deputies standing around, like eager puppies waiting for a pat on the head. As soon as we neared the counter, they had Carol surrounded, peppering her with a barrage of questions and flattery; mostly flattery.

Offers to help came from as far away as Germany. One fine bright morning Lt. Root asked if I wanted to go to Germany. The military police had just telephoned him asking if we thought there might be a connection between the EAR assaults and one that had occurred near an American base in Germany. In that instance, a woman had been assaulted in the woods by a man with a knife. Just not enough to go on or I would have accepted the chance to go. Since all transportation was presumably to be provided by the military, I should have accepted anyway.

But the most relevant offer to assist by an outside agency came when they visited our department. That would have been two investigators from the Visalia Police Department.

Chapter 30:
The Visalia Question

If someone in Sacramento were to point their car south on Highway 99, they could expect at the end of a very long, four-hour drive to find themselves in the city of Visalia. Like Sacramento, Visalia benefits from a nearby college and military installation. They can boast of the College of the Sequoias and the Lemoore Naval Air Station. There was another similarity between Sacramento and Visalia however that was not as benign.

Between 1974 and December 1975, Visalia could claim among their population the distinction of a residential burglar and murderer. The hunt for this criminal became very intense, with a large number of investigators being assigned. That intensity, many believe, is what caused that suspect to abandon Visalia and make the four-hour drive north to Sacramento.

Local media attention, focused as it was on the EAR, soon caught the attention of people outside the Sacramento area and especially other law enforcement agencies. Among those paying attention were two of the primary investigators from Visalia; Sergeant John Vaughn and Special Agent Bill McGowan. That was how I came to find those two fine men sitting in my office one morning in early 1977.

They had two reasons for being in Sacramento. For one, they wanted to exchange information about the Visalia Ransacker and the East Area Rapist. Besides wanting to explore the possibility the two were one and the same, they had a person of interest then living in the nearby town of Davis. It was from these two investigators, and the reports they provided me, that I came to learn most of what I know of the Visalia Ransacker series.

Between 1974 and December 1975 the VR committed at least 125 residential burglaries. There was strong evidence this suspect was an avid prowler who spent as much time as a peeping Tom as he did breaking into homes. In September, 1975, these petty crimes turned into an aborted kidnapping and murder. The series seemingly ended in December, 1975, when the VR shot a flashlight out of Special Agent McGowan's hand.

Since Special Agent McGowan had come face to face with the suspect, they had a description. They also had a second witness. The descriptions that came from both was that of a white male, 5 ft. 9 inches to 5 ft. 11 inches tall and weighing 150 to 175 lbs. Rather than muscular or heavy he was described as pear shaped.

He was thought to be older than high school age with "mean-looking" eyes. Clothing seen was a ski mask, dark green pants and a dark colored shirt. His voice was described as high-pitched.

Officials at the Visalia Police Department arranged for someone to compile a criminal profile of the suspect. It is the only criminal profile I've ever read, or even heard about, that actually contributed to an investigation. It was so precise on two points, I had to wonder if maybe the author should be investigated.

The profile depicted the suspect as being employed by a utility company. It had been conjectured this theoretical employee lived up to ten miles outside the city limits and rode a bicycle to work and back every day. These two investigators quickly learned there was such an employee for Pacific Bell Telephone Company. This employee had, in fact, ridden his bike to work and back ten miles each day.

By coincidence, it was only two days after the shooting of Special Agent McGowan that this employee requested and received a transfer. That employee was now living in Davis, a small college town about fifteen miles from Sacramento. The suspect-employee continued to ride his bike to work and back every day.

I escorted the two investigators to the Davis Police Department where we met with a detective supervisor and a patrol officer. A plan was hatched; the patrol officer would make contact with this employee and get him to step outside to explain physical damage to the front end of the suspect's car. In the meantime, the two detectives and I would wait in my car. In effect, a street-side lineup.

The Davis patrol officer made contact at the suspect's house, asking him to step outside to explain the (obvious) front-end damage to his car. It ostensibly matched that of a hit and run. As this individual walked up to his car, he appeared to be very nervous. Apparently he had been riding a bicycle the fifteen miles to Sacramento and back every day, as his calf muscles were huge.

As the man inspected his car with the patrol officer, Special Agent McGowan began to squirm and in general, became upset. This witness detective, who was seated behind me, was not able to identify this man with the huge calf muscles as the person who shot him. Looking me in the eye, Special Agent McGowan said he had seen too many faces and heard too many voices to be able to identify the suspect.

From what little I knew of their investigation, I felt they had their suspect right there in front of us. I still think they did. If this guy was the VR, then he most certainly was not the EAR. The EAR was slim and this guy was not. He was tubby with elephantine leg muscles. I imagine bike riding thirty miles a day, five days a week, will do that to a person.

Chapter 31:
Victim Draws First Blood

February 7, 1977
Heathcliff Drive
Carmichael

It was early in the morning when those electrons, sputtering their way to freedom, caught my attention. That sputter was the forerunner to the announcement there had been yet another attack by the East Area Rapist. This time the attack was on Heathcliff Drive, a two minute or less drive from where I was at the moment. It was from this investigation that we would learn the suspect's blood type, plus, at least in my mind, confirm the physical description of the suspect known as the East Area Rapist.

As I arrived, I noticed a small parking lot which jutted into the park right behind her house. The lot was probably just large enough to hold a half dozen cars at most. The only vehicle in it was a white van. The parking lot was also on the edge of the Del Campo High School Campus. 300 or 400 feet across the campus were the school buildings.

I went straight to that van, parking my car behind it so as to block it in. It was occupied by a WMA, who appeared to be about 25 years old. After I identified myself, and explained what I was investigating, he was totally cooperative. He explained that two other patrol officers had spoken to him about 4:30 that morning, so he was getting used to it.

I searched both him and his van. The reason for his being there was a little unusual. Working for the railroad, he often found himself up nights. With a fondness for watching the stars, he simply found an out-of-the-way lot where he would park. He had fallen asleep only to be awakened twice by patrol officers. About then, another officer joined us. Apologizing, he said Chief Fred had ordered him to investigate the same man I was in the process of interviewing. This would make the third time the guy in the van had been investigated that morning, with no change in the results. By now, he was becoming an expert at being a person of interest.

Ultimately, Fred and I found a way to get along. The last time we crossed paths it was not by either of our design. With the briefest of glances, we turned and without comment walked away.

Right after I was relieved from investigating the driver of that van, I made contact with Carol Daly, who was by then talking to Brenda, the victim. Brenda turned out to be one of my heroes.

She was a young wife and mother working on her master's degree in social science at Sacramento State College. Her academic studies were focused on corrections. Her internship was at two childcare centers, one of which was located in North Sacramento.

While speaking with Brenda, we made a cursory examination of the crime scene as well as an injury to the top of her head. It was a very small cut with some blood around it. She told us she got the wound while struggling with the suspect for his gun.

Maybe two inches off to one side of the injury, there was another spot of blood. Looking closer, we could not find a second injury, so we decided to take this sample to the crime lab for typing. From the top of the dresser in her bedroom, Brenda picked up a pair of scissors and handed them to Carol, who cut off the lock of hair with blood on it. Carol and I wondered about the possibility the daughter had been injured as well. We did not examine her, but her mother said she was unhurt. When Carol and I spoke with the two of them again, in 2011, they reaffirmed the daughter had not been injured. All of this, examining and collecting the sample of her bloodied hair, was occurring at the same time Brenda was telling us what had happened. A more detailed interview was to be done later by Carol.

Brenda was in the kitchen with her husband helping him prepare for work, when he became agitated. Just before he left for his job at the Cobble-Dick Glass Company, he said he felt something was wrong. She thinks maybe his instincts, developed in Viet Nam, picked up on the suspect who must have been just outside their back door. As he was leaving, he called out to Brenda, telling her there was a van in the parking lot near their house and to be sure all doors were locked. She checked all the locks, but assumed the slider door at the rear of the house was locked. That turned out to be her mistake.

About five minutes after her husband left, a man wearing a mask, gun in one hand and a knife in the other, rushed through the unchecked door. The first thing he did was order her to sit in a chair there in the kitchen.

"Don't scream or I'll shoot you. I just want your money. I don't want to hurt you." Ordering her into a chair, he began to tie her up. He threatened to kill her if she resisted.

Shaking like a leaf in the fall breeze, Brenda did exactly as ordered. Using shoelaces he brought with him, the suspect tied her hands behind her back. After tying her hands, he held a knife to Brenda's throat telling her to shut up and do what he said or he would kill her. When he told her to get up and go into the bedroom she replied, "No!" His response was to hold the gun to her head and tell her all he wanted was to tie her to the bed.

On their way to the bedroom, Brenda noticed the suspect had closed the door to her six-year-old daughter's bedroom. Although still shaken, Brenda once again had her wits about her.

Once in the bedroom, he shoved Brenda onto the bed. It was when he began tying her feet that Brenda began to actively resist. She stopped resisting when he placed the knife against her throat. The pause in her resistance was only temporary.

She quickly began to move off the bed while yelling at her useless dog, "Get the man," and at the man, "Get the fuck out of here." While trying to keep his gloved hand over her mouth, he tried to force her into submission by beating her on the top of her head. By now, she was flat on her back on the bed, and the suspect was sitting on top of her telling her to shut up.

Brenda could feel the gun in the suspect's right-hand jacket pocket. As they struggled, she managed to get the gun out of that pocket. Right there, she became one of my personal heroes and remains so to this day. Here she is with her hands tied behind her back, blindfolded, gagged, recovering from a very recent very major medical procedure, and she is whipping this psychopathic puppy's ass. There is no limit to my admiration for this woman.

As the suspect realized he no longer had control of his penis-extender, Brenda had her thumb on the trigger. She could not be certain which way it was pointed. Fear of sending a bullet into her daughter's bedroom kept her from pulling the trigger.

They struggled over the gun for a few more moments with the suspect finally regaining control. Right after he regained control, he began to angrily and repeatedly stab the bed next to Brenda's head.

From that point on, the assault tended to stick to the pattern of the other's.

The suspect was interrupted by Brenda's six year-old daughter, who first spotted him in the bathroom. To her he said, "Be quiet or I'll cut you up." Then he tied her with cords cut from something in the house and laid her next to her mother.

The six year old's response was to yell, " No!" and to shout as loudly as she could that he was going to kill them both. As the two lay there side by side, tied up, they each began to make as much noise as they possibly could. That was when the suspect ripped the cords from both telephones.

Once they were sure he was gone, they both scooted to the back door and yelled at a neighbor for help.

Throughout this ordeal the suspect spoke through clenched teeth in a harsh whisper. As in some of the other assaults, he ran the tip of his knife blade up both the victim's legs and laid it on her abdomen.

The combined description of the suspect was a white male, 19 to 23 years old; 5 ft. 11 inches tall, weighing 185 lbs. His legs were hairy and very white. He was wearing a sweet-smelling after shave lotion. Brenda described his slick wick as extremely small.

The suspect's clothing consisted of white jockey shorts under black pants and a dark-blue waist-length nylon jacket. The gloves were a cheap black leather and his mask was dark green. This time he wore red, white, and blue tennis shoes, a shoe that would have been more popular among teenagers than adults.

The gun was described as a "thin" gun with a long barrel and dark wooden grips.The knife they described as four to five inches long and dull.

Brenda said their house had been burglarized about a month prior to the assault. Not at all surprising, they had also been honored with a number of hang-up phone calls during the past several weeks.

While Carol was conducting a more detailed interview, I did the required door-to-door contacts. I gained more information on that day than I had from any other neighborhood canvass.

As expected, I learned that prowlers and hang-up calls were common. It was just around the corner, on Crestview, where the young woman doing her laundry in her mother's garage was assaulted. In that neighborhood canvas officers located a neighbor who had seen a skinny blond teenager in the backyard of a house on Heathcliff Drive.

One of Brenda's closest neighbors reported seeing a white male climbing a fence between 7:30 and 8:00 that morning. The fence bordered a large cement drainage ditch near the park. There is a popular spot along the fence where kids climb over, and that is where the young male had been seen. He was about 20 years old, dressed in a blue jacket and pants, giving the impression he was dressed in a blue leisure suit. His hair was light-brown and short. It was right after seeing the kid in blue that the witness was contacted by the victim, who said she had just been raped.

The day before this incident this witness and his wife were working in their yard when he spotted a man who was acting strange. His wife told him that every time she looked, the man in the park was staring at her. However, when he looked at the man, he was staring at the trees and birds or maybe just air.

He described the man as a thin WMA, with short, brown hair, dressed in a blue leisure suit. When he walked away, he did so in an awkward manner.

A high school student, who normally walks down Heathcliff and then across the park to Del Campo High School, made an interesting observation. Just as she and her friend turned onto Heathcliff from Crestview, she saw a white male running fast.

He appeared to have come from the corner house on Heathcliff, which would have been Brenda's house. She watched until he disappeared into the park at the end of Heathcliff.

She described him as a white male, 5 ft. 8 to 5 ft. 10 inches tall, with a medium build—but not skinny. His hair was short and a light color. He wore a blue jacket, which appeared to be heavier than a wind breaker but not bulky. His pants were darker and may have been Levis. She guessed his age as early 20's.

Another lady, who lived about three or four doors from the victim and her daughter, was looking out her kitchen window at about 6:45 the same morning of this assault. Being aware of the EAR attacks, she idly wondered if maybe the young man she was watching walk down the sidewalk might not be the EAR.

She described him as a WMA, 23 to 25 years old, 5 ft. 11 inches tall, with a thin build. He was light complected and had neatly trimmed collar-length hair and a full mustache. When she saw him, he was walking in the direction of the victim's house.

There was another couple who, a few weeks earlier when returning home from a walk around the neighborhood, saw three squad cars turning from Heathcliff onto northbound Crestview. As the three squad cars pulled away, a person 5 ft. 9 inches tall, dressed all in black (which included a ski mask), stepped out from behind a short thick bush. The bush was in the middle of the front yard of the house on the northeast corner of Heathcliff and Crestview. It was the only bush in that yard and was about half way between the sidewalk and the house. Completely ignoring the couple, he stepped out onto the sidewalk, and with hands on hips stood there watching the squad cars drive away.

If the couple told me what they or the man in black did next, I have forgotten. But I do know they did not call the Sheriff's Department. They probably figured why bother; if the cops didn't see him the first time, what were the chances they would the second time around?

Someone contacted the staff at Kelly Grammar School, which is located on the edge of the park and very close to the victim's house. They reported seeing someone dressed in blue running quickly across the park towards Del Campo High School. The direction and positioning of this running person would have him heading straight for the high school parking lot, located on the opposite side of the campus buildings.

Another witness lived diagonally across the street from the victim. It was about the same time the suspect was leaving the victim's house, when this neighbor saw a white male, about 5 ft. 9 inches tall with a slender build, blond hair, and in his late teens or very early 20's, coming from beside the victim's house, walking rapidly as he went straight to the area with all the pine trees, next to Kelley Grammar School. He was lost from sight as he entered the small grove of pine trees near the school. It was the opinion of this witness that the man he saw had just come from Brenda's house.

When first seen, he was just in front of Brenda's house, passing within a foot of her front yard. He could have been walking along the edge of the park and never have been any closer to the victim's home. The timing was perfect, for his having just left Brenda's house.

Going to where the witness pointed, I found a visible trail leading into the center of the grove of trees. There, in the midst of the trees and clearly visible in the dirt, were tennis shoes prints with a herring-bone pattern. Marlboro filter-tip cigarette butts, plus a few empty beer cans, were scattered about as well.

It is probable that afer leaving Brenda's house, the suspect went straight to that group of trees, then cut across the park to the Del Campo High School parking lot, where he used what ever kind of transportation he had waiting to make his getaway. It is not likely he would have left any kind of transportation near the scene, or for that matter Kelly Grammar School, as it was full daylight and it would have been seen by someone.

Between 6:00 and 6:30 on the morning of the assault, a neighbor living on nearby Moraga Way heard her dog growling in her backyard. Standing on a table for a better view, she spotted two white males in their 20's, about 200 yards away. When they saw her, they ran. Then one of them turned and ran back, where he lay down behind a pile of asphalt. One was wearing a knit cap, a dark-blue pull-over sweater, and dark pants.

As soon as Carol and I finished with the scene of the crime, we took the bloody hair sample straight to the crime lab for typing. I clearly remember handing it to specialist Gilmore while explaining to him where it came from. Just as clearly, I remember him telling us he had already typed the victim's blood and it was type B, which is what this sample would be. At the same time he was telling us this, he was typing the sample we brought in. He looked puzzled for a moment, then called his co-worker over to double check his results. They tested it again and got the same results.

We already believed the EAR to be a non-secretor, which means his blood type could not be determined from body fluids. It was because of the Band-Aid left behind, during the assault on Ladera Way, that we suspected he had blood type A+. Now it was confirmed, the EAR had type A+ blood.

For years, the secretor vs. non-secretor status was used to eliminate persons of interest as being the EAR. It has since been proven a person can be both a secretor and a non-secretor. All those people removed from the list as possible suspects, due to their secretor status, are back on it.

Within days of this assault, neighbors of the victim noticed a man who routinely parked his black-over-red sports car near that same grassy area. For over a week he would park his car, about 10:00 P.M., then disappear on foot into the grassy area. At 6:00 A.M., he would return to the car and drive off.

Finally, after more than a week of this, a neighbor confronted the man as he returned to his car. The neighbor told the driver not to return, and if he did, he would give his car description and license number to the Sheriff's Department. With a snarled comment, about it not being okay to park on the street anymore, he left. He was not seen again.

The vehicle description and license number was given to a patrol officer. What became of that information is not known.

Chapter 32:
Pursued Shoots Pursuer

February 17, 1977

It was a quiet evening at home when a noise on the patio caught the attention of both the 19-year-old athlete and his father. Together they stepped outside to investigate. Immediately a prowler took off running. Just as immediately the teenager was hot on his tail. The prowler was over the fence into the neighbor's yard and out of sight in no time. The young athlete was right on him. As the young athlete reached the top of the fence, he heard a click. He recognized the sound of a gun being cocked, but it was too late. There, waiting for him below the fence, was the prowler, gun in left hand, pointed directly at him. The shot knocked the youth backwards off the fence. There was a second shot, but no idea where it went. The father of the injured youth dragged his son to safety. The first bullet had burrowed into the boy's mid-section. To this day, he suffers from the effects of that wound.

They described the prowler as about 20 years old, 5 ft. 10 inches tall, and 170 lbs. He had on a blue watch-cap, blue sweatshirt, dark pants, and white tennis shoes. A composite of this suspect is at the end of this book. A 9 mm round was found at the scene. It is all but a given, this was the East Area Rapist.

The only information I gleaned from any neighborhood canvass that might have been done was that a witness saw three men running from the area. When seen, they were about two blocks away. Nothing connecting them to the shooting was ever developed.

Chapter 33:
Revered Suspect

Of the many questions left unanswered in this investigation, there is one that still haunts me. It was one of those leads I wanted to dredge out of the old reports, to which I no longer have access. It was a lead that Lt. Root had assigned the moment I walked into the detective division early one morning in 1977.

There was a small Irish tavern with a typical Irish name. Maybe it was "Murphy's". This tavern, no longer in existence, was situated on the southwest corner of Fair Oaks and Eastern. What occurred here gave us a very viable suspect, who still remains a viable suspect. The parking lot behind the bar bordered Eastern Avenue on the west side. This parking lot was bigger than one would expect for a small neighborhood tavern. Scattered around it were several light standards, of which some worked and some did not.

The father of a waitress who was employed at that bar was a California Highway Patrol officer. On this particular night he chose to park at the back of the lot to wait for his daughter to get off work, then to follow her home. She had no idea he would be there waiting for her.

While parked beneath a standard with burned out lights, the CHP father watched as another car pulled into the same lot. It parked in a far corner which was also unlighted. As his daughter was walking from the bar to her car, the driver of the second car got out and stood by his open car door watching her. He stood there until she got into her car then he got back into his. As she drove out of the parking lot she was followed by this second car, and right behind that second car was her father. The young lady made it home with two cars following her and she never had a clue. Once home, she remained there for the night. I no longer recall how long the father followed the suspect afterwards, but you can bet he wished he had his patrol car right about then.

This was the information that greeted me the moment I walked into the detective division that morning. The registered owner of that second car was a preacher whose church was located on Whitney, right off Watt Avenue. He lived with his wife and children not far from his church, no doubt where he preached about loving thy neighbor.

I spent a great deal of time learning what I could about this so-called Man of God. A search warrant was served on him for samples of hair from his head, his eye lashes, and his pubic area, along with a blood sample.

For a while, I was inundated with calls from citizens, which included other CHP officers, telling me what an upstanding citizen this preacher was. The preacher was a dud and not a pillar of the religious world. I still don't know what he was up to and don't expect I ever will. We were never able to put him anywhere near a rape. But today, obtaining a DNA sample would be a good idea, if for no other reason than to cover all the bases.

Chapter 34:
Suspect's Stash Found

March 8, 1977
Thornwood Drive
Sacramento

This psychopath's next selection for spreading terror was on Thornwood Drive, a short street like Heathcliff, which was also laid out in an east/west direction. By coincidence, it was not far from the house of the preacher who had followed the girl home from work.

At the east end of Thornwood Dr., and a block or so from this assault, is a thick stand of coniferous trees. Directly opposite these trees is, or was, the Conan School Park. A cyclone fence separated the park from the conifers. Opposite the fence was an athletic field with a track paralleling the fence.

Carol Daly, Lt. Root, Sgt. Bevins, Sgt. Irwin, and I all arrived at the victim's home close to 7:30 A.M. After a quick briefing, we each set about our routines. The normal routine was to call Mr. Krupicki and his bloodhound, but this time that was not done. New to the Sacramento Sheriff's Department was the use of a patrol officer's dog named Prince. So instead of the tired old bloodhound, a young and energetic German shepherd was made available.

This time the EAR chose as his victim a young, unemployed mother and her young son. Her estranged husband, whom she would later call for support, was employed as a teacher at

Florin Elementary School which was located in the southern end of Sacramento County.

Entry into the home was gained by first breaking a small corner of window glass. Then bending the window pane back just far enough to reach in, he flipped open the lock. How he managed to break just a small corner of glass, without breaking the whole window, is another mystery .

As in the other assaults, the EAR announced his presence when he rushed into the bedroom where the victim was fast asleep. His whispered remarks were similar, "Do you feel this butcher knife? If you scream or anything, I'll kill you. All I want is your money. I won't hurt you if you don't scream." To the investigators it sounded like a broken record, with little or no variation in his whispered rantings.

Nor were there any variations in his actions leading up to the rape. Again he used vulgar language; for some reason it seemed to excite him.

First exception was he fondled her breasts, but only briefly. He had touched two of his previous victims on their breasts, but also briefly. In those instances, as in this one, he seemed to have no real interest in touching them. This time, he removed his gloves during the sexual assault. In one other assault he had removed one glove during the sex act.

One other, and a very unusual action he took was to squeeze the lady's thumbnail very hard between his fingers. Later, blood was found on her thumbnail, but it was not hers. The results of any analysis of that blood are not available.

When being interviewed, this latest victim commented the suspect's performance in the sex acts was notably lackluster when compared to his actions when tying her up. She felt the act of tying her hands so brutally tight, along with his constant threats, was a form of sadism he enjoyed far more than he did the sex.

We learned from footprints found in the backyard that there had been prowlers over the past days and possibly weeks. Apparently the prints had been made by the same person responsible for this assault, as they matched perfectly.

Besides the prowler, this victim had also been the recipient of multiple, annoying phone calls. The calls were the type where the caller does not speak or hang up but instead just leaves the line open. About a week or so before she was assaulted, the calls stopped.

We also found Salem brand cigarette butts outside the victim's house. The bindings used to tie the victims hands and feet were again standard, black, and also brown shoelaces. So far there was really nothing new being discovered. Then there was the neighborhood canvass. That was to be a whole new story.

Long before this latest assault, I had learned that if one were to go back a day or two later and contact the neighbors a second time, one could usually obtain more information. It seemed if given a little time to think about what had happened, memories tended to churn out other tidbits of information. That certainly happened here.

The corner of Northwood Drive and Thornwood Drive was two or three doors west of the victim's house. Stepping around that corner onto Northwood Drive, you will find yourself standing next to a tree. Short, as trees go, it is perhaps 20 feet high, and at the time it was heavy with foliage. Right next to the tree, perched on a driveway was a full-size pickup camper. It was here on this corner that we were fortunate enough to fill in a gap in the EAR's method of operation.

Immediately beneath the tree were a number of tennis shoe prints with the wavy, zig-zag pattern. Cigarette butts, with light colored filter tips that had either one or two stripes on them, lay scattered about. There were enough cigarette butts to indicate someone had spent some time there, probably over a matter of days.

The house that belonged to the driveway was set back from the street about 30 feet. A long, low hedge bordered the wall that faced the driveway, then it wound around to the back of the house running the full length of the house.

A young man about 20 years old answered my knock at the front door. When I asked about any incidents, phone calls, or anything out of the ordinary, he had an answer for me. Escorting me around the corner of the house he pointed at the hedge and said, "We found a bag inside that hedge." A few weeks earlier someone in his family found a cloth bag hidden inside their hedge.

In that bag had been a ski mask, a pair of gloves, and a flashlight. Here was proof the EAR stored his equipment where he prowled.

Realizing they had something important, they called the Sacramento Sheriff's Department. Whoever answered the phone that day gave them an answer that upsets me to this day. "Throw it away," were the instructions they received. Some people credit the EAR as being real smart. Maybe, but he did not always need to be.

The family, having no need for a used ski mask and gloves, threw them away. However, they did keep the flashlight. This silver colored flashlight used one "D" cell battery. The lens was one to two inches in diameter and gave off a bright beam. As the girl Marcy had said, "You could hide it in your hand."

I, and a few others, spent weeks chasing that flashlight all over the United States. We stripped it inside out and were never able to discover even a smudge of a print nor any identifying mark. Had internet been available, it might have been a different story, but we never located the source or even who manufactured it. Some have called it a navigator's flashlight, but it was most definitely not a navigator's flashlight.

In recent years, I have tried to locate that flashlight again, but it is a part of history now. At some point after I retired all the old files, which contained a list of possible suspects, were destroyed, and that flashlight was stored in the same file cabinets that as they. My best guess is that it is now languishing in a nightstand or someone's garage.

Following this bonanza of information, I continued down and around the next corner, eventually making my way to the house directly behind the victim's home. There on Wood

Crest Drive, I spoke with two young men who also had some interesting information to share.

These two reported seeing a WMA, about 5 ft. 9 inches tall, in his 20's, park an old yellow pickup by the curb between their house and their neighbor's house. They saw this pickup at the same location several nights in a row. Each time they saw the driver, he was walking towards the back of their neighbor's yard where they assumed he was going to visit.

A description of a rounded cab, hood, and fenders, with rubber tubing over the tailgate chains, placed this vintage yellow pickup in the 1940's to possibly very early 1950's.

Like the two young witnesses on Primrose, these two agreed to undergo hypnosis in hopes of pulling some more details out of their deep memories. When I called to make an appointment, they too had changed their minds.

These two boys were not the only ones to spot that pickup. A 15-year-old girl had seen an old yellow pickup three or four times over a period of three weeks, parked near 3828 Wood Crest, which again was behind the victim's house. She usually saw it a little past 7 P.M.

Thinking it was a visitor of her neighbors, she thought little of it. It was old with a rounded roof and a small dent next to the right headlight. The tailgate had chains with rubber tubing on them. The last time she saw it was during the week of February 28 − March 4. The California license plate had the letter "J" followed by either a "1" or "L". There was no rear bumper.

DMV investigators were contacted with this information. To help us, they provided the registration information for every pickup of 1940's and early 1950's vintage pickup that was registered in California.

The information was passed on to every law enforcement agency in California, as well as all branches of the military. A large number of detectives, myself included, spent untold hours going to these registered owners. Obviously, nothing ever developed.

About 6:30 on the morning of the assault on Thornwood, another neighbor saw a man standing on a porch looking into the window of 3148 Montclair (the corner of Thornwood and Montclair). She described him as 5 ft. 8 to 5 ft. 9 inches tall, and not a large build. He was wearing what looked like a gray sweatshirt, suited for jogging.

A woman, who worked for Hubert/Hunt/Nichols Construction, and her two daughters, had been receiving some rather strange phone calls. They were of the variety where the caller never spoke, nor was the phone hung up on the other end. Pretty much what this latest victim had experienced. The last time they received a crank phone call, it was answered by one of the daughters. The caller was a woman asking for her mother. By the time her mother got to the phone, the caller had hung up.

The usual routine of contacting the paper boy and the delivery man was done by Sgt. Irwin. What he did learn was the man who delivered milk to this victim lived very close to where the previous assault had occurred on Heathcliff. The day of that assault he found a screen had been removed from a rear window of his own home. Apparently this psychopath really covered a large area when he reconnoitered.

Not much of a description could be given by this latest victim, for as the others, she never really had much of an opportunity to see her assailant. She figured he was a white man who spoke in a clear but hostile whisper. She did not detect any accent or other characteristic to his voice or speech. All she saw of his clothing was a shiny jacket and gloves that felt like rubber.

It was no more than a couple of weeks later when a viable suspect for this particular assault was developed. This person of interest was a professional photographer who mostly photographed women. Sgt. Bevins obtained a search warrant for this man's house where he found nude photos of the victim. As it turned out, she had hired him to shoot the photo layout, so it was just one more false alarm.

That short barreled flashlight may have been the one lead we were looking for. As stated already, we knew navigators were being trained at Mather Air Force Base, but this small flashlight was not part of their issued equipment. With its chrome case, it would not have suited special forces.

Everybody knew a bomber squadron was assigned to Mather. Few knew that atomic bombs were moved in and out of Mather AFB on a semi-regular basis. Nor did that many know all navigators were trained at Mather AFB. Thanks to Russ Oase and his rummaging around on the internet, I now know considerably more about Mather AFB and its mission as a training base for aviation officers than I did at that time. Even the OSI failed to give us much information about the responsibilities of the base.

When responsibility for training navigators was moved to Mather AFB in 1976, the Marine Corps also transferred their MANS (Marine Aerial Navigator School) to Mather AFB.

Originally MANS was based out of the El Toro air station near Irvine, California. A personal contact, who was there among them at the time, believes there were never more than 20 or so Marines stationed at Mather AFB. Information from the internet indicates 130. Their training was done independently of the Air Force. None of them were members of the military police. Marine navigators included enlisted personnel, with the highest rank that of warrant officer.

In 1976, the TWENTY-NINE (VT-29), a squadron responsible for training naval aviation officers then stationed in Corpus Christi, Texas, was decommissioned. In January, 1976, the VT-29's responsibility was transferred to the 3535 FTW squadron at Mather AFB. There the Navy established a unit, designated NAVAIRTU Mather (Naval Air Training Unit Mather). Like the Marines, this unit was under its own command but housed at Mather AFB.

Most surprising was to learn that during this period of the Cold War, responsibility for training navigators at Mather extended not only to all U.S. Military, but to all of America's allies as well. Considering Mather had 7,600 assigned personnel, toss in all of NATO and personnel from other friendly nations, plus the other four military bases close by, the pool to draw on for suspects increased beyond my ability to count.

March 18, 1977
Benny Way
Rancho Cordova

Answering the telephone with, "Hello," she was greeted by a male voice she did not recognize. That voice identified himself as a roofer wanting to speak to her father. After telling the caller her parents were out of town for the weekend, she hung up the phone. Later she asked her father if he had expected such a call and he said he had not.

This call reminded her that for the past couple of weeks, she, her sister Amelia, and her parents had been receiving telephone calls where the caller would hang up without uttering one word. Once it sounded like a woman or girl in the background was coughing. There were so many of these calls that her mother twice blew a whistle directly into the telephone. It had been over a week since the last call, so there was probably no connection to this latest one. There would be three more phone calls that day, but Amelia's sister would not know about them as they were not for her or her family.

"I'm the East Area Rapist," followed by laughter then the telephone connection abruptly ended. That was the first call. The second call was a repeat of the first. Then a third call, "I'm the East Area Rapist, and I have my next victim already stalked. You guys can't catch me." More laughter and again the connection abruptly ended. These three calls were made between 4:15 P.M. and 5: 00 P.M. on March 18, 1977, to the Sacramento Sheriff's Department.

As it turned out, this was an "in your face" declaration by the suspect. That same evening he struck for the 15th time, the 4th time in Rancho Cordova. This particular assault was on Benny Way. Benny Way connects with Dolecetto Drive, smack in front of the house where the dog was beaten to death in 1974.

An opportunity to prevent this assault and maybe even catch this psychopath presented itself later that same evening, but as happened before, the opportunity was ignored.

About 9:30 P.M., a 15-year-old girl who was home alone watching TV happened to look out a window. Across the street was a man she did not recognize, walking across her neighbor's front lawn and into their backyard. Scared by what she had seen, the 15-year-old closed all the windows, locked them, closed the blinds, and then returned to watching TV. She never called anyone to tell them what she had witnessed.

An hour later, 16-year-old Amelia, walked through her front door. She had just gotten off work from the local Kentucky Fried Chicken establishment and had plans for the night. With her parents leaving town for a few days, she was going to spend the night with a friend. Picking up the phone, she placed the receiver against her ear and began to dial her friend's number.

The forced whisper she heard did not come from the receiver in her hand but from behind her. She was being greeted by what you now know was the EAR's way of a formal introduction, "Don't scream or I'll kill you. Don't look at me or I'll kill you." Amelia turned to see a ski masked freak holding a green handled hatchet above his head. It was aimed straight at her face.

What followed was right out of the East Area Rapist's text book. All the forced whispering, tying, blindfolding, leaving the room, ransacking, quickly returning to check on the victim, eating, leaving the house for a few moments then coming right back inside; it happened as it had in all of the assaults. Same statements, lotion applied to self; it was all there. None of it was any different. He seemed to enjoy tormenting Amelia with vulgar statements while clicking a pair of scissors near her face each time he walked by her. Tormenting his victims appeared to be far more enjoyable than sex to this psychopath.

After an hour of this torture there was a knock at the front door. The knock caused the suspect to run out the back door. Later Investigators found a green handled hatchet on the backyard fence. They also found two empty Dr. Pepper soda cans beside the garage. Since Amelia was the only one in the family who drank this type of soda, and they were not her cans, then it had to be assumed the suspect brought them and consumed them. Two real estate signs for Kastoras Realty were also lying in the backyard.

In keeping to our own MO, a tracking dog was brought to the scene. As always, it was hoped that in determining the suspects route of travel, we might stumble across someone who had seen the suspect. The dog led investigators out the backyard, across the front lawns, and around the corner. The trail ended at the curb of 2626 Ellenbrook.

When interviewing the neighbors, we learned a prowler wearing a stocking mask had been seen on February 21, 1977. Unfortunately, while the blonde color of his hair could be seen, his features were so blurred any further description was not possible. Here again, the hang-up calls to the neighbors were common.

Besides prowlers, the neighbors also noticed vehicles they did not recognize as belonging in the neighborhood.

One was a 1966 or 1967 four-door Bel Air which was parked near the SE corner of Ellenbrook and Malaga. This car had a school decal of some kind. It was seen there several times by some residents, yet never seen once by those living right next to where it had been parked.

A teenage boy living on nearby Garrett, arriving home about 11:05 P.M., saw a white Chevy station wagon with brown wood trim pulling away from a residence on Ellenbrook.

Another neighbor saw a older model gray sedan, California license plates 413 MTK, parked on Benny Way for several hours. There is no record available for what became of that information.

The last car, unknown to the neighborhood, was seen at noon on the day of the assault. It was a pickup, yellow in color, parked on Malaga near Benny. It was occupied by one male, in his early 20's, who appeared to be writing something down.

Amelia was the first to get an albeit brief face-to-face look at the suspect. The composite she made was the one circulated: A man with wide eyes and a wide mouth, wearing a ski mask. This is exactly what she saw when she looked at him. Nothing identifying at all. She probably had more pressing things on her mind at the moment than looking for details.

She said he had a young round face, putting his age in the late teens to early 20's.

The description given to us by Amelia, at the time, was a white male, 25 to 35 years old and 5 ft. 9 to 5 ft. 10 inches tall. She based this on the fact his mouth came to her nose, and she is 5 ft. 7 ¾ inches.

He wore a dark, Army-green nylon jacket and the mask. He wore dark shoes with soft soles and no heels.

Amelia had no frame of reference for the size of slick wick's slick wick. Comparing it to the common frankfurter, she said it was just slightly larger.

It was a day or two at the most when Carol and I met Amelia at her home. There we showed her photos of people known to be associated with sex crimes. The best she could do was say the "eyes are similar." So we brought yearbooks from 1970 – 1974 for Cordova and Folsom High Schools. After going through the books she pointed to one photo, saying it looked a lot like the suspect. She went on to say she was not saying it was him, but it looked a lot like him. After thoroughly going through the yearbooks, she returned to that one photo and again said it sure looked like him. The photo was of a kid named Jamison who graduated in 1974 from John Kennedy High. Finally, we had a real person of interest to investigate.

I spent a number of days running down the background on Jamison. With a birth date of 11-23-56, and a physical description of 5 ft. 10 inches, 160 lbs., with sandy-brown hair, he was right on. His father was a Tech. Sgt. assigned to Mather AFB, where they had their family home. Jamison himself was frequently seen wearing military fatigues as he wandered around Rancho Cordova.

I started at Folsom High school where the principal gathered the various teachers who knew Jamison, so I could interview them all at once. They agreed that while he was not close to any one person at school, he did associate with other students. He was generally considered as bright but troubled.

I managed to get a copy of his high school transcripts which is where I learned once he transferred to Folsom High his grades fell from A's to F's and D's. He even failed Physical Education. Transferring back to Kennedy High, his grades bounced back up to A's and B's.

While at Kennedy High he was a member of both ROTC and the track team. He graduated in 1974 and according to some who knew him, joined the Marines only to be kicked out a few months later. Some of those people speculated it was because he was half nuts. I never confirmed anything about his military record. The Air Force Office of Special Investigations (OSI) was going to investigate his military record, but failed to come through, or if they did, the information never reached me.

After the family left Mather AFB, they moved to Georgetown Drive in Rancho Cordova. This is where he was living when being investigated for this series of crimes. The OSI was unable to find any record of Jamison's father ever being stationed at Mather AFB, much less living on base. In retrospect, I am not sure the OSI was of much assistance to anyone – in this investigation.

Sergeant Mike Henretty learned Jamison was employed at a gas station on the corner of Auburn Boulevard and Orange Grove Boulevard. What better place for a late streetside lineup, where the suspect has to wait on the public? From someplace Sgt. Henretty acquired a van for this purpose. With Mike driving, me riding shotgun, and Amelia in the back, we headed off to buy some gas. Once we confirmed our target was on duty, Mike pulled up to the pumps and asked Jamison to fill it up. While he pumped the gas Amelia sat in the back seat. Peering intensely at him from a distance of less than three feet, for the time it takes to fill a gas tank, she could not identify him as her assailant.

Jamison was arrested by Sacramento Sheriff's Department for rape and sex perversion in 1990. He also had seven aliases. Pancreatic Cancer took him at age 54.

Of interest is that KC discovered Jamison's in-laws lived, and still may live, in the same areas where the Original Night Stalker went on his insane rampage. She even discovered Jamison has relatives living in or near all the areas in California where the EAR struck.

In 2013, Russ and I learned there had been no further investigative followup on Jamison because he was 6 ft. 1 inch, and considered too tall. He was not 6 ft. 1 inch tall when I talked to him. With that in mind, Russ and I contacted his daughter in October, 2013.

We learned from her that her father was indeed 6 ft. 1 inch tall. However, based on her own observations and family photos, he always wore his dark hair long. There were a number of tattoos on his neck, back, and on both upper arms.

He was employed as a truck driver which took him all over California. She did not recall any tattoo in particular. His style of dress was not western, nor was he inclined to corduroy pants.

As she explained it, her father and a cousin (who was also his best friend) enlisted in the military together in 1977. After being caught stealing from a vending machine, they were both kicked out of the military. That cousin was identified and described as 5 ft. 10 inches, and on the pudgy side.

While investigating this latest assault I received a call from a local body shop about a car Folsom PD had impounded in January 1977. So on March 30th I was at the Folsom PD to ask officer Connors about a 1961 light blue Valiant found abandoned by one of their officers.

On January 16th their officer ticketed a 1961 Valiant abandoned beside a road. Returning to duty the next day, the officer found that during the night the Valiant had been moved just down the street. In the officer's mind abandoned was abandoned so he impounded the Valiant. Sunrise Body Shop towed it to Sunrise & Folsom Blvd., Rancho Cordova where they stored it in their yard.

On March 29th, while removing personal property preparatory to a mechanic's lien sale, the body shop employees discovered property they found suspicious. That was when I entered the picture.

In the 1961 light blue Valiant they found:

1. Several new pairs of pants, shirts, socks, shoes and coats. All identifying information had been removed.
2. One wig
3. Two automatic riot shotguns. Both the kind used by law enforcement and illegal for public use.
4. A quantity of double-ought (00) shotgun ammunition.
5. Two boxes of .45 ammunition.

Immediately adjacent to the Valiant was a black over yellow Ford, CA license TOM 461. This car was also being prepared for a mechanic lien sale. Inside it were three banana clips for a .45 caliber Machine gun. Officer Connors traced this ammo and learned it was made in 1944 especially for the Marines' Riesling submachine gun. The Marines have since discontinued use of this gun and sold them all. Only small police departments and prison systems were using them in 1977.

The owner of that Ford was the known girlfriend of a man wanted for bank robbery.

Because both cars were parked so close to each other and they could be accessed by the public the question was raised: Does this property belong to both car owners, just one, or neither?

I traced the light blue Valiant to Ralph, living in Citrus Heights. In general he fit the physical description of the EAR but so did some thousands of other men. He did have a lot of facial hair, which would have taken him weeks to grow. At the time we did not think the EAR had any facial hair.

Ralph said he placed an ad in *The Sacramento Bee* offering the car for sale. On December 21, 1976 a slender white male about 20 years old bought it. The clean-shaven youth had light colored shoulder length hair. He was eloquent, affable and very soft spoken. At the time he was wearing a dark blue ski jacket, blue denim pants and waffle stompers.

Later I spoke with Ralph's girlfriend. She said when the youth arrived to buy the car he just seemed to appear from across the street (They lived on Center St., in Roseville at the time). He never really looked at the car but pulled out an envelope and paid for the Valiant in twenty-dollar bills. When the conversation turned towards him, he became very evasive. He did say his name was Dennis Allen.

She described him as a white male, about 16 years old, with almost shoulder length dishwater blond hair cut in a shag and parted down the middle. His teeth appeared to be spaced but not widely. He was wearing a blue nylon coat and white tennis shoes. She was not certain but thought his eyes were brown.

The Valiant obviously was not abandoned but parked. Which tends to indicate he was living close to others and most probably with someone. Which ever, he clearly did not want to be associated with that car. It can also be implied that he did not live far from there. Almost certainly within walking distance. Folsom prison grounds maybe?

Chapter 35:
East Area Rapist Ups the Ante

April 2, 1977
Richdale Way
Orangevale

As I turned onto Richdale Drive in Orangevale, another Sacramento suburb, I was reminded of a typical scene from a cops and robbers movie: Police cars, lights flashing and sirens screaming, screeching to a stop in front of a crime scene hours after the crime has occurred. The cops are always seen walking around talking quietly among themselves. What is really happening are a bunch of actors repeatedly mumbling "Peas and carrots, peas and carrots."

On this morning, at a real crime scene, there were a few police cars parked at or near the scene of the crime—none of which had arrived noisily. Indeed there were a number of officers walking around talking, but they were not discussing dinner menus. They were knocking on doors. Armed with a list of specific questions which had been formatted months earlier, they were conducting the first neighborhood canvass. There would be a second canvass in two days in which I would participate.

It was a little after 6:00 A.M. when I arrived. As I was stepping out of my car, Lt. Root, walking briskly across the front lawn, greeted me with, "There was a man in the house this time, but it was not her husband." My first thought was, "Oh, oh. Now it hits the fan." He quickly added the victims were girlfriend and boyfriend. Filling in the picture a little more, he added that there were two small children in the house who slept through the entire assault.

This was becoming typical of the EAR: brutalize the adults but take care that any small children were unharmed or at least undisturbed. What I found troubling was the question; at what age would he consider a child a child, and not available as a target? Would age even matter to him? So far, 15 years was not too young. It would be another year before we got a definitive answer to that question.

This, his 16th assault, is when the EAR put a couple of twists in his MO. One of those twists was to attack when a man was present. I'm sure in his mind this elevated him to some special level of skill and courage. One has to wonder just how brave he would have been if his victims were not caught off-guard and were armed.

As Lt. Root unfurled the story, I learned the victims, Katie and Bob, both clerks at a Kaiser pharmacy, were asleep when attacked. Katie was the first to awaken to a bright light shining directly into her eyes. A controlled whisper coming through clenched teeth, from behind that bright light asked, "See the gun in my hand?" Katie replied that she could, but all she could really see was a bright light.

"Don't move. Turn over onto your stomach. I have a .45 with 14 shots and two clips." By then Bob was awake as well. Tossing Katie some shoestrings, he ordered her to tie Bob's hands and feet. Katie did as told, but then she was told to do it tighter. He then re-tied them both.

As soon as he had his victims securely tied, he went straight into his routine of going from room to room, ransacking drawers and closets. It was right after he left the bedroom the first time that he returned and kinked his MO just a little more.

When he came back in that first time, he had some dishes, which he stacked on Bob's back, telling him if he heard the dishes rattle or the bed squeak, he would kill Katie. Then claiming he was afraid to leave them together in one room, he escorted Katie into the living room where he made her lie down. Then he placed dishes on her back.

Apparently, after satisfying one appetite, he returned to Katie to satisfy another. When he asked if she and Bob had had sex that night, and that she better tell the truth, Katie said, 'No." Katie lied. In fact, they had had sex, but Katie had not yet cleaned herself. It was her secret, and one that possibly gave her some satisfaction, when the suspect orally copulated her. Before the second assault on Katie, the suspect placed a pair of high-heeled shoes on her feet.

After the unpleasant eternity was over, the suspect wandered back into the kitchen where he again could be heard eating. Evidently eating regenerated his torqued libido for he returned to Katie where he once again assaulted her. Two times he actually stopped in the middle of the sexual assault to partake of the kitchen contents. At other times he stopped in the middle of a sex act to wander around the house or check on Bob. Once he asked Katie if she had any candles and matches. He never gave any hint why he wanted them.

As the psychopath was leaving, he leaned over Bob and whispered, "Next place, next town." As soon as Bob felt he was alone in the bedroom, he worked at getting the cup and saucer off without making any noise. He figured it took about ten minutes, but he did it. Sliding out of bed, he hobbled as quietly as possible to the bedroom of Katie's son. It was then that he determined the suspect was actually gone.

Other statements whispered by this psychopath were: "I'm going to my camp by the river. If I hear a rattle I'll kill everyone one in the house...I don't want to hear bed springs...I was in the Army and I fucked a lot when I was there...Don't make any sudden moves or I'll kill you like I did some people in Bakersfield."

Because of an expected delay between the suspect leaving and the arrival of a tracking dog, some articles known to have been handled by the suspect were placed in a sealed container in an effort to preserve his scent. It was about 7:30 A.M. when the dog was ushered into the living room. The dog's response was immediate when the container was opened. He headed out of the house to the sidewalk, then around the corner for a short distance. There the trail ended.

Where the trail abruptly ended was the same type of location as in the other assaults. Whatever he was riding had been parked a short distance from a main thoroughfare (in this instance, Bullion to Main Avenue) in such a manner it was not directly in front of any one residence. If he was riding a bicycle, it would have been in hidden in shrubbery.

The ID technicians actually observed a fingerprint from the suspect on Katie's wrist, but they were unable to lift it. This observation would soon give us a different investigative angle to follow.

The suspect description was that of a WMA about 5 ft. 10 inches, with a medium build. He was probably in his mid 20's. His thighs were heavy with abrasive hair, as if shaved. When speaking, it was always in a controlled manner and he whispered through clenched teeth. Bob was sure he picked up a hint of a German accent. The suspect knew precisely what he was about, and by now, he should have.

The inevitable question came up about the size of his male organ. It was described as five inches long and thin.

His mask was constructed of a white material, and it may have been a ski mask. The jacket he wore was a dark-colored, nylon windbreaker. Gloves were skin tight leather.

The routine of contacting those who delivered the morning papers and milk was incorporated along with contacting all the neighbors. We learned this whole area had been a beehive of activity for several months as a plethora of information was developed. Little if any of it had been reported to the Sacramento Sheriff's Department.

Katie and Bob were assaulted on the 2nd of April between 3:20 and 5:00 A.M. That morning, between 4:30 and 5:00, a neighbor heard a small foreign vehicle circling the block several times.

A house next door to Katie and Bob had been on the market for less than a month. It was for sale by the owner, so the owners personally met each potential buyer.

The first day a couple in their early 20's stopped by to look at the house. The man was described as WMA, blonde and slender. They were driving a 1976 Chevrolet station wagon. A day or so later, a man stopped by who said he was transferring from Las Vegas to work as a civilian employee at McClellan AFB. They described him as thin, short blonde hair, and blue eyes. He was estimated to be in his 20's.

On April 1, the day before the assault, a neighbor saw a primer-gray station wagon passing back and forth, about five times, on nearby Winterbrook.

Then about 6:00, on the morning of the assault, another neighbor saw a dark-colored car backing out of Katie's driveway. It was described as full size and possibly brown or even purple in color with a loud exhaust. We considered the possibility this was a sheriff's unmarked car, but none of them had a loud exhaust nor were they purple.

As anticipated, we learned Katie had received a few of those hangup-type phone calls. One of her neighbors, a woman and her two daughters, had been receiving them for some months. In most of those calls, only breathing could be heard on the other end. These three were probably on the EAR's hit list.

Nearly three months prior to this assault, a neighbor happened to look out his back window to see a man he did not recognize standing in his neighbor's backyard. The backyard belonged to a single woman living alone. He gave chase, but the suspect, who was described as very athletic, cleared fences in single bounds, quickly leaving his pursuer behind. He was described as a WMA, 25 to 30, 5 ft. 9 inches to 5 ft.

10 inches tall, with a stocky build, collar length, light-brown hair, wearing a white or tan shirt and dark pants.

Besides the usual prowlers and hang-up calls, there had been a few burglaries on Richdale and neighboring streets over the past three months as well.

Phony meter readers had been spotted on at least three occasions in the neighborhood. The utility company had been contacted by the neighbors who asked about meter readers, which is how they knew these were phonies. One occurred on March 23rd. The "meter reader" was wearing dark pants, and a blue nylon windbreaker, and was clean shaven. The woman who spotted him noticed his hands. They were empty. Not even a notebook on which to jot down the meter numbers.

Every neighborhood seems to have one person who always makes it their business to know who comes and goes. One of these was deep into weeding her flower beds when she glanced up. Peering through the weeds and flowers she could see a man wearing jogging clothes walking down her street. She watched as he crossed the street several times, stopping each time to stare at a house. One of those houses was Katie's. This man did not know he was being watched until he was in front of this witness's house. When he saw her he said, "Good evening," then headed straight down the street, turning north onto Bullion. Seconds later she heard tires peeling rubber and saw a light colored sedan, possibly bluish-gray, leaving. She did get the license number but did not have it at hand for the investigating officer. She was never able to locate it.

This woman gardener described the man in jogging clothes as a WMA, 18 to 20 years old, about 5 ft. 10 inches, and 165 lbs. He was slender, but well developed, and was average looking. He wore tennis shoes with several white stripes—similar to the Adidas brand. He wore a blue-gray, two-piece sweatsuit with a hood. She almost certainly got a good look at the face of the EAR. I don't know if she ever made a composite or not.

Two days after this assault, Sergeant Henretty and I conducted a second canvass of the neighborhood. I remember very clearly talking to one man who kept his dog in the backyard. He said a week or so earlier he found an empty meat wrapper in his backyard, as well as a tennis shoe print on the top of a 2" x 4" railing of his fence.

Desperate to try something new in order to move the investigation along, I contacted the California State Department of Forestry. I knew they sometimes caught arsonists on film, so asked how they went about spotting people behaving badly in the woods.

It seems the Department of Forestry employs Big Brother tactics. Disguised cameras, that will operate continuously for a week or more, are placed in specific locations. Today they are called game or trail cameras. These may be at ground level or in trees. Considering the area we were interested in at the moment was bordered by Main Street on one side, and the American River Canyon on the other, it was more or less contained. In my opinion, if it worked for the State Forestry Department, and they were willing to provide the equipment and manpower, then what did we have to lose by trying? At my request, they agreed to install a number of these cameras in the general area of the latest assault.

It was years before I learned if they carried through with their promise. In any case, I would soon be transferred and it was guaranteed no one else was going to follow up on the project. Sixteen years after I retired, I encountered the same agent I had spoken to about that project. Although he thought the cameras were installed, he could not remember what the results were, if any.

Another scheme I was kicking around was to involve the military. I never acted on it, but I did wonder if it might be possible to arrange for a military helicopter crew to assist—maybe make it routine for a helicopter crew to respond to a sexual assault report with the rest of us. I'm sure the idea of catching this psychopath would be all it would take to entice a crew into going for it. Little things like communication between the pilots and the ground troops, not to mention cost of flying the rig or noise generated, would be issues. It was a great idea, but I never made the suggestion.

Chapter 36:
East Area Rapist or Not the East Area Rapist?

To add to the busy month of April, 1977, there were two incidents that occurred in Rancho Cordova which at the time were accredited to the EAR. One was a sexual assault, the other an apparent preparation for a sexual assault.The EAR was not involved in either of them. I know for certain Art Pinkton was responsible in one and would bet my life he was responsible for the other as well.

The sexual assault occurred in the evening when a woman visiting her boyfriend in his downstairs apartment stepped outside to her car parked just to the right of his front window. She was accosted by a ski masked man right there on the sidewalk next to her car.

Struggling at first, then when it looked like she was losing, she acquiesced making some statement to indicate she was giving up. Her assailant relaxed his grip which was when she made a break for it. He grabbed her, then sexually assaulted her on the sidewalk, within feet of her boyfriend's apartment window.

The only difference between this sexual assault and one Pinkton was arrested for in 1968 was the victim, the physical location, and the year. The scenario, even the words spoken by both the victim and the suspect, were the same. I know because I had copies of all the sexual assaults for which he had been arrested. The next day the local newspapers screamed the EAR had struck yet again. It was later removed from the list of those assaults believed to have been by the EAR.

This young woman was unable to identify her assailant, and with no evidence, the investigation was pended. I did not respond to the initial call.

About two weeks after this sexual assault, and just a few blocks further east on Coloma Road, preparations for another sexual assault were underway when they were interrupted. The intended victim, a woman in her 60's, was the one who interrupted them. She was coming down the stairs when she saw a man standing in her kitchen ripping towels into strips. When she yelled for her male friend, who was upstairs, the man dropped the towels and ran.

As I entered her apartment, I was met by the intended victim as she descended those same stairs. She seemed a bit upset, but not really all that excited. After hearing what happened, I placed a stack of big shot photos in front of her to look through. These were photos of men who had been and were suspected of sexual assaults.

For those who do not know what was known as a "big shot photo," it was made with a Polaroid camera designed for a close up photo of people. In a word, a mug shot. Almost immediately she yanked a photo from near the top of the stack; handing it to me said, "That's him." She was absolutely positive—it was Art Pinkton.

This lady, a near victim, was also very insistent there be no report of the incident. Her reason was not at all well thought out; it was out of a concern for her married boyfriend who was upstairs at that moment. She was afraid his wife would learn where he was, and she wanted to avoid making trouble for him. Even after I explained he could remain upstairs, out of sight and out of mind, she refused. This is one of those "do over" situations that I would do differently in a heartbeat. Let her explain to the District Attorney why she did not want to file charges. Like I said earlier, Art Pinkton just wouldn't go away.

April 15, 1977
Cherrelyn Way
Carmichael

It was about 2:45 in the morning when the East Area Rapist made his presence known on Cherrelyn Way in Carmichael. In all respects it was a repeat performance of the assault on Richdale Way.

The young couple was asleep in bed when a large, round, bright beam of light, aimed at their eyes, brought them suddenly wide awake. Debbie, thinking it was her boyfriend Gary playing around said, "Gary, knock it off and go back to sleep." The response she got was not what she expected.

The unexpected response, "Roll over on your stomach or I will blow your brains all over," was whispered through clenched teeth. The whisperer continued with, "Do you know what a .45 magnum is?" At the same time Debbie could feel a knife blade pressed against her neck. As he continued with his peculiar style of self-introduction, the suspect told them all he wanted was their money and no one would get hurt. From the tossing of shoe strings to Debbie, to personal threats, to the separating of Debbie and Gary and placing dishes on their backs, nothing much varied. This time, however, he did not gag Debbie. Other than that, like a carbon copy, it was all there.

A number of times the suspect stopped in the middle of a sexual assault to go into the kitchen to eat or to wander around rummaging in closets and drawers. More than once, after sexually assaulting Debbie, he went into the backyard only to return and sexually assault her again.

Twice, when trying to alleviate the pain in his hands, Gary rattled the dishes stacked on his back. Each time the suspect responded instantly by returning to the room. Upon his return, Gary heard the gun being cocked as it was placed against his head amid new threats, "Kill the girl."

When the radio dispatcher announced there had just been an EAR assault on Cherrelyn Way, Officer Stincelli and his partner paid attention. They were ready.

Their shift had been dedicated to the EAR task force, so they took a pre-arranged position near Sunrise Boulevard and the on-ramp for Highway 50. It was not long before a small yellow car came off Sunrise and onto Highway 50, headed westbound towards Sacramento. The driver, a white male, was the only occupant. On went their red lights as they sped after him.

With each of them taking a side, they walked up to the car. Shining their lights inside, they quickly spotted a container of hand lotion on the front seat. The two officers were definitely interested now.

In response to routine questions, the male driver explained he was on his way to work at a rice mill in Sacramento. Turning this guy loose, without further investigation, was just not going to happen. Officer Stincelli requested and got permission to look inside the trunk of the car. After looking inside the trunk, they took the driver into custody and asked the radio dispatcher contact me.

As I arrived at the traffic stop, I could see the still open car trunk, the flashing red lights of the squad car illuminating the contents. A coil of rope was the first thing I keyed in on, and it was the first thing I examined. It was narrow gauge and still in an unopened cellophane wrapper.

I felt a small bit of disappointment that the rope did not come even close to any of the bindings used thus far by the suspect. However, I was aware of the attack on Merribrook where rope had been used, and I was very cognizant of the fact that I had not personally seen that rope.

Along with the rope were two zippered bags, a pair of tennis shoes, a gun, and a knife. The knife was short-bladed, and the gun was a pellet pistol. They did not match any used (that we knew of) by the suspect. There were other items, but at this point in time, I have no idea what they were. It looked like the driver had just about every type of survival gear ever made in that trunk.

The driver was 5 ft. 9 inches, with brown hair and brown eyes, about 160 lbs. His hair was short, but not especially short. At that moment we were still thinking the suspect most likely had blue eyes. There was not much else about him that I can recall, other than he did not stand out. But over the years, when recalling him as a person of interest yet to be eliminated as a suspect, the image that always comes to mind is brown; I simply remember him as just plain brown. No facial features even.

The "all brown" driver gave me a signed consent form to search his residence. He lived in an old, weather- beaten trailer designed for hauling camping materials—not people. It was something like eight feet long and definitely not tall enough to stand up in. It had been abandoned on a steep Fair Oaks Hillside, where brush had grown up all around nearly covering it. His sister, who owned the hillside, kindly let him call it home.

The trailer was so small only one person at a time could get in to search. Nothing could be located in or near that small trailer that even began to resemble any clothing or articles of property taken from any of the victims. Pretty much it only held a small bed and a few items of clothing. If there had been anything else, it would have needed to have been hidden in a hole in the ground, in which case the only way to find it would have been to stumble into it.

The search of his car and trailer did not turn up any ski masks, shoe strings, or military garb. He had never been in the military. The fact he had the hand lotion on the front seat with him cast doubt in my own mind. So far as we knew, the suspect normally would use lotion belonging to the victim. When he did take it from the house, it was always found nearby.

I left there feeling he was not the psychopath for whom we were searching. There were just no strong indicators connecting him to the rape series.

The rice mill where he worked as a janitor was in Woodland. Although I did not think he was the EAR, Lt. Root, the task force commander, was not going to rely on my opinion alone. As it turned out, this person of interest had been at work when the assault occurred on Woodpark Way.

What evidence we did have consisted of black hairs and brown hairs. The black hairs were recovered from the beds of two victims. The black hairs were later determined to be canine hairs. The light brown hairs had been found on either the victims themselves, or on cloth articles touched by both a victim and the suspect. Those hairs have never been identified as belonging to any one person.

One of the reasons I wanted access to the EAR reports was to find out if the suspect stopped by Stincelli that night had been cleared. I remembered much about that night, but there was much I did not remember.

To that end I contacted Carl Stincelli about this person of interest, just to be sure I knew what I was talking about. Carl said neither has he ever forgotten the man nor his car. The only thing he cannot remember is the man's name. He also remembered the trunk of the car had just about every kind of survival equipment available, including a pellet gun. The equipment was kept in two, large, zippered bags. Considering his living conditions at the time, he needed just about every piece of survival equipment on the market to survive.

Homicide Detective Ken Clark, of the Sacramento Sheriff's Department, works the EAR investigation when time permits. He read the supplemental reports that Carl and I had written. Loaded with the information provided, he went in search of that driver. Detective Clark located him, and after obtaining a sample of his DNA, had it compared to that of the EAR/ONS. Unfortunately, another dead end.

After searching the location where the POI was living, I made my way to Cherrelyn Way. By the time I arrived, Debbie was being interviewed by my partner, Carol, and other officers were about the business of contacting as many neighbors as they could locate. I took that opportunity to look more closely at a house that was for sale directly across the street from where Debbie was assaulted. There was an R.R.W. Real Estate sign in the front yard of the unoccupied house.

Since it was unlocked, I wandered inside. There was a laundry room at the SE corner which provided a clear view of the house Debbie occupied. That the suspect had been there was a given. Among the appliances were a number of filter tipped cigarette butts. Partial prints of tennis shoes were also visible in the thick dust.

About two days after the assault, I returned with Sgt. Henretty to re-interview Debbie. While Sgt. Henretty busied himself snooping around the crime scene, I explained that I had some questions for her. To put her at ease, I explained those questions had nothing to do with the sex acts themselves, for once established there was no need to go over them again. Instead, I was interested in details about sounds, smells, appearances, intuitive feelings, specific actions, personal routines, social connections, etc.

Debbie worked for the state of California as a typist, on S Street, in downtown Sacramento. Her sister worked for Pacific Bell Telephone Company on J Street. She spent her off time playing softball for the American River Construction Company.

When asked about unusual phone calls or circumstances, Debbie said for the past few weeks she had been receiving phone calls in the mornings, noon, and evenings. Each time the caller hung up without a word being spoken. Only breathing could be heard from the caller.

The beam from the flashlight that woke her up was large and round. When he announced he had a gun, she also felt the knife, which he did not announce, at the back of her neck. She described the knife as seven to eight inches long, with a thin blade sharpened on both sides. She said he sounded like he was gasping for breath when he rapidly sucked in his breath through clenched teeth. She had the impression her assailant seemed to get more enjoyment from using the coarsest language he could, then ordering her to repeat verbatim what he had just said, than he did any act of sex.

The blindfold on Debbie came loose, and if she had tilted her head up she could have seen her assailant's face. Fear of losing her life kept her from taking that chance. So instead, she did what she could and paid close attention to what she could see, and that was the hair on his legs and arms − of which there was not much. It was light brown, medium in texture, and definitely not coarse

She had gotten a brief glance at his eyes, which she was certain were brown. His head hair was cut to collar length and dark-blonde in color, straight, but also of a full-bodied texture. As far as she could determine, he did not have any facial hair.

It seemed to her, when he whispered, there was a slight hint of an oriental accent. Even when whispering close to her ear, the hint of accent remained consistent.

Debbie had recently been undergoing a series of serious dental procedures. As a result she had a prescription for codeine, but the codeine was a generic brand. After going through her purse, her assailant said he was in real need of a fix and asked where she kept her codeine. That was when he started to gasp which she took to be how he thought an addict would act.

After he took the pills from her purse, she heard the sound of running water in the kitchen. Later the ID techs found the empty prescription bottle in the kitchen sink. The next day a plastic bag with wet pills was found in a neighbor's backyard. Also, two empty beer cans were found just outside the house.

What I took from that bit of information was that the two previous EAR victims both worked at a pharmacy. Also, the suspect knew the proper name for a drug listed by its generic name.

His pants may have been corduroy, but were definitely dark colored and he had a light green jacket with nylon straps in front. He covered his face with a ski mask, and he had gloves of well-worn, black leather with large stitching on the sides. His shoes were military boots badly in need of a shine.

To try for an estimate on the height of the suspect, Debbie lay on the bed for a moment. Then she stood, and comparing her mental image to Sgt. Henretty and my height, she settled on 5 ft. 9 to 5 ft. 10 inches tall.

Then Debbie launched into a description of the size of the suspect's penis. I really was not interested, but she seemed determined not to be deterred from the subject. As she ended her dissertation she pointed to a coin in a nearby ashtray saying, 'It was no bigger around than a quarter and maybe five inches long." It was apparent she considered herself something of an expert on this topic, so I have always accepted her description as accurate.

Later Lt. Root and Sgt. Bevins arranged for Debbie to undergo a hypnosis session. They were hoping it would help her recall more details. It did.

She was outside washing her car when a light colored Valiant drove by very slowly. The driver was the only occupant and he stared intently at her as he passed. That night she was assaulted. She was able to remember a license number but it was not registered.

After I retired from the Sacramento Sheriff's Department, I did as so many retirees do, and that was go back to work as an on-call reserve. It was in that capacity that I worked in the work-release program. This program allows people to serve community service, as opposed to actual jail time. They sweep floors, pull weeds, etc. It was while supervising a group of "weekenders" at a high school that I met a former sister-in-law of Debbie.

Per this former sister-in-law, Debbie gave a different account of what happened to her family. She told them she was certain there were two rapists. During the first sexual assault the suspect, as in all the other assaults, did not allow his full weight to come to rest on her. This was the guy with the small penis. After he was finished assaulting her, he stepped out of the house and into the backyard. Then he came back in and climbed onto the bed to assault her again. This time the bed sank down much further than the first time, and he allowed his full weight to bear down on her. Not only that, but he had a normal sized penis. There was more than one trip out that back door, and more than one sexual assault that night.

She was positive there were two suspects, with one noticeably larger than the other. This particular assault occurred about the same time I told Lt. Root I could make a case for two suspects in the East Area Rape series. In a heartbeat, he responded with, "I don't want to hear about it." He went on to explain that to make that public would create more confusion and panic, in a public which already had a plentiful supply. "Go arrest them, then tell me about it," was his response.

My only issue with what Debbie allegedly told her family is that none of the victims I spoke with, nor with whom Carol spoke, ever told us they thought there was more than one suspect.

Chapter 37:
Fingerprinting the Human Torso

The assault on Richdale gave rise to a unique change in our investigative protocols. Some of us had noticed the suspect kept his gloves on at all times; that is except during the actual rape, and then the gloves might come off, but only for a moment. Since we had been unable to find his prints at any scene, it would be necessary to come up with another way to get them. Carol and I sat down one day and discussed just what would be a good way to go about accomplishing this goal. We were aware in the Richdale assault a fingerprint had actually been seen on the victim's wrist.

Sometime in early 1977, Carol and I again approached Gilmore, of the coroner's crime lab, only this time we asked if it was possible to actually lift prints from where a person had been touched by another. Gilmore thought about it for a moment, then said he would find out and call us. No more than a day or two later, he called and asked us to stop by his lab; he had something to show us.

True to his word, Gilmore had checked with the FBI lab and not only learned how to lift prints from a person's body, but he acquired the equipment for doing it. There was enough equipment to outfit two or three patrol cars. The method required using a silver plate, a small piece of equipment, and iodine or a similar substance. But first a fine powder had to be blown gently over the area of the body to be tested.

Lt. Root, the task force commander, and the few women patrol officers we had at the time, accompanied Carol and me to watch a demonstration of this new technique by Gilmore. Although she helped brainstorm a way to collect the suspects prints, Carol was not entirely in favor of this new procedure. She defended the victims saying they were going to feel much like the rape crisis personnel had described—objects to be poked and prodded. But we were desperate, and it was decided to give it a try.

At the time there were only four or five women patrol officers. Naturally, they would be the ones to utilitze this new technique. I clearly remember telling them what I had been saying to everybody all along. That is, the suspect seemed to know what we were doing and when we were doing it, but they were to keep this new procedure to themselves. Above all, they were told to stay off the radio with chatter about the investigation. To paraphrase the East Area Rapist, "Shut up!"

Within two days of that meeting, there was another rape. This time the suspect's gloves did not come off.

I soon learned my warning had been totally disregarded as the police radios were alive with conversations about the details of this new procedure. Today, Carol clearly remembers two things about the new procedure for developing fingerprints.

Because there was only a short window of opportunity to apply this procedure before the prints faded, Carol had to drive at a rather excessive speed to get there in time. Once there, the first step in this new technique was to have the victim lie down so she could apply a fine powder over her body where the suspect touched her.

To do this Carol had to lock everyone, except for her and the victim, out of the room. Then using a straw she was to gently blow a very fine powder over the areas where the suspect had touched the victim. Only after this powder was present could any attempt be made to develop any prints. The whole idea of this process, plus blowing the fine powder over the victim, struck both Carol and the victims as funny–funny enough they would both be giggling like school girls. Never were any prints developed.

This procedure has since been done away with as it is now believed to be carcinogenic.

Chapter 38:
Second Stash Found

May 3, 1977
La Rivera Drive
Sacramento

The next assault by someone believed to be the East Area Rapist happened on May 3, 1977. This time it was on La Rivera Drive, which is within the jurisdiction of the Sacramento Police. I had absolutely nothing to do with this investigation. What I do know of it came from talking to the SPD detectives, Carol, who spoke with all local and some not so local EAR victims, and of course reading the report. From that, I can lay out the scenario for this assault.

The victim was a 6 ft. tall housewife and part-time student at Sacramento City College where she was taking a course in real estate. She was employed at Mather AFB as was her husband, an Air Force major. She, her husband, and her two small children lived in a two-story house in an upper middle-income neighborhood close to the American River levee. This was the first time an assault attributed to the EAR had occurred in a two-story home.

About 1:00 A.M., a neighbor heard someone walking on the gravel in her yard. The next day when she checked to see if anything was amiss, she found her gate was open.

Close to this same hour, the victim-to-be heard a thump which sounded like someone jumping a fence. After ensuring all windows and doors were locked, she went to bed alongside her husband.

About three in the morning, something caused her to wake up. That's when she saw a strange man standing in the doorway to the bedroom. He held a flashlight in his left.hand and a small gun in the right. She is certain on this because he shined the light onto the gun while announcing it was a .45 caliber, and for no one to move. If they did he would kill everybody.

From that point on, it was a virtual repeat of past performances. First, he told them all he wanted was money and if they cooperated he would not harm anyone and be gone. After the ritual of tying his victims, he began with his usual threats. The threat he repeated a few times was that he could kill them and "get away to my camp across the levee," or across the levee and into his camp.

He made one statement which, because of the possible suspect developed in the assault on Benny Way, might have been relevant. "I got kicked out," was a statement the suspect made in reference to being in the military. I'm fairly sure that lead was never followed up. Did the suspect know about Jamison and was he telling the truth?

After covering the major's head with the sheet, he placed a jewelry box and later added a cup and saucer. With this, he gave the warning about not making a noise upon pain of death.

In keeping with his routine he made frequent trips to the kitchen to eat. On one trip to the kitchen she could hear him unzip and zip up what she took to be a bag. In previous assaults the rustling of paper bags could be heard.

There was another notable difference in his behavior. This was probably the second or third time he fondled his victim's breasts and stomach when assaulting her. This time his touch was gentle and not at all rough, which was totally out of character.

Twice the suspect shivered and just as suddenly stopped. The victim had the feeling he was pretending to be an addict, as he had earlier asked for cocaine.

His voice was soft, clear, and articulate. With the possible exception of the assault on Woodpark Way, this was the first time he had not whispered. To both the victim and her husband he sounded like an actor reading from a script. He definitely gave the impression he was bored and had been through all of this before. When he did seem to be on the verge of becoming nervous, he breathed deeply as if trying to keep control.

Wearing a puffy ski-type jacket, he was described as a white male, 5 ft. 8 to 5 ft. 9 inches tall, 165 lbs., with a slight build. She described his gloves as form-fitting leather, soft and smooth. Her husband, on the other hand, said they were a construction type glove, made of heavy canvas. His mask was described as brown or beige, beige being just another shade of brown which means it was light-brown.

She said he had a very small penis but did not give an estimate on length and width.

The SPD brought in a tracking dog which led them to the levee behind the victims' home. There they found a knife at the base of the levee that was later identified as belonging to the victim. On the levee they found two empty beer cans, but it was not confirmed they had been left there by the suspect. Several large puddles of water were observed on the levee, none of which had been disturbed, indicating no car had been used for the escape.

This victim and her family had been receiving hang-up phone calls for two weeks or more. They usually occurred just after she arrived home from school, which was early in the afternoon.

During their on-scene investigations, the police learned six neighbors had been receiving hangup calls for a period of three weeks. Two of them had suffered burglaries of their homes as well.

The more interesting incident happened just before Christmas. A woman found a plastic bag in the bushes, under her window, that contained a flashlight and pair of gloves. It would seem the EAR liked this method of keeping his shop at the ready. The description of the flashlight is not available.

May 5, 1977
Winterbrook Way
Orangevale

While some people were preparing for their Cinco de Mayo celebration, I found myself walking through the front door of a house on Winterbrook Way in Orangevale where another EAR attack had just occurred. Again it was a man and a woman who had been targeted. This attack was only a couple of blocks from the assault on Richdale. I was soon to learn that although the suspect had studied this area thoroughly, this assault may have been a crime of opportunity. No doubt if Sgt. Bevins heard that, he would turn those big soulful brown eyes on me and quietly beam a big warm smile.

Winterbrook is a neighborhood that had a lot of new construction going on at the time. Like nearby Richdale, access to the American River greenbelt was only a few blocks distant. With so much natural river habitat along that river, a herd of elephants could have easily hidden from view.

While gathering what information we could, Patrol Officer Gabe Bender approached us. She told us the suspect never took his gloves off at any time during the actual sexual assault. There went our chance of developing the suspect's prints off the victim. I took that bit of information as a clue that there could be no doubt the suspect knew all about our new technique for fingerprinting the human body.

After getting a more or less synopsis of what had occurred, we briefed the officers assigned to assist. These officers, referred to as X-ray units, began contacting the neighbors. Carol transported both victims to the medical center where I was to meet them. At the hospital, while Carol accompanied Sherry through the procedures, I interviewed her friend, Carl, in the office of the campus police which were assigned to the hospital.

Carl moved from the 5600 block of Manzanita Avenue ten days earlier, which explained the lack of window curtains. He was still moving in.

Both he and Sherry (the rape victim) worked at a local stockbroker's office in downtown Sacramento, where she was a sales assistant. It was about 8:30 P.M. when Sherry stopped by Carl's house to discuss some business matters over dinner. Their relationship was purely platonic and cordial.

Sherry brought her two dogs with her. She ushered them inside the house, but then set them loose in the backyard. As soon as the dogs were out the door they began barking in the direction of a large oak tree on the neighboring property. A neighbor's dog was already barking in that direction. Looking out the door, in the general direction of the oak tree, and seeing nothing, both Carl and Sherry put the incident out of their minds and went about their evening.

At exactly 12:15 A.M., as Carl walked Sherry to her car which was parked in his driveway, a man wearing a ski mask stepped from around the corner of the garage. Pointing a .45 caliber handgun at them, he ordered them both to go back inside the house.

Once inside, the ritual of only looking for money and tying the victims took place. Again the dishes and the ransacking were accompanied by a multitude of threats.

Carl described the suspect's voice as slightly high pitched. It was his opinion the suspect was speaking through clenched teeth in an effort to sound mad. Even though he was speaking with his voice lowered, he did not speak in a definite whisper.

The description given by Carl was of a white male, 25 to 35 years old, 5 ft. 10 inches to 6 ft. tall, with a slender build, weighing about 160 lbs. The suspect wore a dark navy-blue mask which fit loosely, hanging just below his chin. His gloves were dark as were his tennis shoes. The thought struck me that the way the descriptions of the suspect's shoes varied, he must have had access to a shoe store.

Once they were sure the suspect was gone, Sherry managed to cut the bindings from around Carl's feet. Leaving her in the house, Carl made his way to a neighbor's house where they cut him free. By then his hands were turning black and Carl felt he needed medical attention.

My conversation with Sherry did not take place for another few days and that was when she showed up at my cubbyhole. Sherry repeated her story of how she and Carl worked together for a local stocks and bonds broker, and how she happened to be at his new house that night. She then told me they had sex on the living room floor in front of the uncovered window.

When Sherry compared the suspect's height to her own, she felt he was definitely no more than 5 ft. 9 inches in height. Contrary to what Carl had said, she thought the suspect spoke in whispers through clenched teeth. Still, she thought his voice was a little high-pitched. He kept taking deep breaths, but she was not sure why. Her friend Carl thought maybe it was because he was trying to build up some courage.

Sherry repeated something that at least one other victim had said. She thought she picked up a hint of a Mexican accent but she could not be sure. She also described his penis as about 5 inches long with the circumference of a quarter. To her he did not seem to enjoy what he was doing and had trouble maintaining an erection.

When he was rummaging around in the house, she heard the sound of a zipper being zipped open then closed a number of times.

During the sex acts the suspect kept his gloves on at all times. In order to orally copulate her, it would have been necessary to remove, or at least lift his ski mask. In any case she did not feel any facial hair when he did this.

The next morning I was back at the scene looking for evidence and talking to the neighbors.

The oak tree mentioned by Carl was next to his property and not that far from the living room window. There were scuff marks on the trunk and what appeared to be some tennis shoe prints in the dirt nearby.

A Zippo lighter was located on the floor of the master bedroom. There was also a piece of plastic found under the living room couch that had "075" typed on a piece of paper stuck on the piece of plastic.

Although anyone could buy a Zippo cigarette lighter, they were endemic to the military. So, my first thought was that we had just one more indication the suspect might be military.

An empty Coors beer can was discovered lying by the back door, a knife behind the living room couch, and a piece of chewed gum, with hair stuck in it, on a clothing hamper.

There were two possible witnesses developed by the officers during the initial neighborhood canvass that were of especial interest. One of these witnesses gave me reason to contact Lt. Engellenner of the Placer Sheriff's Office.

Through his department Lt. Engellener had become a certified hypnotist. As a trained hypnotist he offered to help with our investigation. It was through his skill that we hoped a possible witness might recall some details of a particular car and the driver.

On May 2nd, as our witness was opening the garage door for her husband, she noticed a car parked across the street, the driver being the only occupant. Almost immediately she became suspicious and therefore tried to get his license plate number. Before she could get the number, the driver drove off. It was this observation that we felt might just be a good lead in our investigation.

On May 9th, the meeting between Lt. Engellener, the witness, and members of her family took place in his office. I was present as well.

During the session both the witness and her sister went into a relaxed state of mind. That relaxed state resulted in a number of details about the driver and the car.
She described the driver as a white male, late 20's, fair complexion, dark-brown, shoulder-length hair, no mustache, but a full well-trimmed short beard. His eyes were large and attractive. The arm hanging outside the door window appeared to have very little hair but the arm hair was lighter in color than the hair on his head. His build was medium to slender. All she could see of his clothing was a well-worn, white T-shirt.

She described the car he was driving as square in body style. It was a sun-bleached pinkish-grey with a white undercoat beginning to show through. There was a lot of chrome on the front end of the car. It had single headlights. The tail lights were single, small, round and protruding out from the body of the car. A recessed area on the body stretched from one tail light to the other.

The paint on the front license plate frame was all but gone. Still visible on that frame was the word Mercury. It was the old California black and yellow license plate. ?HD? - 951. She felt the missing letter was J, or maybe even an I, T, or L.

All possible combinations of letters and numbers were run through DMV. Only one combination was on file. It came back to a 1962 Ford. A photo of a 1962 Ford was shown to the witness who said it most definitely was not the car she had seen.

After the session with Lt. Engellener, the 11-year-old son of the witness said the description sounded like the man who drove the ice cream truck in their area.

Carol Daly learned the driver of that yellow and white ice cream truck was a Robert William Lee. He was described as a WMA, in his 20's, with a short, well-trimmed beard and no mustache.

Carol and I located Mells Ice Cream Company, on Dry Creek Road in Sacramento, and we confirmed Lee was employed as an ice cream truck driver.

The second witness developed during the neighborhood canvass lived on Dredger Way which connects to Winterbrook.

The teenage daughter of the family living there had, on at least one occasion, seen a man driving a rusty looking older model four-door Chevy in the area. The car looked as if it had no paint on it at all. The second time she saw it, the driver stopped at her house and told her he worked for Stone Plumbing and had been sent to make a repair at her house.

As far she knew there were no repairs needed, nor had her parents called for any plumbing repairs. She described the man as a white male, early 20's, 5 ft. 1 inch and very muscular, with short curly brown hair and a pock-marked face.

The next time she saw him he was again parked on Dredger Way near her house. As she walked outside to check the mailbox, he drove away. That was the last time she ever saw him.

The day after the session with Lt. Engellener, I was contacted by Mr. and Mrs. Irish and their 17-year-old daughter, Bonnie. They felt they had information that might be pertinent to our investigation.

In December, 1976, the Irish family was living on Hartnell Place in Sacramento in a home that was for sale. While still living there, they experienced what they felt were suspicious circumstances. The first occurrence was when Bonnie arrived home at 1:10 A.M. As she was parking her car in the alley behind their house, she noticed a whitish-colored Datsun or

Toyota, with a man in the driver's seat, parked in the alley. As Bonnie got out of her car, the driver got out of his car and started towards her. She quickly got back into her car and drove away.

After leaving, she telephoned her mother who told her to drive by again and if the car was still there to honk. Bonnie did as instructed but the car was gone.

Bonnie arrived home about the same time the next night and there the man was again, only this time in a different car. This car was described as pinkish/ grayish/ whitish with a square body style. Again she drove away and as before telephoned home. Her father answered the phone. He quickly stepped outside and headed straight for the car which the man was still occupying. As he did, the single occupant jumped out of the car and ran from the area.

When he got a close look at the car, he saw it was a pinkish-grey 1960 model Valiant. His impression was someone had been sleeping in the car. The CA license plate was ZGL 357 registered to a 1965 Chevrolet reported junked on 11-20-1976 in Lodi, California.

Bonnie's dad reported the circumstances to the city police and that the car had been abandoned. The officers who responded left the car as they found it. By 4:15 P.M. the next day it was gone.

A few days after the car was abandoned, Bonnie arrived home about 11:30 P.M. Again the same man was sitting in the Valiant which was now parked in a different location but still in the alley at the rear of her house.

I contacted the SPD records section searching for a report, but no report had been made. Without the records at hand I cannot say precisely what steps I followed or who I spoke with, but I did trace that car back to the Stockton area. No specific address or name was ever developed. It just seemed to fade into nothingness much as the suspect had.

Bonnie described the man as a white male, 5 ft. 9 inches tall, with a slim build, dark hair to his shoulders, fair skin, and a small, short beard. She did not see a mustache.

On May 11th, I made contact with the ice cream truck driver who identified himself as Robert William Lee with a home address in Orangevale. Thomas did not seem even a little surprised that I was talking to him about the investigation. He assumed it was in response to his contacting the SPD and asking for a description of the suspect being sought.

Robert was then living with his wife on Alma Mesa and drove a maroon 1960 Chevrolet with California license plate AJD 777. Drivers license information showed Robert to be 6 ft. tall and 143 lbs., with a Lincoln address. He had brown hair and green eyes.

I noted that he did have light-brown hair with a full Van Dyke type beard about four inches in length. He also had a very thin mustache with the ends drooping down. His eyes were large and dark, but I could not testify to as whether or not they were attractive. He did not appear to be more than 5 ft. 10 inches in height (his weight was about 140 lbs.) on a thin build. Thomas told me his blood tested A positive. At the time of the interview, he was wearing size nine tennis shoes. The soles were of the zigzag pattern but the pattern was very nearly gone due to wear and tear.

Robert was never fully eliminated as being the East Area Rapist but that was mostly due to the fact there was no evidence available, making it impossible to eliminate him. He left California sometime in the late 1970's or very early 1980's, and now lives in Arkansas with his wife. A DNA sample from Robert would bring closure to the question of whether he is or is not the EAR.

A Poem

1977 – a poem purportedly written by the East Area Rapist.

This poem was allegedly written by the EAR himself. There is NOT, nor has there ever been, a way to authenticate who wrote it. According to some, there is reason to discount it as being written by the EAR.

"Excitement's Crave"

All those mortal's surviving birth
Upon facing maturity,
Take inventory of their worth
To prevailing society.

Choosing values becomes a task;
Oneself must seek satisfaction.
The selected route will unmask
Character when plans take action.

Accepting some work to perform
At fixed pay, but promise for more,
Is a recognized social norm,
As is decorum, seeking lore.

Achieving while others lifting
Should be cause for deserving fame.
Leisure tempts excitement seeking,
What's right and expected seems tame.
Jessie James has been seen by all,
And "Son of Sam" has an author.

Others now feel temptations call.
Sacramento should make an offer.

To make a movie of my life
That will pay for my planned exile.
Just now I'd like to add the wife
Of a Mafia lord to my file.

Your East Area Rapist
And deserving pest
See you in the press or on TV

This was received by *The Sacramento Bee* and a local TV station via mail sometime in early 1977. Assuming this was written by the EAR, then the essence of this poem validates my opinion. He was a career criminal with rape being his specialty. He was pursuing this goal as much as if he would have an academic major.

Two other points of interest are his use of the word "leisure" and "planned exile." He most certainly had a lot of free time to pursue his "career" as he wandered about both day and night around the state. The word exile might just explain why he suddenly disappeared from the radar. He may well be an expatriate, or maybe he was never a citizen to begin with. It's those kinds of possibilities that make mysteries what they are: mysteries.

Chapter 39:
EAR Gets Careless

May 14, 1977
Merlindale Drive
Citrus Heights

It may have been in February or March, 1977, when rumor reached me of a foot pursuit on Merlindale Drive, another residential street close to Primrose where an EAR assault occurred. In this incident Officer Ackerman and a reserve officer were on routine patrol when they spotted a man walking down an alley.

This is what officer Ackerman personally told me happened. In this incident he and a reserve officer were on routine night patrol when they spotted a man walking down an alley.

Pointing the squad car down that alley was all it took to fire up the walker. He was immediately in full sprint mode. Just as the squad car aimed in his direction, he turned and disappeared through a gate. As he slammed down on the brakes, officer Ackerman told his partner, "Get 'em." His partner did not clear the squad car until Ackerman was out and running.

By the time they were through the gate, the man they were chasing was out of sight. Concluding the only way he could have disappeared so quickly was by entering the house directly in front of them, they decided to go in after him. All they found was the resident of the house on his couch.

A search of the front yard turned up a baseball cap with the logo of a local company called Overhead Doors. I was told there was no other identifying information in that cap.

In 2013, I learned there was indeed additional information in that cap which included the name of an employee of Overheard Doors. A patrol officer, temporarily assigned to the EAR task force, had allegedly taken it upon himself to follow-up on the lead. Interestingly enough, in 2013 this lead was also news to both Sgt. Bevins, the lead investigator, and Lt. Root, the task force commander. Apparently the cap was stolen from the car of the employee of Overhead Doors; the cap owner was eliminated as being the East Area Rapist.

The reserve officer who partnered with officer Ackerman that night was well known to me. He was the same individual I suspected of emulating the Early Bird Rapist–the same individual whose polygraph test results strongly indicated deception.

I was already aware of active prowling in that area and had been on the alert for any evidence of more. Enough information had surfaced that it was possible to make an educated guess when and where the next assault would occur. The odds were good it would happen on the weekend of May 14-15, in the neighborhood near the Birdcage Mall. The closest intersection would be Sunrise amd Greenback Rd.

Had I been aware of the information about to come to our attention, there would have been no question of when and where he was going to hit. As it was, I approached Lt. Root in his office the morning of the 14th with the prediction there would an assault by the EAR that night or the next. Extending my neck a little further, I said it would happen on one of three streets: Guinevere, Farmgate, or Merlindale Drive. All three were close to the earlier assault on Primrose Drive.

I proposed the five officers delegated to Rancho Cordova be re-assigned to the neighborhoods in question. After some discussion, he agreed to cut one officer loose. It would be up to me where that officer would be assigned.

Where to place that one officer was the question of the moment. The fact was, I was a bit conflicted as to where the EAR would strike next. It was considered by a number of investigators the EAR would stick to his pattern and strike near Thornwood Dr.

Somebody borrowed trip alarms, used in Viet Nam, from the military. These consisted of spikes stuck in the ground and others designed to look like dog poop. In theory, the vibrations caused by anyone walking by would set them off. They were placed in every spot around Thornwood where it was thought the EAR might prowl. They were left in place for several days, but none ever went off.

While I still thought the area of Birdcage Mall was highly likely, I was not opposed to the possibility of Thornwood Drive. Because a lot of resources and thought had gone into that plan of action, I decided that was the place for the one officer's assignment. There was also the safety factor to consider, so that was where I left it.

While we were wasting time setting up a neighborhood wide surveillance system near Thornwood Drive, Pam and Mike were about to become the next victims of the EAR.

What follows is a timeline of events leading up to and including the assault as it was pieced together:

A couple of weeks earlier, a young girl, playfully riding on the shoulders of her brother in their Merlindale backyard, spotted something suspicious. From her higher than normal vantage point, she saw a short, stocky, white man, dressed in dark clothing and crouched behind some bushes in the backyard of 6140 Merlindale. When the crouched man realized he had been seen, he immediately took off, clearing fences as if they were hurdles on a track.

12:45 A.M. on May 13th, Mr. and Mrs. Martin heard someone on the roof of their Merlindale home. At the same time, neighborhood dogs south of their house began barking. At 1:00 A.M., a neighbor called the Martins saying they heard someone on their roof. The Martins then called the SSD.

1:04 A.M., the neighbors who called the Martins about someone being on their roof could still hear the prowler walking around on their roof.

1:05 A.M., the SSD squad car arrived. The roof crawler was gone—not surprising since he would have seen the squad car approaching.

2:00 A.M., the family who called the Martins heard someone trying to force open their slider door.

By coincidence, the names of this family were the same as a future victim of the EAR, plus a witness to yet another EAR assault. Both of those assaults occurred outside of

Sacramento, and nothing was ever found to show these three families were aware or connected to each other.

Late night, May 13th, a woman thought she heard noises in her garage. She did not investigate. Neighbors told her they also heard loud noises coming from her garage, but assumed her husband was working in the garage. These same people had their home burglarized in December, 1976, just prior to moving to Merlindale Drive. Where they lived prior to Merlindale is not recorded.

6:30 A.M., May 13th, another resident on Merlindale Drive reported a suspicious person to the SSD. She told the officer because she had been receiving a lot of hang-up phone calls, she was on the alert for anything out of the ordinary. This is why, when she looked across the street at that early hour, and saw a white male between 5 ft. 8 inches to 5 ft. 10 inches tall and weighing about 165 lbs., she called the SSD. He had short, light-brown hair and was wearing a blue shirt and pants. The man was long gone by the time the SSD arrived.

6:30 P.M., in the general area of Merlindale, a young woman saw an older black car with a battered paint job that was being occupied by one man. To her it looked like an ex-California Highway Patrol car. The man was dressed in what appeared to be a dirty, rumpled, brown uniform. At first she thought it was some kind of stakeout. After about two hours, the car's loud exhaust announced its departure.

Then it happened.

On May 14th, at approximately 3:15 A.M., someone forced entry into the new home of Pam and her husband on Merlindale Drive.

5:15 A.M., the telephone call to report that a sexual assault had just occurred was made to the SSD.

5:20 A.M., a twelve-year-old paper boy at the corner of Sunrise and Birdcage watched a van with wide wheels speeding north on Birdcage. When it reached Greenback Lane, it turned west. The van was blue, and looked like it had been sanded.

Recent arrivals from out of town, Pam and Mike had just moved into their new home on Merlindale Drive. She was a waitress, and he was a manager of another popular restaurant.

As soon as they moved in, the hang-up phone calls began. There had been a prowler in their backyard days earlier.

As most victims of the EAR, they were in bed sound asleep when awakened by a bright light in their eyes. Pamela awoke to a man, his head stuffed into a nylon stocking, standing in their bedroom doorway. "You make a sound and I'll kill you. I have a .45 and I'll kill you if you move." Then from the stuffed nylon came, "I'm going to take your money and I want some food. Then, I'll leave in my van." After the introductions were over, the contest of who could tie whom the tightest was on, followed by his other sick games.

Absolutely nothing was any different in his program of terror. In between his, "Shut up's," he told Pam what a beautiful body she had and asked if she would like to go to the river with him. He mentioned she was so beautiful, and said, "I'm going to take you in the van with me. How would you like to be in the river?"

Pam and Mike described the suspect as a WMA, 5 ft. 9 to 5 ft. 10 inches tall. He was a little on the stocky side with dark-brown shoulder or collar-length hair. No facial hair was noted, but Pam did say his legs felt very hairy.

The woman who sold the house to Pam and Mike arrived while the investigators were still there. She did not live far away and when she learned of the assault, she wanted to share information with the deputies.

This woman, Mrs. Simmon, said she and her family were living in the house when they sold it to Pam and Mike. For several weeks they had been receiving hang-up phone calls. Even after she sold the house and moved, the calls followed her. Not being a realtor, she had hired Bohannon Realty to handle the actual transaction of selling the property.

But all of that information was, to Mrs. Simmons, coincidental. What she really wanted to pass on was information about a real estate agent who struck her as suspicious.

He was an extremely well-dressed white male, 5 ft. 9 to 5 ft. 10 inches tall, about 25-years-old, styled light-brown hair, with a darker complexion. The car he was driving was an older brown car in very poor condition. This man introduced himself as Frank William Dubbins, Jr. He claimed to work for American Realty with offices on American River Drive. Mrs. Martin found that a bit odd, as a Mr. Parker, from the same company, had already toured the house twice. Also, Dubbins, Jr. had not called ahead for an appointment, as all other realtors had done.

But even that was not what made her uneasy about this alleged salesman. When he first arrived he wanted to look at the outside of the house. There he focused primarily on the south and east sides of the house. Once inside the house, he never looked at the same points of interest as other real estate sales people typically did. While touring the house, his questions mostly were about her husband and daughter and asking why they were not home. Their family schedule was something in which he seemed very interested.

Mrs. Simmons became very uncomfortable when she tried to look Frank Dubbins, Jr. in the eye. It was almost as if he were glaring at her. In short, he scared her.

Coincidentally, Sgt. Querin of the South Lake Tahoe Police Department called me, two days after the Merlindale Drive assault, with information about an individual he felt we might want to investigate as a possible suspect. It turned out this new person of interest was the same one Mrs. Simmons told us about.

Dubbins lived in the South Lake Tahoe area where he worked as a security guard. It was while employed as such that he became a suspect in a series of break-ins where women were sometimes assaulted. The assaults did not include rape, or at least I was not told so if they did. The suspicion arose when Dubbins would just show up, after each break-in, just as an officer arrived on the scene. He was always out of breath claiming he chased the suspect, but had lost him.

Sgt. Querin said Dubbins was known to have a police monitor and a .357 handgun that he bought in 1975.

Dubbins was known to be an alcoholic. He had two scars on the right side of his face, close to his mouth. It was thought he may have been in the military, but that was not confirmed.

Sgt. Querin's thought Dubbins was a coward, but if he caught a woman off guard, he would be capable of rape. He was going to find out if Dubbins had an alibi for the night of this assault and contact me with what he learned. I never heard from him again. In the meantime, I turned the investigation of Dubbins over to officer Fred Mason.

Officer Mason contacted the American River Realty Company where he learned neither Parker nor Dubbins had ever been employed. Information later came to him that both were employed by American Marketing and Development Company, which was located in Rancho Cordova.

As with many of the POI's, the case on Dubbins was left hanging for a numer of years before he was eliminated as a suspect. Homicide detectives of the SSD were able to document his presence in another state at the time of an assault by the EAR.

It was right after the assault on Merlindale when I received a call about another suspicious acting person. This actually took place in Rancho Cordova, but it had to be followed up regardless of where it happened.

The day of the Merlindale assault, a young woman riding her bicycle in Rancho Cordova saw a man in a white compact station wagon. Later that afternoon, she saw him again. This time she saw him close to where she lived. Then for a third time that day, this same man in the station wagon showed up. This time she was with two other girls in a car. The man idled his car beside them. Each time they moved forward or backward, he would do the same. All three girls made it obvious they were writing down his license plate number, UOC 572. He did not seem to care, and after a while he drove off.

Except for one thing, the girls might have thought the whole episode was some form of juvenile flirting. That one thing was his physical appearance. The first time seen, the driver of the station wagon had shoulder length dark-brown hair, a beard that stretched from ear to ear (which was not over an inch and a half in length), and he was without a mustache. A short time later she saw him again.This time he was without the beard. The bearded description closely matched a possible suspect described for the Winterbrook assault.

The compact white station wagon was registered to USCG LORSTA, San Mateo Street, San Clemente, California, a Coast Guard base. The registered owner lived on Armory Street in Imperial Beach and was shown to be 5 ft. 9 inches, 130 lbs., with brown hair and blue eyes. The second name found for the car lived on East Rose in Paramount, but there was no other identifying information.

No response was ever received from the Coast Guard when asked for information about the car or the name associated with it. Without access to the original reports, there is no way to know what came of this lead.

Chapter 40:
Wife of a Mafia Lord

May 17, 1977
Sandbar Circle
Carmichael

"Look at me. Look at me. Do you hear me?" It was the soft voice whispering those words, not at all deep but young-sounding, that brought Wanda wide awake. As she turned her head towards the source of the words, she caught a brief glimpse of the clock by the glare of the light shining on her and her husband who was beside her. The clock glared back showing it was 1:36 A.M. May 17th, exactly three days after the assault on Merlindale Drive. Her two small children and their grandfather, visiting from Italy, were sleeping soundly in other rooms.

The first Patrol officers to arrive found Joe and his father standing outside the house. Joe was extremely irate. Waving his arms he said to the officers, "What's the hurry? He's gone. Just come on in and…" The rest of his comments were lost in a flurry of part-Italian and broken English.

As soon as I saw Joe, I recognized him as the man strutting around the public forum—the one I had asked what he was worried about, saying he was not going to get raped. I don't recall any comments from him to show he recognized me. But contrary to the popular rumor, the assault on him and his wife did not occur the next day. That night in the forum was then seven months in their past.

Joining me at the crime scene was SPD Officer Vin Sant, and a short time later Lt. Root, the task force commander. When Lt. Root arrived, he was challenged at the front door by a rookie patrol officer assigned to guard the crime scene from outside the house. Lt. Root, personally offended, loudly announced his identity, then walked around the officer and relieved him of guard duty.

The assault was a carbon copy of the ones preceding it. There were some minor variations, but even they were copies of the other minor variations. For example, during the sexual assault, the suspect took his gloves off briefly when he was caressing Wanda's legs.

His statements were along the same lines as before, except this time he was probably trying to extend his control towards both the police and media. To quote him, "Those fuckers. Those fuckers, those pigs. I've never killed before but I'm going to kill now. Listen, do you hear me? I want you to tell those fuckers, those pigs, I'm going home to my apartment. I have bunches of televisions. I'm going to listen to the radio and watch television, and if I hear about this, I'm going to go out tomorrow night and kill two people. People are going to die."

Wanda sensed the more he boasted, the more excited he seemed to become. The more excited he became, the more a tendency to stutter showed. She did not feel he was pretending. We all knew this guy was nuts, but this outburst just told me he was not so mature after all. It was something I would expect from an uneducated, not overly bright, immature teenager−or a psychopath.

Here again, a virtually identical program was repeated. He was heard going in and out of the kitchen. Sounds of him eating, as he wandered around ransacking the house, could be heard. Yet the two children and Wanda's father-in-law never woke up. Then, precisely as he did in the assault on Woodpark Way, he said he was going into the kitchen to cook something to eat and he quietly left. by the back door. In the victim's backyard, investigators later found three partially-empty containers of three types of cheese crackers, along with some empty beer cans.

When describing the whole horror-filled experience Wanda said her impression was the man was crazy and had an obsession to eat. Surprisingly, he was never rough with her, but he seemed to vent a feeling of anger towards her husband. Maybe he had been at the same forum as this family.

Wanda gave his height as 5 ft. 8 to 5 ft. 9 inches tall, and of this she was certain. He never spoke except as a whisper through clenched teeth, which he often punctuated by deep breaths. She thought the suspect had a very small penis, and again, going only by feel, she thought he had very hairy legs.

When first seen, he held a gun in his right hand, which he claimed was a .45 caliber, and a flashlight in his left hand. His flashlight was 12-15 inches long with a very bright round beam.

Throughout this ordeal, he repeatedly held a knife to Wanda's neck. His knife came from their kitchen, as Wanda had heard him when he picked it up.

What she saw of his clothing was a beige ski mask with knitted ribbing that ran from side to side. His gloves were light-brown leather with rough seams. The seams were split on the top at the sides at the wrist and to the center of the back of the hand. From the sounds of squeaking when he walked, she thought his shoes were probably hard-soled.

A tracking dog was brought to the scene and immediately began to follow the suspect's trail. Ultimately, the trail led to the corner of Sandbar and Canebreak Circles where it ended at the curb.

About two weeks prior to this assault, someone shot two BBs through one of Wanda and Joe's house windows. Sometime later, they discovered their garage door had been pried at the top making it difficult, if not impossible, to open.

The damage to the garage door was exactly where, if a proper tool were inserted, the catch could be slipped and the door opened—something of which the average home owner is not aware. It had since been repaired and both of the incidents were reported to the SSD.

Hang-up calls, while they had occurred, had not been frequent for Wanda and her family. But this was not so for some of her neighbors. They had been experiencing crank calls and prowlers for a number of weeks. In one case, since January, 1977.

A day or two before the assault, Wanda was standing at her kitchen window. Looking out, she saw a man who was holding something in his hands, walking across her neighbor's lawn. When the man went to the side the neighbor's house, she lost sight of him. The neighbor had recently been widowed and the neighborhood was looking after him.

The night before the assault another neighbor saw a man shining a flashlight into all the cars parked on Sandbar Circle. It was about then that the neighborhood dogs joined in a chorus of barking.

About 10:25 P.M., as a couple was walking down the street, they found themselves following a white male who seemed to be looking closely at the houses as he passed them. He walked as if he had no real purpose. They lost sight of him at the intersection of Sandbar and McClarn Circle. The couple described him as being close to 6 ft. tall, with a slight slouch. This made the fourth time the description of a slight slouch had come up.

The night of the actual assault, another neighbor saw someone, between the hours of 9:00 and 9:30, shining a flashlight near Wanda's house. Naturally they did not notify Wanda, or her family, or the SSD for that matter.

Two weeks earlier, yet another neighbor heard someone in their yard. When they investigated, they discovered a window screen had been pried off. They did not deem it worth calling the SSD.

One neighbor, however, had a lot to report. Early in the evening on the day of the assault, they saw a brown 60's or 70's Dodge Charger in front of their house. It looked out of place.

Twice in the past two months these neighbors had been approached by census takers who wanted to know how many people lived in their house. This seemed okay, except census workers only collect data during years ending in "0" as by the decade. Also, they typically do not visit the same house twice. For that matter they seldom, if ever, work in pairs.

Harassing phone calls were received by these same neighbors, both at home and at work. Once they found their slider door ajar when they got home. Another prowler was seen in a backyard on February 9, 1977.

This same neighbor reported another car, not known in the neighborhood, that caught her attention. She described it as a Plymouth, California, license --. Patrol officer, Pat Flood, responded to the scene.

The license plate came back to a Clarence Edward with a birth date of 10-3-1950, 5 ft. 8 inches, black hair, and brown eyes, The address given was on 42nd Street in Sacramento. Again without access to the "Holy Grail," I cannot report what action was taken with the information.

Another vehicle was seen near the victim's home on the day of the assault. It was a new model, brown El Camino, California license plate 366T??. It was parked on the river levee behind the victim's house. The driver was a white male, 25 to 27 years old, with collar-length brown hair and deep-set eyes.

The neighbor who saw the El Camino was asked to undergo hypnosis, which she did. I was not presented at the time, but did receive a picture of a decal that she had seen on the El

Camino. It bore the picture of a parachute with a missile suspended beneath.

I took the drawing to the OSI at Mather and asked them to ensure it was dispatched to all military bases in California, or anywhere else they could think of. They agreed, and that was the last we heard from the military on the subject. Copies went to other law enforcement agencies as well.

In 2014 I received a suggestion as to the source of that decal. As it turns out it was representative of a drone recovery. The drone program, a highly classified military operation, was not declassified until about 1975. The AF 4200 Support Squadron, assigned to Beale AFB, was responsible at that time for the drone recovery program.

The military attempted to recover these drones while still in flight. Sometimes that did not work out. So as alternative some personnel were given jump training. That is they used parachutes. When a drone was successfully recovered a picture of a parachute with a drone suspended was painted on the drone fuselage. Exactly like the decal seen on the El Camino.

There was one more significant point to come from the neighborhood canvass. A nearby neighbor of Wanda's had their house for sale. The sign in the front yard was for JB&H Realtors. The company was based out of Modesto, California. Wanda's family lived in Modesto. This was also the same company that sold the house on Primrose where the EAR had struck a few weeks earlier. However, no connection was ever made between this series of sexual assaults and that company, nor for that matter, any company dealing in real estate.

The very next EAR assault to occur would be against a ranking member of the Sacramento water treatment plant, which was almost within throwing distance of Sandbar Circle. Today the treatment plant is the site of the Sacramento Sheriff's training academy.

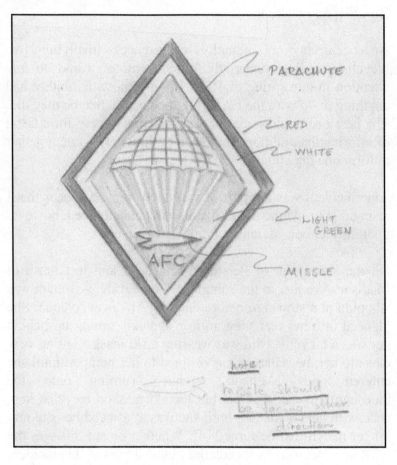

Drawing of the decal seen on an El Camino parked near Sandbar Circle.

Chapter 41:
Two Bicyclists and One Car

Bicyclist on Pershing

An occurrence or actually occurrences involving two bicyclists falling under the title "remote" came to my attention in late spring of 1977. I don't know that either had anything to do with the EAR But, then again, maybe they did. The best one could hope for was to collect every little tidbit of information and hope they would ultimately come together to form one big chunk.

One incident was a report of suspicious circumstances that I responded to. At the time I dismissed it as unrelated, however upon further consideration, it may have beeen.

On the side-street of Pershing, off Hazel and just north of Madison Avenue, in the suburb of Orangevale, a woman was stopping at a stop sign before entering Madison Avenue. She glanced into her rear view mirror. Quickly oming up behind her was a bicyclist who was wearing a ski mask. Getting very close to her, he remained, as if glued to her bumper, until she entered onto Madison Avenue. Turning onto the thoroughfare, she sped up, but the ski masked bicyclist kept pace with her. It was not until she was at a speed he could no longer match that he turned off. Whether or not this was the EAR is wide open to speculation, but I do know this incident was not very far from the assault on Richdale.

The other incident involving a bicycle occurred just off of Dawes Street, in Rancho Cordova. This time two detectives were the witnesses.

Chapter 42:
Bicyclist in Rancho Cordova

It was early in the evening as the sun was just setting when Sgt. Irwin and I were parked less than a block from Dawes Street. We were right in the middle of the area where there had been five sexual assaults associated with the EAR. After following up on some leads, we decided to remain in the area for a while to see if anything caught our attention. A couple of things did. Sgt. Irwin's vibrating in place behind the steering wheel caught my attention. A speeding bicyclist caught his.

The speeding bicyclist was a man dressed all in black, heading south on Dawes Street towards Folsom Boulevard. As he sped through the intersection behind us, Sgt. Irwin commented, "That's him. There he goes." I asked how he knew, and he replied, "I just know."

A few minutes later the same bicyclist returned only now he was speeding north on Dawes Street towards Dolcetto Drive and Los Palos Drive. He was quickly out of sight.

Within minutes of losing sight of the bicyclist, there was that brief burst of escaping electrons from the radio, followed by the announcement that someone had just attempted entry into an occupied home.

Inside of one minute we were at Dawes Street and the drainage ditch. The attempted entry had been made on the second house from the corner of Dawes and Los Palos. With that ditch behind the house a quick escape was all but guaranteed. Even if we had gone after the bicyclist, we would not have been able to catch him in the act, and quite possibly we couldn't have even have caught up with him.

May 1977
South Sacramento

May, like the previous months since we responded to that first call on Woodpark Way, was a very busy one. Detective Rick Martin and I found ourselves sharing an unmarked car on a daytime surveillance. This late in the game, I have no idea what we were doing there, but it was in South Sacramento on a residential street which paralleled the main thoroughfare, Florin Road, on the north side.

From where we were parked facing east, there was a short street to our left. It was not more than a few blocks long. About midway down, there was a small tag football game going on in the middle of the street.

Moments after we had parked, a car headed east bound came by very slowly as opposed to typical neighborhood traffic that whizzed by. What really caught my attention was how focused the driver was on that tag football game. After he was gone, I looked more closely at the composition of the group. It was composed of all boys except for one attractive young woman with long hair. She was about 20 years old. She was very active in the game. Looking back, I think she was playing the quarterback position.

After enough time to circle the block once, the car returned. The driver was as attentive on that game as he was before.

This time I noted the make and model of the car. After all these years I can only say it was a light colored square shaped car that was possibly a Datsun or even a small Chevrolet.

With time to circle the block for a third pass, the driver was still intent on the group. I wrote down the license number, as did Detective Martin. Reading from that piece of paper I radioed in the license number asking for a quick registration check. I commented to Detective Martin if that car came by again we were going to pull it over. It never returned. The license plate we called in was not on file. I am certain we copied those numbers down correctly.

The driver was a pencil-necked blond male about 19 to 22 years old. Was he the sick pencil-wick for whom we were looking? It was his intense focus on that group of young people that caught my attention. Typically, when investigating a case, I try not to overlook any detail—no matter how remote. I can promise you I most definitely was not about to overlook anything that even hinted at the possibility of leading us to the identification of this psychopath. It was only weeks after this incident that the EAR took his show to South Sacramento, about a mile from where we observed the car with an unregistered license plate.

Chapter 43:
Exactly Who is Chasing Whom?

May, 1977

Where the American River flows from the town of Folsom to Sacramento, it is bordered on the north by steep cliffs. The south side is a different story. During the gold rush of the 1800's, huge gold dredgers were put to work. These football-field size machines dug their own pond in which to float. They managed to travel by digging the pond ahead of them. It was by that method the pond moved ahead with the dredger still floating in it.

What was left.behind were countless tons of river rock. Piled high in places and low in others, they made homes for small ponds that housed some of the best bass fishing in the state of California, something very few people knew. However, they also presented an excellent corridor for people like the EAR to move about unseen.

Today, having been smothered under concrete and asphalt, the fish and ponds are all gone. In the 1970's they existed from the American River to more than a mile south of Rancho Cordova proper. Near the intersection of Coloma Road and Sunrise Boulevard, lay a neighborhood perfectly matched to the type the EAR preferred.

El Manto Drive is three blocks long. At the east end of El Manto is the beginning of an "L" shaped park. On the south side, El Manto runs parallel to the long part of the "L." Each end of that "L" shaped park hosts a school. On the east end is the John Mitchell Middle School and at the other end an elementary school. My family and I lived at 2308 El Manto at the time, right smack in the middle of the park's "L" shape. It was here that I believe late one night we were visited by the EAR.

The fact we lived in the type of area the EAR seemed to prefer had not escaped me for an instant. My primary sense of security, for the nights I was away, was our dog Squire, a German shepherd. He was an unusually intelligent animal and extremely protective. Never outside alone, he neither had the opportunity to make friends with strangers, nor did he seem partial to the idea. Once, my sister-in-law babysat for us. She, a very frequent visitor in our home and friends with Squire, was unable to enter our sons' rooms after we left for the evening. Squire simply sat in the hallway and would not let her pass.

His presence, and the fact my wife was armed and quite willing to shoot any prowler or potential prowler, gave me some feeling of peace when away. Even then, I would drive by as frequently as I could. They were never entirely alone or unprotected for the patrol officers in that area knew her and also made periodic drive-bys. If all the lights had been turned out, we would have known something was amiss.

But still the EAR may have made a visit to our house one night. We have two sons and each had his own bedroom. The older son slept a normal eight hours while the younger rarely slept more than four or five hours; a habit which he has to this day. It was the younger one lying there in his bed who saw somebody looking in his bedroom window.

As it was told to me later, it sounded like someone on the roof was deliberately making as much noise as possible. Listening to this, our son became very scared. Then a head covered with some sort of mask was suddenly hanging upside down looking through his window. Had it not been for a small cloth ball bobbing around, as it hung straight down from the covered head, he might not have seen it. That is until a flashlight beam passed once around the room. Then the covered head was gone. Now thoroughly frightened, the about-to-turn five year-old boy came into our room and climbed into bed with us.

He must have caught us in our REM sleep because neither of us became wide awake. We both recall him crawling in between us and telling us he was scared, but either he did not mention any details or we failed to pick up on them. Had I comprehended what he was telling us, I can absolutely and without any reservation guarantee the entire park and surrounding area would have been crawling with cops and tracking dogs—either that or I would have had a leaky roof.

But I was not fully cognizant of what happened until morning when I awoke and our son told us the story in more detail, probably for a second time. Today he still vividly remembers the incident because it scared him so badly. In his memory, he came into our bedroom and climbed in between his mother and me telling us what he had just experienced, then huddled down for the rest of the night.

The first thing we did that morning was to check for footprints and any other signs of a prowler, but we found none. Not surprising, considering he spent much time on top of houses. This incident reminded me: I often wondered if some items, stolen by the EAR, were found on roofs not because he tossed them there, but perhaps they fell out of his pocket.

We never had any indication that anyone had been inside our house when we were gone. I'm certain that was because the houses in our area had roll-out windows, as opposed to sliders. That is probably why there were no reported illegal entries in our neighborhood. I'm certain I would have picked up on it if there had been.

As I was about to retire from law enforcement a *Sacramento Bee* reporter interviewed me about this case. Some misunderstandings happened and the news article reported my son was so traumatized by that event he would not sleep in a room by himself. That was incorrect. He would not sleep in a room with the lights off until he was 15 years old. Today it no longer bothers him in the slightest to have the lights off.

May 28, 1977
4th Park Way
Sacramento

The next EAR assault, and the last investigation I was to formally participate in, occurred on May 28, 1977, at about 12:20 A.M. This time the suspect moved further out from his usual area and into South Sacramento. There was a lot of speculation about why he did this. Here is one possibility to consider.

The EAR assault immediately before this one was on Sandbar Circle. Sandbar Circle is separated from the American River greenbelt by a levee. As stated before, just opposite this levee was the water treatment plant for Sacramento. The husband of the next victim was a top level supervisor at that plant. There could be a connection, but then again maybe not. The husband was also a marine reserve, assigned to the army depot on Fruitridge Road. Maybe there was a connection.

Two or thee weeks new to the neighborhood on Parkway, Cindy and her husband Fred were in bed engaged in sexual foreplay when they were interrupted by a light shining on them. From behind that light came a harsh raspy whisper, "Lay perfectly still or I will kill all of you. I will kill you, I will kill her, and I will kill your little boy." Their young son was asleep in his bedroom where he would sleep through the entire assault. As the nightmare wore on, they each noticed the suspects voice seemed to rise to a higher pitch when he was excited.

Nothing occurred or did not occur in this assault that made it any different from all the others. But before the suspect left, he told Cindy he wanted her to give the pigs a message. Twice he told her, "They got it mixed up last time. I said I would kill two people. I'm not going to kill you. If this is on the TV or in the papers tomorrow, I'll kill two people. Are you listening?" He then made her repeat what he said.

The dog used to track the suspect led us across a small lot then to a low fence bordering Highway 99. This time we hoisted the dog over the fence. Immediately the dog was hot on the suspect's trail. But it was only a short distance before that trail ended.

For those who don't know California Transportation (CalTrans), it is the department responsible for the highway maintenance and landscaping. They have beautifully landscaped the freeways in some areas. Where the dog lost the trail was close to, but not among, tall trees bordering the north bound lanes of Highway 99.

Right where the trail ended, we spotted tire tracks. Their spacing indicated a small car, such as a Volkswagen or even a Porsche. One of the officers present used a measuring tape to figure out the wheelbase of the car. I have long since forgotten what it was, but I do not think it was a VW.

The sale of the victim's house had cleared escrow two or three weeks earlier, but the "for sale" sign by AIM Realty was still in the yard.

As with his other victims, Cindy could provide only a partial description of her assailant. She figured him at 5 ft. 9 or 5 ft. 10 inches tall and weighing 165 or 170 lbs. His build was slender as was his short penis.

Every time he spoke, it was with a harsh raspy whisper through clenched teeth. She thought he was a bit hyper because he kept loudly breathing in and out. At times he seemed to stutter, especially on the letter "L". His clothes consisted of a dark-colored, bulky jacket and dark pants. His gloves were black leather. The mask he wore was a red, knit ski-mask with oval holes for his eyes and mouth.

The flashlight he used was a small two cell with a bright beam. All she knew of his gun was it looked like a large caliber semi-automatic made of blue steel. To Cindy it looked like a military gun.

At approximately 5:00 A.M., Russ Oase, Special Investigator for the Federal Government, was on duty. He had been following a car he had an interest in when he spotted a white sports car, possibly the larger VW model, stopped at the intersection of Fruitridge Road and Stockton Boulevard.

Something about the driver caught Russ's attention. It was when Russ motioned for that driver to proceed through the intersection that he began to really take notice. The driver would not look in Russ's direction but instead stared straight ahead, returning the motion to move ahead. A couple of motions and horn honks later, Russ found himself thinking how out of place a man wearing a sport coat and tie was in that area, especially at five in the morning. It was not until the next day Russ learned of the assault on 4th Parkway. His encounter with this driver occurred about one mile from the scene of the assault.

Interviews of the neighbors turned up the generic nonsense phone calls, but nothing of note.

Nearby was a small fenced off building that housed some sort of utility equipment. From the number and varied descriptions of cars seen parked there, almost every day and usually at noon, one would have to assume people chose that spot for a car-picnic. Although there were a number of vehicle descriptions, none of them had license plate numbers copied.

One man was seen in a white station wagon on nearby Sky Parkway. He drew attention because of the impression that he was living in it.

Several solicitors had been in the neighborhood recently. They were selling vacuum cleaners and kids books. The Mormon missionaries had also been through the area.

Chapter 44:
East Area Rapist in the Crosshairs

June, 1977

Sometime in early June, a lot of discussion about a recent development in the investigation suddenly broke out around the office, and especially over the departmental radios. It seems a man living on a street called Cedarhurst Way had been unable to locate the work schedule for his new job. While searching for that slip of paper, he discovered his handgun, which he kept in a nightstand, had been unloaded and the gun replaced.

Interest was further whetted when tennis shoe prints, similar in size and design to the ones believed to belong to the EAR, were discovered along a path behind his house. The only problem with those prints was they were on a path used by students going to and from a nearby school. There was also a report of a man with thick black curly hair seen on that path which even further heightened the interest of some.

I knew little beyond what I had overheard; and there was a whole lot of chatter about this new information. In the meantime, I continued with my own efforts of reviewing reports−looking for any hint of where and when the EAR would strike again.

Probably no more than two days after the discovery of the unloaded gun, I came across an illegal entry report I felt might be the work of the EAR. Even though nothing seemed to be missing, the people who lived there were certain someone had been inside their house. They reached this conclusion when they noticed some items had been disturbed. Naturally my only option was to visit them.

As I started out the office door, I nearly ran into officer Syd Curtis who was coming through, announcing as he did, that he had been assigned to the task force. Did I need any help? Perfect timing, so I invited him along.

The information we were to glean from that morning excursion provided us with a very neat and concise picture of how the EAR prowled an area and learned about his intended victims. None of it was new, but for the first time I was able to confirm his steps before he actually assaulted anyone.

The house where the illegal entry occurred was located on Templeton Drive in Carmichael. Templeton Drive is a relatively short street paralleling Madison Avenue. Essentially a frontage road.

Nobody was home in this small one-story stucco home, so we invited ourselves to look around the outside. The very first thing to catch our attention was a shoe print.

There, on the wall just below a small window, and about five feet above the driveway, was a faint shoe print with the herring bone pattern. It appeared to be about the same size as the other shoe prints found at the crime scenes.

With no one home to dispute it, we determined this shoe print was at the point of entry. Based on this print and the illegal entry report, we felt we had identified an area where the EAR was active. Sensing investigative treasure in the offing, we set out to confirm our opinion.

Directly across the street from where we stood was Cedarhurst Way. Cedarhurst Way, more or less, cuts a curve from south to the northeast, with the south end butting up against Templeton Drive. As fate would have it, the man with the missing work schedule lived at the other end of this street. A fact of which we were not aware.

Based on what we had learned over the past few months, we chose to start with the second house from the SE corner of Cedarhurst Way and Templeton Drive. If that failed to elicit any results, we would switch to the second house from the opposite corner. There was no need to be concerned.

A knock on the door brought about our introduction to an attractive, single, young mother and her daughter. As she recounted some recent events to which she had not attached much importance, Syd and I exchanged glances. We knew we were on a roll.

On more than one occasion this young mother and her daughter returned home at the end of the day to find their front door unlocked, and at times slightly ajar. Other times she thought, but was not sure, some items in the house had been slightly moved. One time, she said, she noticed a large floor plant had been moved. That time she was sure someone had been inside while she and her daughter were away.

She had been receiving an unusual number of hang-up phone calls. It had been a week or two since her last phone call. We pretty much knew the answer to our question before we asked it. Question: where do you keep your spare house key? Answer: under the front door mat.

This young lady was squarely in the crosshairs of the psychopath known as the East Area Rapist, and she had no idea. I'm certain she was very high on his hit list.

Before taking our departure, we gave her a heads up on what was happening, plus a number of suggestions on how to be more secure. Then we did the only logical thing.

We went straight across the street and knocked on the front door of that house. Like the house on Templeton Drive, no one was home, so we invited ourselves into the backyard. More investigative treasure awaited us there.

In a far corner of that backyard was a tree. It was much like the one around the corner from Thornwood where evidence of the EAR had been found. Heavy with foliage, it was about 15 feet tall. Scattered beneath it were tennis shoe prints and cigarette butts. They were filters with a double yellow stripe around them. We left them in situ.

Then we contacted the neighbor whose house was immediately next door on the north side. This man said it was about 10 P.M. a week earlier when he looked out his window to see a young blond man walk through his neighbor's gate and onto Cedarhurst Way. The neighbor had no idea which way the man went after he reached the sidewalk. He added that the man he saw was definitely not as tall as the fence. He mentioned that twice, with emphasis on the second statement. In fact his last statement was one of those that has remained with me over the years. "I don't know who he was, but he wasn't as tall as the fence." The fence was a typical fence made of redwood standing about 5 ft. 10 inches to 6 ft. tall.

It was crystal clear the East Area Rapist had the woman, who lived in the second house from the corner, in his sights. We chose not to broadcast this information for what I considered a good reason.

As indicated before, I suspected the EAR might know what we were doing and possibly even planning. One of the reasons he might have been so well-informed was because of all the chatter being passed back and forth over the police radios. This was of course speculation but I never heard any better theories.

 An incident near Sunrise Boulevard and the American River, directly across from Rancho Cordova, that tends to support this radio-chatter theory. A woman called the SSD one night to report a possible prowler near her house. I was the first to arrive. When I made contact, she seemed surprised. She had heard what she took to be a police radio prior to my arrival, and therefore assumed the police were already there.

When we got back to the office that day, I heard more chatter about the incident of the missing work schedule and the unloaded gun at the opposite end of Cedarhurst Way. Knowing every detail of that incident had been passed around over and over again, we chose to wait two or three days before we made the world aware of what else we had discovered.

Other than the patrol officers assigned to that area, we told no one of what we had discovered. Both ends of Cedarhurst Way were a perfect setup for a stakeout. In view of the amount of radio chatter about the work schedule and unloaded gun, we felt a stakeout would have been a moot issue. Too bad, because it would have been a perfect situation.

Sure enough, all of the suspicious activity in that area immediately ceased. I was sure the EAR was aware we had been on Cedarhurst and would not return.

Chapter 45:
Color Me Gone

July, 1977

Captain Stamm, as Commander of the Detectives and by default commander of the investigation of the EAR, was under a lot of heat from Fred and the Sheriff. My relationship with those two just turned up that heat, in particular, my relationship with Fred. Fred was, to put it mildly, my biggest detractor. As time wore on, our conflict began to flare more openly. So it was anticipated, when I took vacation time in July, 1977, I would be immediately transferred. Apparently Captain Stamm was only too happy to accommodate, as he had me transferred to patrol as watch-commander almost the day I began my vacation. It was an assignment that many sought to have. It was also among the most boring jobs in the department.

There was another reason for Captain Stamm wanting me out of his nest. He was not overly impressed by my investigative skills. As it was explained to me, it was because of the occasional assignments he gave me. At those times he would lean across his desk, handing me a slip of paper while rumbling, "Check this guy out." My response was usually, "He isn't the one, but I will check him out," then I would proceed to do exactly that. Being candid does not endear one to others.

None of his suspects ever needed more than a day or two, at the most, to be thoroughly investigated. In fact few persons of interest took more than two days. I would respond the same to Lt. Root, but he could not complain for it was he who taught me how to investigate. Captain Stamm was not overly impressed with Lt. Root's investigative skills either—and mostly for the same reasons.

Chapter 46:
Color the EAR Gone

September 6, 1977

Less than two months after my transfer and three months after the revelations we had received on Cedarhurst Way, the EAR struck on Portage Circle in Stockton. There was—and is—a lot of speculation as to why he left Sacramento only to strike an hour away. His reasoning could have been as simple as he just felt like going for a drive that night. Bottom line, one guess is as good as another.

Here are three possible scenarios to consider:

Scenario One

In three of the EAR assaults in Sacramento, the suspect left behind blue paint smears. These have been likened to architectural paint. I have to assume that means there is a high likelihood construction was involved. It was soon after these assaults the suspect moved out of town. Possibly his job, if he had one, was in construction and it took him to Stockton.

Scenario Two

It was getting very hot for the EAR around Sacramento. Law enforcement was right on his tail as evidenced by the prediction of his assault on Merlindale and the two revelations discovered on Cedarhurst Way. It was also about this time the Sacramento Sheriff's Department was publicly talking about acquiring a helicopter. Not until early 1978 did they actually acquire one.

Scenario Three

He brought the paint with the intent of leaving traces behind.

Scenario three is my choice.

Up until now, all the information in this narrative came from what I personally witnessed, logs, discussions with both retired and current investigators, and from reading reports—many of which I wrote. From this point forward, what will be reported comes from other sources, without my personal participation.

September 6, 1977
Portage Circle
Stockton, California

It was the sound of drapery hooks hitting each other that awoke Doreen. Looking in the direction of the sound, she saw a man in the doorway. As she watched, he reached back through the door and picked up an old style medical bag, the satchel type that is opened by pulling the handles apart. Realizing he had been seen, the man said, "Don't say anything." With a thud, the doctor-like satchel hit the bedroom floor giving both Doreen and her husband the impression it had cans in it.

This time the psychopath selected a couple who owned a local business. The assault was pretty much the same old story for the EAR. Other than one alteration to his MO, he stuck to his standard.

Doreen was sure the man had a rubber penis strapped to his waist. Not only could she tell by feel it was artificial, but it was much bigger and firmer than what he was packing naturally. According to Doreen, he was not very successful with either instrument.

The best details for the description of this suspect came from a six-year-old girl who got up in the middle of the night to use the bathroom, As she walked down the hall, she spotted a man standing in the kitchen doorway eating. As she paused to figure out what she was looking at, he said to her, "I'm playing a game with your parents. Do you want to help?" The child, not really comprehending what she was seeing, did not reply and continued on with her business.

She later described him as a white male adult wearing a purple short sleeved shirt with a zipper instead of buttons. There was a pocket on the shirt. His gloves were black knit and he wore a brown ski mask. Around his waist he was wore a belt that had a gun holster on the left side and a "sword' hung from the right. A metal banded wristwatch was on his right wrist. He was not wearing any pants or underwear.

A later hypnosis session with this rather astute child brought out even more details. She remembered a tattoo, similar to the Schlitz Malt Liquor bull, on his left forearm. This bull was black with white horns. She also recalled a belt buckle with two revolvers imprinted on it, their barrels crossed over each other. There was something about a large black ring on his right hand, but that detailed information is not available.

Doreen and her husband added this description of their assailant a white male, 5 ft. 9 inches, weighing about 150 to 160 lbs., with a slender build. The suspect had a very strong body odor which was quite unpleasant. During the sexual assault, Doreen felt a small holster, or something similar, on the belt that a beeper might fit into. Noticing it was rough plastic, she thought of a policeman's belt.

The suspect tried to disguise his voice by talking very quickly in a low, hoarse whisper. When excited, his voice took on a much higher pitch. The impression he managed to convey was one of nervousness. Neither victim noticed any stutter, and both felt he was role playing.

Within a few minutes of the suspect leaving, a Volkswagen engine started and then the area. It is worth noting that the neighborhood had been experiencing prowlers for a few weeks prior to this assault. Dogs barking, footprints in yards, and frequent banging of fences between 10:00 P.M. and midnight indicated prowlers.

Some of the neighbors may have seen the prowler the night before the sexual assault. It was late evening when a man was seen walking in the neighborhood. Apparently when he realized he was being watched, he began to jog, however he was not dressed for jogging.

A "strange" vehicle was seen driving slowly around Portage Circle between 10:30 and 11:00 the night before this assault. The description given was a ligh-blue or green two-door Datsun or Toyota. Several neighbors had received a phone call that same night. Instead of hanging up, the caller said, "Go to hell, babe."

Dogs were barking around 1:15 in the early morning hours of the assault. Maybe 15 minutes earlier, the neighbors heard what sounded like an small older-model vehicle driving around their cul-de-sac. Yet another neighbor reported the sound of a car the night of the assault. It was between 1:00 and 3:00 A.M. when a car with a big engine squealed the tires as it drove around Portage Circle.

One woman neighbor was on the phone when she heard someone trying to open her back door. Quickly hanging up, she crawled to a bedroom where she retrieved a handgun. Gun in hand, she waited for somebody to either break in or her husband to come home. Nobody broke in. She was a wise lady indeed.

For the past couple of weeks that same wise woman had seen a white station wagon parked at the public park on nearby Cumberland. On the previous Tuesday or Wednesday she saw the same car with the same driver going slowly around their cul-de-sac, not once but twice. She described him as a WMA, 20 to 27, with brown hair over his ears. He had a rough, ruddy complexion.

The following Tuesday or Wednesday, on two occasions, she watched as the same car and the same driver passed through the cul-de-sac. There were two houses with real estate signs located in the cul-de-sac.

While checking the yards of neighbors for evidence, the officers found footprints which indicated the suspect had traveled through those backyards, confirming what the neighbors had reported. Impressions from some of these prints were taken to a local shoe dealer who positively identified them as belonging to a Converse All-Star tennis shoe.

During my turn with this investigation, I had managed to arrange telephone traps to be placed on some of the victims' telephones. None of them ever received a suspicious call. We stopped this effort and still none of the victims received phone calls from the suspect. In Stockton, it appeared the suspect may have actually telephoned one of his victims after the assault.

For the next three days, at mid-morning, the victim's telephone rang but the caller never spoke. Why do we think this was the suspect? Who else would it be? Besides, soon after this assault he began calling a number of the women he assaulted.

Very soon after Doreen was assaulted, she came home to find a note from Stockton police, Sgt. Grude. The note said they had been trying to call her, but her phone was not working properly. She was told not to worry, that the police would notify the telephone company of the problem.

Later Sgt. Grude called to say her telephone had been repaired. Right after that conversation, her mother used the phone, only to have it go dead in the middle of the conversation.

After a conversation between Doreen and an older man at the phone company, it was decided her phone was repaired. Only it wasn't. Each time she made a call, there would be a click in the middle of a sentence, followed by a disconnect, then after a moment a reconnect. It was like someone was listening in and plugging and unplugging the line whenever they felt like it.

Officer Pat Noble, from the Stockton Police Department, stopped by just as Doreen received another phone call. A young sounding man confirmed her phone number, then said, "Our office has been" and something about, "your having trouble with your phone." The victim looked at Officer Noble who immediately understood something was wrong. To stall the caller, she asked him to repeat what he just said. That was when the young sounding man hung up.

On the 13th of September, a trap was placed on the victim's telephone. It was no surprise the calls ceased immediately. Kind of a "been there, done that" sort of thing.

Chapter 47:
An Accomplice?

October 1, 1977
Tuolumne Drive
Sacramento

Petite Donna, a maid for the Six Pence Motel in Sacramento, was the first to learn of the EAR's return to Sacramento. Like a number of others before her, she made his acquaintance from the receiving end of a bright flashlight. Forced whispers through clenched teeth told her who he was and what she was in for. Later she and her boyfriend would recall he held a handgun in his right hand and a light in the left.

Donna had been living with her boyfriend on Tuolumne Drive for several weeks, before finding her own place to live. That was two weeks earlier. Since moving out, she had undergone a major medical procedure at a hospital in North Sacramento. That was two days ago. Not feeling well, she was back at her boyfriend's house to spend the night.

At the time the intruder woke Donna and her boyfriend, there was a rifle leaning against the bedroom wall. For the first minute or two, the suspect only made threats but did not come close to them. She felt this was probably because the intruder was afraid her boyfriend might go for the rifle. Apparently, the intruder's courage grew exponentially as he realized her boyfriend was not going to go for the rifle. It was then he stepped close with the shoestrings and began his game of who can tie whom the tightest.

Some claim the intruder pointed at the loaded rifle, telling her boyfriend, "Go for it." I found no such evidence in the actual report, but that is not to say it did not happen.

Donna was moved into another room where she was tied and blindfolded. Then her assailant returned to the master bedroom to place a tray and a salt shaker on the back of the boyfriend. As soon as he was alone, the boyfriend began working at silently removing those dishes. In all, the intruder returned eight times to check on him.

The boyfriend was not sure when, but at one point he heard a doorbell ring. The intruder went outside and was gone for several minutes.

Donna heard that same doorbell but also other sounds connected to it.

Right after he sexually assaulted Donna, the assailant was in the kitchen, responding to what was probably an eating neurosis, when a car horn honked twice. After a few moments it honked twice again. A few more minutes passed, then the doorbell rang five times. Then, whoever rang the doorbell knocked not on the door, but on a window. Donna could hear muffled voices—one sounded like a woman's voice.

Donna did not recognize the voices, nor did she learn who they were. It was right after hearing those voices her assailant left by way of the back slider door.

While all this was going on, Donna's boyfriend was still diligently trying to maneuver out from under that tray-supported salt shaker. Once free of this burden, he rolled onto the floor where he managed to retrieve a pocket knife from his pants pocket. After freeing himself from the bindings, he pulled a revolver from between the mattresses.

The boyfriend was no longer the hunted; he was the hunter. Unfortunately for the world, the assailant was already out the gate. After freeing Donna, he stepped into the backyard and hoping to attract attention, fired one round into the air.

Donna had been sexually assaulted by a white male, 5 ft. 9 inches tall, around 170 lbs., between 21 and 35 years of age. His breath was bad, but worse yet was the bad odor about his whole body. It was as if the bad odor emanated from every pore.

His clothing was described as a black vinyl or leather jacket with four pockets that came below his waist. His shirt was either dark-blue or dark-brown, and his gloves were black leather.

Interestingly enough, his mask was a nylon stocking with a knit cap on top of it. The knit cap seemed to match the one my son saw hanging upside down outside his window.

In this assault his weapons of choice were again a knife and a .357 revolver. The loaded shotgun that had been leaning against the bedroom wall was found beneath the living room sofa by the Sacramento Sheriff's Department ID technicians. It had been unloaded.

One has to wonder why the EAR would hide a shotgun under a sofa. In the assault on Kipling he left a bent spoon beneath a sofa. When I was very young, I put things in the oven. But I was two or three years old. Today, I passionately believe ovens are for making cheesecakes. What kind of kink in this guy's mind made him hang onto childhood actions?

Now it was confirmed. The EAR was back! Was he here to stay, or was he leaving again? The question now facing law enforcement was: where will he strike next? Stockton? Sacramento? Or …? No one had been tracking his movements since July, so there seemed no way to know.

October 21, 1978
Gold Run Avenue
Citrus Heights

This time, a 32-year-old wife of a cement contractor was assaulted. As in several of his assaults, there were children asleep in the house at the time. Her ten-year-old daughter woke up long enough to go the bathroom. Other than it was the middle of the night, she had no idea what time it was. The sound of someone walking in the hallway caught her attention, but she assumed it was someone in the family and was soon back in bed soundly sleeping.

The usual way the victims became aware of the intruder was the same. This time there were some, possibly significant, changes in his behavior. I say possibly because I personally am not at all convinced it was not an act.

Typically his first trip to the kitchen was immediately after sexually assaulting his victim. This time, instead of hearing him smacking down food or gurgling a beer, she heard him sobbing. After assaulting her a second time, he walked away crying.

Apparently his sadness was not so overwhelming that he could not take time to enjoy a beverage with the meal he stole from their kitchen. Afterwards three, empty, Miller beer cans were found just outside the house. The victim did not drink alcohol, and her husband did not drink Miller beer. Although he did have a six pack of small cans, these beer cans were not his.

Not so unusual for the assailant, he failed to reach a sexual climax. What was unusual about this attack was his failure to force her to hold his penis or to refer to it in any way.

There were other changes in his behavior—three major ones, in fact.

In addition to the "sobbing" in the kitchen, a second change was the treatment of his victim. As usual, he directed a lot of verbal threats, liberally laced with profanity, at her. But where he differed in his contact with this lady was the gentleness when he touched her. Something similar to this had been witnessed in one other assault.

The real kicker was the third major change. When providing the investigators with a description of her assailant, she described his penis as, "Fairly large around with a very small head." She was certain he had been circumcised. Strange as it sounds, the description of this man's penis had actually become relevant.

Up until this time, it had been thought he was not circumcised. This particular subject had been discussed early on when trying to ferret out the identifying details of the suspect's appearance. Someone said then that he was not circumcised. A strange thing to remember, but I do recall the subject under discussion and someone making that comment. Whoever it was probably just wanted to bring an end to an unpleasant topic. At the time we were all quite happy to accept that pronouncement as fact.

In every assault, the suspect was known to make statements to his victim. Usually he would say he had seen or met them before. We took all of his statements to be an effort to mislead the police. This time he said something else, "My buddy is in the car waiting. Tell the pigs I will be back New Years Eve." When saying 'pigs' he stuttered on the letter "P." Because he seemed to be groping for the words to say, his victims felt this stutter was genuine. Once before there had been mention of a possible stutter.

The description provided for this suspect was pretty much like the others. He was a WMA, 5 ft. 10 inches tall, in his 20's, fit with no potbelly or any flabby skin. When he spoke, it was a whisper through clenched teeth. Both the victim and her husband felt the suspect was very nervous and hyper-active. They even thought they may have detected a slight accent.

There was not much of a description on the suspect's clothing. His gloves were possibly smooth plastic or leather or even the surgical type.The mask was a dark a colored ski mask with plastic trim on it.

Interviews of the neighbors found the similar reports of crank phone calls and prowlers. The bulk of these occurred two to three weeks prior to the assault.

However, this time the crank calls to the victims did not stop prior to the assault. They continued right up until the assault. On two occasions the victims arrived home to find their garage door standing open. Just a couple of days prior to this assault, their daughter had discovered the sliding glass door, from the kitchen to the garage, standing open. It was open enough that the wind was blowing the curtains. They just assumed one of them had been careless.

October 29, 1977
Woodson Avenue
Sacramento

Early in the evening of October 28th, a young car salesman and his wife stopped off at Rico's Pizza on their way home. Having become friends with the couple who bought their old house, they planned on sharing a pizza with them. It had only been 2 ½ weeks since they moved out and the other couple moved in. Already they were good friends.

After sharing their pizza, the young car salesman and his wife returned to their new home where they watched television before retiring for the night. The house belonging to this young car salesman and his wife happened to be the only house on that street not under construction. Some were near completion and others not so much.

The young car salesman had been hospitalized for two weeks following surgery and had only been out of the hospital for three or four days. His wife visited him twice a day at Sutter General Hospital in downtown Sacramento for those two weeks. While he was hospitalized, his wife moved into their new house and began turning it into a home.

About 1:45 A.M., the young salesman woke up to some idiot tapping on the bottom of his foot with a hand gun. The sound of voices and a light in her face brought his wife awake.

Later she would say she could sense that the man with the gun and light was as afraid of them as they were of him. But once they were tied, she could no longer sense his fear.

In what she described as a low, whispery, desperate-sounding voice, he kept telling them that all he wanted was money and food for his van. When she offered to cut him a check, his response was, "Shut your fucking mouth."

While the two were being tied, the suspect kept repeating, "I know you've got a gun in here." There was one in the night stand next to the bed. Later, investigators found it on the floor underneath the comforter that was hanging over the edge of the bed. It had been unloaded. The ammo for it was found in the backyard of a neighbor who happened to be a state police officer.

It has been said more than once that rape is about anger and not sex. This pervert proved it that night. After forcing her to orally copulate him, he tried to sodomize her. Her response was exactly what he hoped for. She screamed in pain. After that, he would rape her briefly, then briefly sodomize her. He did this repeatedly, knowing full-well that she found it agonizing.

As usual the psychopath spent some time in the kitchen. This time he was not heard eating. Instead he could be heard sobbing, "I'm sorry Mommy. Mommy, please help me. I don't want to do this, Mommy. Someone please help me." To her, his sobs sounded genuine as his breathing and speaking were consistent with someone crying. Then he began walking around staying close to his victim. She had the feeling he was lost and stumbling, as he again was crying, "Mommy, I don't want to do this. Someone please help me."

This assault was one of those where the suspect wanted his victim to talk dirty to him. As with all the others, when she did try to speak, he told her to shut up. The second time he told her to shut up, he held a knife against her throat, then stood up and repeated his crying act.

From the bedroom where he lay tied, the young salesman could hear the suspect crying, "Oh Mom," followed by sounds of hyperventilation, as if he were angry. To him the suspect's voice sounded feminine. He, too, felt the emotion being shown by the suspect was genuine.

The victim said he maintained an erection, but he was unable to remain inside of her because of the movements necessary to sexual intercourse. His penis was described as bigger around than described by the media, but short. There was no comment about his being circumcised.

During the earliest assaults, sounds of something being placed in a paper bag were heard. Eventually those sounds were described as a zipper. This time the sounds sounded like canvas, as if in a duffle bag.

A new phone service had been installed just two days earlier, on October 26th. On that day or the next, there was one hang-up phone call. For the suspect to have gotten this new phone number so soon should have been a heads-up for someone—assuming, of course, it was the suspect who placed that call.

There had been indications of prowlers, although it was after the fact they became aware of that possibility. On two occasions they arrived home to find their garage door open. So often this had happened to people and very nearly 100% of the time it was written off as nothing could be done about it. They were right, except it would have been a heads-up on what might happen. Merlindale and Cedarhurst come right to mind.

Their description of the suspect was a WMA, 5 ft. 8 to 5 ft. 10 inches tall. His legs were very white with light-colored hair. Clothing again consisted of corduroy pants with burgundy colored socks. It was mostly the sounds of the cloth rubbing together that made the victim think he was wearing corduroy. His jacket was made of nylon and his tennis shoes were badly worn and dirty. But, the colors of medium-blue with white soles and a white stripe across the toes could still be seen on his shoes.

When his victim's legs brushed up against him, she felt a holster for a gun on his right side.

As had become protocol, a tracking dog was brought to the scene. The trail led to 4400 Whitney where it ended at the curb in front. There was one male occupant in that house who was contacted and eliminated as a suspect.

The house next door was nearing completion and the new owners made a point of driving by every evening to check the progress of the construction. It was dusk, on the evening of

the assault, when they noticed a blue, two-door 1964 Ford
Falcon driving slowly through the cul-de-sac. This same car
had been seen driving through on two other occasions. There
is no record available to show that anyone contacted the other
new home owners, who were having houses built in that cul-
de-sac. Perhaps they, as well, had been checking on the
progress of their new homes.

At 4:45 A.M., on the day of the assault, a nearby resident was
preparing for work when he noticed a man walking slowly
past his house. The man appeared to be looking at the houses
as he passed by. He passed directly under a bright yard light
giving this neighbor an opportunity to see his face clearly.

As he walked by, the two stared at each other. The man
continued to walk until he neared a large pine tree between
4507 and 4512 Whitney. There he stopped and looked back at
the man. It appeared he was about to cross the street.

The man, who was about to leave for work, looked away, but
just for a moment. When he looked back, the man by the tree
had vanished. As he left for work he made a point of looking
by that tree for the man. There was no sign of him.

This neighbor was certain the man he saw walking did not
cross the street nor continue in the direction he had been
going. Most probably the man just stood behind the tree,
pressing himself tightly against it until the annoying resident
left. According to the reports, a composite was made using an
identikit. I have been unable to locate this composite.

The description given of the man was a WMA, 5 ft. 8 inches
to 6 ft., and 20 to 25 years old. Weight was about 180 lbs.,

and he had medium-brown, neatly cut, collar-length hair. There was no noticeable facial hair. He wore a shirt with several brown stripes around the chest. His pants were darker than his shirt and his shoes were sot-soled, as they were noiseless. Even though the weather was cold, he was not wearing a jacket.

The interesting part came later in the morning when the owner of a local beauty shop on Whitney called Sgt. Jim Bevins to tell him about something she had seen that morning.

It was about 6:30 A.M., while she was preparing to open for the day, she casually glanced out the window. Across the street from her business was a dump truck with a trailer attached. As she looked out the window, she watched a man pull a bicycle out of the back of the trailer. She shifted her gaze for a moment and when she looked back he was riding the bicycle eastbound on Whitney Avenue. The bike rider was dressed in dark clothing with a hood over his head. He may have been dressed in a jump suit, but, in any case, it was all dark clothing.

Three things came to mind when I learned of these two witnesses' statements. My original theory was, self-taught or not, this suspect had some training in special forces. For him to be seen standing and then suddenly vanish takes a practiced skill.

The second thought was the tracking dog used must have had allergies. How could the dog have missed his scent in that trailer? The other possibility is that the bicycle rider had nothing to do with the rape that had just occurred—he just happened to have his bicycle stored in that trailer. I have not seen any report where the owner of that truck and trailer was contacted. This late in the game, it is all speculation.

November 10, 1977
La Rivera Drive
Sacramento

Although it is my intention to avoid a blow-by-blow account of each assault, this one deserves some attention because of the spunk shown by the two ladies living on La Rivera Drive. The suspect left early and it may well have been because they managed to keep him from accomplishing his self-appointed mission of terrorizing defenseless people. I'm not so sure he was not intimidated.

It was about 3:30 in the morning on November 10, 1977, that the suspect known as the East Area Rapist reached a new low—even for him. After breaking into a house on La Rivera Drive, he tied up the 56-year-old mother of his next intended victim; a 13-year-old child.

Like the broken record he was, the EAR woke the mother up with a light in her eyes. Her immediate response was, "What do you want with me? I'm an old lady." Again he claimed that all he wanted was her money and no one would be harmed. Following his usual routine of tying his victim's hands and feet, he set out to locate his real target which would be the child asleep in another room.

Someone shaking her brought the child wide awake. Not realizing what was going on, she muttered, "Leave me alone," then opened her eyes to see a ski-masked nut standing over her. Holding a sharp knife against her throat, he said, "This isn't a joke." When he ordered her to turn over and put her hands behind her back, she simply said, "No." His response was to threaten, "Do what I say or I'm going to stab you with a knife. I'll slit your throat and watch you bleed to death."

This child, although frightened, kept her cool enough to notice things about her assailant. Besides how he was dressed, she picked up on a lot of "S" sounds in the vicious whispers directed at her. Those whispers were at a medium pitch and at no time did he use his normal voice.

Once, while threatening her, he slid a knife down behind her ear then asked if she wanted him to cut it off. She had already figured out who her assailant was, and that his biggest goal was to terrify his victims. She had read an article in the newspaper about him saying how he wanted his victims to be afraid of him and to have total control. Having no intention of giving him any kind of satisfaction, she replied, "I don't care." Surprised, the man stopped threatening her for a few minutes.

After tying her hands, but not her feet, he told her he wanted her money. She lied and told him she did not have any money. To her way of thinking, if he couldn't find it, then she wouldn't lose it.

Failing to terrorize this child, the suspect left her bedroom and went back to her mother's room where he could be heard threatening her. She could hear her mother's replies which parroted her own, "I don't care."

Returning to the child's room, he tied her feet and left.to do whatever it was that he did at those times. When he returned a few minutes later, he found the child had managed to get her feet free. Retying her, he told her that if she did that again, he would kill her mother.

After a few more trips around the house, he returned. Straddling her back, he placed his little slick wick between her tightly bound hands saying, "Grab it. Squeeze it. Do you know what this is?" She said, "No." He asked her if she had ever fucked before. This time she said, "I don't know." Not getting a satisfactory answer, he ordered her to turn over and she came back with, "Why?" After threatening to kill her, if she did not comply, she again refused, saying, "Don't want to." Getting no cooperation, he physically rolled her over himself.

After she had been forcibly rolled over, the suspect tried to penetrate her vaginally. Later, after an explanation of what an erection was, she said that he was erect when he tried to penetrate her, but with repeated attempts and no success he finally gave up. To him it probably seemed things just weren't going right.

When the assailant returned to her room, a breeze from the area of the front door was making her cold. While telling her he was going to pack some groceries, he noticed she was shivering. Retrieving a sleeping bag from the floor, he placed it over her then left.the house.

The collective description of the suspect from these two was a white male 5 ft. 6 inches to 5 ft. 11 inches tall, about 25 years old, with a medium to slender build. His shirt was a long-sleeved plaid, with red, blue, and green colors. His gloves were dark and tight-fitting, as were his pants and ski mask. The young girl described his legs as slender.

Although the child had never seen a penis, she had seen pictures of them in her sex education class. Based on that, she described his organ as no more than five inches long.

The child was a student at a private school. Her mother was employed at The Department of Employment Development at 800 Capitol Mall. Yet again, a victim with a connection to downtown Sacramento.

During the neighborhood canvass, it was learned there were numerous joggers at all hours on the nearby American River levee. Several of the neighbors said they had found evidence of prowlers around their houses at various times during the past year. Once, a woman woke up to a light shining on her through her bedroom window. Many of the neighbors experienced the hang-up phone calls.

December 2, 1977
Revelstock Drive
Sacramento

About 11:00 P.M., a complaint clerk at the sheriff's department routinely answered a phone call to hear a male voice whisper, "I'll commit another rape tonight." There was nothing further said, and the call was not recorded.

Thirty minutes later, a group of four or five young kids, on Revelstock Drive, were outside making a lot of noise, as young kids sometimes are wont to do. Their noise making could be clearly heard inside the house where, in spite of it, Veronica and her two small children were sound asleep. Her husband, an Army Lt. Colonel, assigned as an advisor to the National Guard at the Sacramento Army Depot, was away and not expected back before late morning.

It was late when Veronica awoke to a bright light aimed at her eyes. From behind that bright light a whispered voice said, "Hush, or I'm going to gag you." These whispers included threats to harm the little boy asleep in another room if she did not do what he said. That little boy was actually a little girl with very short hair. At least we know he had not prowled that house or family to any real extent prior to the assault.

Veronica was then gagged, blindfolded, and her hands and feet were tied. There was never any attempt at a sexual assault, although the suspect did remove her panties and throw them into the hallway. Nor did the suspect apply any lotion to himself or force Veronica to masturbate him. Basically, all he did was threaten her, wander around the house while repeatedly looking out the window towards the noise-making kids. This was the same thing we had arrested Richard Boren for a few months earlier.

Right after the suspect left, Veronica was certain she heard a car motor start, then a vehicle drive away. For whatever reason, she felt it was a van. There was a good likelihood that she was correct in her assumption of it being a van. A week earlier, a dark blue van, with a Sacramento Army Depot sticker on it, was seen in the area near Veronica's house. No one in that neighborhood was ever connected to that particular van.

No weapon was ever seen or even mentioned. The suspect description was given as a WMA, 20 to 25, shorter than 6 ft., with a medium to thin build. When he spoke, he whispered through clenched teeth. Veronica was certain his natural voice was high-pitched. His clothing was all dark. Veronica thought his gloves were the kind used by doctors. She based that strictly on how they felt against her skin.

The only correlation between this attack, and any of the others considered to be by the EAR, was what occurred prior. For example, for several weeks Veronica had been receiving hang-up phone calls. The last one was a few days prior.

Sometime during October, Veronica and a visiting friend left the house for a short while. When they left the door was unlocked, but when they returned it was locked. Looking around for anything missing, they found a jar of pickles in the refrigerator had been moved from one shelf to another. She also discovered a photo of her was missing. Her assailant was the EAR, of that I personally have no doubt. Others in the department had their doubts and treated this report as a false. In the end, they changed their collective minds, but not until Veronica had taken a polygraph test and passed.

The information learned from the neighbors was of the same garden variety. One neighbor, living one street over, had seen a suspicious man the day before the assault. He was a WMA, 5 ft. 9 inches, 25 to 30 with short, light-brown hair. He was wearing a multi-colored print shirt and dark slacks. When she saw him, he was coming from the walkway that leads from Woodbridge School to the Kies area. After reaching the end of the walkway, he just stood there for five minutes, as he and the neighbor stared at each other. Finally, the neighbor became uncomfortable and went inside her house. Her house, as were some others, was armed with a burglar alarm.

About midnight on this same night, a 16-year-old boy, coming home from a ball game, spotted a car parked across the street from his home on Revelstock. What caught his attention were two things: he had never seen this car before and it was the only car on the street without fogged windows. It was a bright-white station wagon with blackwall tires.

There were two girls sharing a house on Kies, a nearby street, who came home to find the power to their house had been turned off. Just before they moved into this house, they received a phone call where a male voice whispered three times, "You are next." Exactly where they lived when they received this phone call was not indicated

One of the girls worked for the State Legislature on Capitol Mall and part-time, evenings, as a waitress at the Woodlake Inn.

A neighbor, who lived immediately next door to Veronica, saw a full-size, beige, four-door station wagon parked between her house and Veronica's house. She managed to get a close look at the car and the license plate, but then she forgot what it was. There was no report available outlining what steps, if any, were taken to help this lady recall that license plate.

There are reasons making a false report is against the law. From start to finish the report process can become expensive as it can involve a lot of resources. It is especially frustrating when those resources are already stretched, as ours were at the time. Our past experience with false reports of rape is what led the investigators to ask Veronica to submit to that polygraph examination.

The first false report of sexual assault that I was acquainted with happened at the end of 1976. No report was made, and there were not that many details to report anyway.

Someone notified Lt. Root a young woman had been kidnapped by the EAR and taken out of Sacramento County, then released in the Sierra Mountains, above the town of Auburn, on a frontage road for I-80. Lt. Root contacted me and, together with Carol Daly, headed off for the Placer County Sheriff's Office. There we were to meet with the victim and Captain Nunez, soon to be elected as Sheriff of that county.

After a brief interview by Lt. Root, the victim accompanied us to the spot where she had allegedly been released. Long before we even left the office, Lt. Root was convinced she was lying. Once on the "scene" she admitted it was a false report. Captain Nunez wanted to arrest her, but Lt. Root declined. As he said, other than wasting a couple of hours no harm was done and, if she was that desperate for attention, then she had enough trouble already.

The next phony report of an EAR attack came a month or so later in Carmichael. A married woman in her 40's was upstairs, and her family downstairs, when she told them she had just been raped by the EAR.

Again the same investigators responded and again Lt. Root, with Carol assisting, got the woman to admit she was lying.

No action was taken by our office, and I have to assume for the same reasons as before.

Then in April or May of that same year, there was yet another false claim of an assault by the suspect known as EAR. This one was also quickly cleared, but with a bit of a twist.

About mid-day, and mid-week, a young woman decided to call the SSD to report she had just been raped by the East Area Rapist. When the dispatcher asked for a suspect description, the young woman only had to glance out her front window to see a man walking by her house. Having such a ready description at hand, why not use it? What she did not know was I just happened to be three or four blocks away and headed in her direction. Just as the suspect's description was broadcast, I spotted the unfortunate pedesterian stepping off the street where the alleged rape had just occurred.

This poor guy was just walking along, minding his own business, when suddenly he was approached by a plain-clothes cop asking him if he just raped someone. Both of us curious, him cuffed and strapped into the seat, back to the "scene" we went.

Imagine how that young woman must have puckered when minutes after she made her report of rape an unmarked sheriff's car pulled up in front of her house with the "suspect" in custody.

Her father, a sheriff's officer assigned to the patrol division and on duty at the time, was home within minutes. She quickly admitted she had made the whole story up. The disposition of that case was left in his capable hands.

Chapter 48:
Missed Opportunity

Sometime in December, 1977, a bit of valuable information found its way to Sgt. Ted Daly. Sgt. Daly was in charge of the Selective Enforcement Detail (SED) which was the forerunner of today's SWAT team. I might add Sgt. Daly was, and is, the husband of my then partner Carol Daly. One night, at the beginning of his shift, he was approached by a member of his team.

This officer had been approached by a patrol officer who wanted to pass on information that he had received from a night clerk at the 7-Eleven store at 10785 Coloma Road, Rancho Cordova. It almost sounded like the "I know somebody who knows somebody who knows somebody" scenario. Considering the topic, it still had to be investigated.

According to this multi-handed information, a man matching the general description of the EAR frequently came into that 711 on Coloma Road. Normally, he appeared around 2:00 A.M., then went to the back of the store where he stood looking at girly magazines. The individual always wore a shiny, black jacket with an image of Viet Nam embroidered on the back. Those jackets were very common in that era.

Instantly seeing this as a priority target, Sgt. Daly assigned two of his men to drop what they were doing, just before midnight, and report to that 7-Eleven. Their orders were clear. Dress in civilian clothes and stay out of sight .

Unfortunately orders were ignored and one officer only placed a civilian shirt over his uniform shirt. To make matters worse, he repeatedly left the storeroom, going to the front counter. The colored vertical stripe down the sides of his uniform pants must have been like a flashing neon light saying, "cop here". The other officer remained outside in an unmarked car.

Sure enough, about two in the morning the clerk answered the phone to, "Let me to talk to the cops in the back." The clerk denied there were any officers around, to which the caller replied, "Don't give me that shit." Shrugging his shoulders, the clerk told the officer he had a telephone call.

Taking the phone from the clerk, the officer said, "Hello. Who is this?" There was a chuckle, then the phone went silent.

The man wearing that black Viet Nam jacket never came back. The 7-Eleven store no longer exists, nor are there any records for that incident filed away in Sacramento County— at least none that either a clerk or I could find.

Not that many weeks after the incident at the 7-Eleven store, Sgt. Daly came across another interesting situation. Being reasonably sure the EAR lived in Rancho Cordova, the same the area where Daly lived, the good Sgt. patrolled the area whenever time permitted.

It was the time of year when 7 A.M. was still dark. Sgt. Daly, just finishing his shift, decided to spend a few extra minutes patrolling said area.

Driving by the intersection of Dolcetto Drive and Chardonay, he spotted a car moving very, very slowly, heading east down Dolcetto Drive, towards him. The slowness of the car was not the only thing that caught his attention. The headlights were barely bright enough to see by and there was no front license plate. The car itself was a boxy, primed white, two-door Datsun. The fact it did not make any discernible noise as it moved along only added to its outstanding features.

Not wanting to spook the driver, Sgt. Daly continued on for a very short distance before making his U-turn. As he did he saw the Datsun turn from Dolcetto onto Chardonay then abruptly onto Lambrusca, where it disappeared around the corner.

From the time Sgt. Daly saw the car and made his U-turn was less than a minute. In that brief span of time that Datsun had totally disappeared. Searching briefly and not finding the car, Sgt. Daly parked and sat with the motor off for some time, but the boxy Datsun never returned.

Who knows? Maybe the Datsun simply drove into an opened and waiting garage. The description of an old white Datsun was to come up again during this investigation.

December of 1977: An Active Month for the EAR.

On December 9, 1977, the 21st victim, living on Sand Bar Circle, received a phone call where the caller said, "Merry Christmas, it's me again," in a hoarse whisper.

On December 10, 1977, a caller told the Sheriff's PBX operator he was going to "hit tonight. Watt Avenue." Two minutes later he called back and said the same thing.

On December 11, 1977 a letter was received at *The Sacramento Bee*, the Mayor's office, and Channel 6. The letter mentioned the wife of a Mafia lord. It may have been in reference to the man who postured at the forum.

Chapter 49:
An Official Analysis

Sometime after I first began to put what I know of this investigation onto paper, Russ Oase and KC provided me with their copy of a six-page report compiled by Hugh S. Penn, a consultant hired by the Sacramento Sheriff's Department in December, 1977. What follows is a copy of his report as I received it. Those who question my analysis and conclusions may feel better accepting the ones of a professional consultant. Had anyone bothered to ask, I would have given them much the same information Mr. Penn did, and in the process saved the SSD some money. I insert Mr. Penn's report here for it was completed in December, 1977, and might be of use as Mr. Penn explains it far better than I do. His suggestion on how this investigation might best be conducted should please Lt. Root.

December 8, 1977
From Hugh S. Penn, Consultant

Subject: <u>EAST AREA RAPIST</u>

INTRODUCTION

Long and laborious investigations of the activities of the offender known as the East Area Rapist have developed a great body of subject matter. However, because of the well thought out modus operandi of the offender, which minimizes the chance of accurate observations, very little significant material can be gleaned from the reports of witnesses. This is true not because of a paucity, but because of an over-abundance of such reports.

Errors of observations arise from variety of causes. (Here the author goes into factors such as personal viewpoints, lighting at the time of observation, etc.)

In this case the subject has been said to be between 5 ft. 6 inches and 6 ft., with short blondish to dark long hair, driving many different makes and models of vehicles. The reported license numbers which have been checked out have invariably led up blind alleys.

The task of following up on each lead in this welter of various information is obviously time consuming and non-productive. An alternative methodology is proposed herein - one which starts with the end event, the attack on the victim and work backward. The key feature of this approach is the formulation of a hypothesis - as in the EAR's mode of operation and the selection of data from the huge body of investigative material which will support elements of the hypothesis. If a coherent explanation can be arrived at, it can be tested experimentally and either confirmed or discredited.

(The author goes on to discuss odds. He gives the hours in which the EAR struck as between 0240 and 0430 with a median of 0325. Over the span of the EAR assaults the times were as late as 10:00 p.m. and as early as 6:45 a.m. He goes further and talks about the days of the week on which the attacks occurred. He concludes it to be most likely the EAR will strike on a Friday or Saturday between the hours of 0240 and 0430.)

> The geographical distribution of EAR attack shows some puzzling factors but others which may be of tactical value. Case 1, 3, 6, 7, 15, and 24 are in the Rancho Cordova area. Except for 24, they are rather tightly grouped. Since this is the scene of his first operations it may serve as the prototype of his subsequent depredations. It shows a tendency to return at roughly regular intervals at the outset and then after longer periods. Counting 6 and 7 as one incident, the intervals are 2, 2, 5, and 6 1/2 months.
>
> Numbers 2, 8, and 21 occurred between Fair Oaks Boulevard and the American River south of Arden Way. The same tendency to a lengthening frequency is evident here, though on a smaller scale. Here the intervals are 3 1/2 and 7 months."
>
> Auburn, and Sunrise Boulevards. Greenback Lane and Madison Avenue the locus of 5, 9,12, and 19. Intervals:1 1/2, 2 1/2, 3 3/4.
>
> A neighborhood near Folsom, between Main Avenue and the American River was the site of 16 and 20, which were 1 3/4 months apart.

The area enclosed by Fair Oaks Boulevard and Manzanita Avenue, and Madison and San Juan Avenues saw incidents 4, 10, 13, and 17, separated by 3 1/2, 1 2/3 and 2 1/4 months.

Between Watt and Howe Avenues, U.S. 50 and the American River attacks 11, 18, and 27 took place 4 and 6 month apart.

Single incidents 25 in Foothill Farms and 26 in Carmichael are removed from the main concentration and may represent the nuclei of new clusters of assaults.

The average time span between attacks in these major groupings is about two months. However there is little interval regularity within groups; about the best that can be said is that the first incident in a new area is generally followed by another in two months or less.

The monthly pattern is continuous from the middle of 1976 to the time of the ----case (Sandbar Cir) May 17, 1977. Then on May 28 the --(4th parkway) incident came to light in South Sacramento, which up until then had been completely outside the habitat of the EAR. The situation remained quiet for over three months when the the subject resurfaced in Stockton with the assault on the ---family.

What follows is a two paragraph discussion on "what ifs."

PERSONAL CHARACTERISTICS

The offender is apparently below medium height, of a slender body build, with either light brown or dark blond hair or collar length hair. The accounts of some victims who seemed rather coherent and who had opportunities to make somewhat objective estimates are as follows: -- Slightly taller than 5 ft. 6 inch, slender to small build but well-proportioned. -- From 17 to 20 years. --The ten year-old son who impressed the investigator as being very observant and rational, was sure the intruder had blue eyes. His mother who walked beside the subject said that his height as about the same as hers, 5 ft. 7 inches -- Slightly taller than victim who is 5-2 3/4. -- thought EAR was about 5 ft. 9 inches, slim build; -- WMA, 5 ft. 8 inches or 5 ft. 9 inches -- neighbor, Ed Hicks saw subject 5 ft. 8 inches, 5 ft. 9 inches wearing brown pants with a red and green plaid shirt standing near home of victim at 10:00 P.M. Victim later stated that her assailant was wearing a red plaid shirt, but was uncertain whether the stripes were blue or green. ---described the loiterer as weighing about 140, of a thin build. -- daughter thought the intruders eyes were hazel. His legs were very white and hairy.

There is a wide consensus among victims as to the paleness of the assailant's skin and heavy growth of light brown hair on his legs. In the main, no distinctive odors were noted. Two victims reported an unpleasant body odor and one or two detected shaving lotion.

As noted before, almost every vehicle in the Blue Book has been sighted near the scenes of the crimes. However the only one that recurs with any degree of consistency is a Volkswagen. Two days before the — case broke a neighbor, Charles Reynolds observed an old VW, dark green with gray rear wide fenders and wide tires, parked in the field behind the – residence at about 6:00 P.M. A neighborhood resident saw what he described as a silver blue VW without lights leaving the area sometime after 4 A.M. An investigating officer measured the width of the tire tracks and found them to be 4' 9". In the —- case footprints led across two fences to a dirt area, where tire tracks were found. These tracks measured 4' 3" center to center. According to the officer who made the measurements VW wheels are 4' 4 ¾"apart in front and 4" 3 ¾" in the rear. Assuming that the vehicle does have wide tires and the measurements in the —- case were from the edges of the tread instead of from the center, the two observations could be reconciled. In the Stockton incident Mr. — heard what he identified as a VW engine start soon after the interloper left his house.

The EAR also has an apparently extensive wardrobe of informal clothing, and a wide assortment of knives, handguns, and flashlights.

Hypothesis as to Method of Operation

A hypothesis is defined as an unproved theory tentatively accepted to provide a basis for further investigation. Modifications in the original thesis may be necessary as the investigation proceeds. However, effort within the framework of the hypothesis generally gives superior results to activity on an undirected basis.

From a reading of the reports the following impressions were gained:

1. The first few cases of the EAR seem to have been conducted on an individual, somewhat opportunistic basis. His attacks were confined to cases of young girls he had apparently determined to be in defenseless situations. Later he refined his technique and began to attack married couples. The remarks below apply to his operations in this later phase of his development.

2. He seemingly finds a neighborhood to his liking in which there is a home for sale or under construction. These specimens may be studied for such features as floor plans, locations, types of window, door locks, etc.

3. Preferably there should be an open field, school grounds, levee, or concrete lined ditch at rear of the development. His getaway through such areas is attended by only negligible chances at being spotted in the early hours of the morning.

4. He next spends some time in prowling and/or burglarizing in the neighborhood, perhaps picking out a suitable victim, studying her and her family's habits, and further familiarizing himself with the interior of the house or houses he intends to break into.

5. In this intelligence gathering activity he studies several residences so that he may operate in the neighborhood at a later date with a minimum of reconnaissance.

"Real Estate Operations" - In the — case there were two nearby homes for sale. This was also true in the — incident. In the —- case a home being sold by Century 21 was directly opposite the victim's house. A neighbor of — was showing his own home for sale. About two weeks prior to the attack on — a prospective purchaser inspected the house. He purportedly was transferring from Las Vegas to McClellan AFB. He is described as being in his 20's, thin, blond, with short haircut and blue eyes. In the —- backyard were two signs from Kastaros Realty. It appears that the house had been shown earlier. The house of the —— had previously been owned by Naomi DeMartini who related that while the house was in the process of being put on the market a very unusual realtor called. According to Mrs. Demartini he paid no attention to the interior to the house but inspected the south and west exteriors. He asked her where her husband worked and why her daughter wasn't home. He is described as extremely well-dressed, light brown hair, darker complexion and medium frame. In the ———— vicinity there were several newly constructed and unsold homes. There was a vacant residence (condominium) for lease near the ———- home. The garage window at this location was open. The ———- had recently moved into their house, which still bore a "SOLD" AIM Realty sign at the time of the attack. A neighbor of the —————— Marilyn Ann Smith was marketing her home through Jones, Brand & Hullin under the multiple listing plan. The ——— home had just been sold and Mrs. ———- was planning to join her husband in the Bay Area where he had already moved. A new home was being constructed next to that of the —————-."

This listing is probably not exhaustive in that other instances of real estate or building activity may not have been reported.

Nearby Terrain - Unfortunately a compilation of locations abutting open areas was not made. From memory only, it seems that a preponderance of victims homes offered escape route through open fields, school grounds, parking lots of apartment complexes, the levees of the American River, or concrete lined drainage ditches. (Every one of the assaults in Sacramento did)

Prowling: There is scarcely a case in the file which does not contain mention of suspicious activities near the victims' houses. Prowlers were sighted through the windows, footprints found, noises late at night near doors and windows were heard, dogs barked at unusual times, non-response phone calls were received, locked doors were found open, minor burglaries were suffered, etc.

The author then goes on to cite 17 examples where the suspect knew details about the victims and their families.

<u>Conclusions</u>

The EAR is a WMA in his late teens or early twenties. He is about 5 feet 8 inches in height with a pale skin light colored eyes (blue or hazel), moderately long dark blond hair or light brown hair and a slender build.

He most probably drives an older VW of a nondescript color sighted under varying lighting conditions and reported variously as dark green, gray or silver blue. It may have expanded rear fenders and wide wheels.

He has a tendency to return in areas he appears to have familiarized himself with. These areas seemingly can be distinguished by homes up for sale and escape routes where he can avoid detection during the hours.

And here my copy of his report ends.

January 6, 1978 – A counseling service in Stockton received a phone call from someone claiming to be the EAR. The caller said he had been in counseling all his life and in the Stockton State Hospital at one time.

January 28, 1978
College View Way
Citrus Heights

On January 28, 1978, there was a sexual assault against two sisters that strongly resembled the one which occurred on Marlborough Way in August, 1976. These girls, 14 and 15 years old, were students at La Sierra High School. Their mother was a teacher at Sacramento City College and their father an insurance broker.

Having spent the day skiing at Boreal Ridge, the girls went to bed tired. It was a little after 11:00 P.M. when a thumping noise awoke Angie. While she was looking out the bedroom widow for the cause of the noise, she heard whispering behind her. Switching focus she quickly turned to see a man standing there. "Get all your money or I'll kill you." After she gave him her sixty dollars he told her, "Go wake up your sister. Don't make any noise and don't look at me."

Having secured his own safety by binding the sisters, he threatened them with, "Don't talk or move or I'll cut your throat and slip away in the fog." At least he changed from his phase, "be gone in the dark of the night."

But what was really different, the first time he returned after his ransacking to assault them, was that he was whimpering like a child, "I don't want to do this anymore. She's making me do it."

Being innocent of sex, neither girl had a realistic frame of reference for describing his penis. But after an explanation by officers, they said it was never fully erect and he never climaxed. In fact the act of forced intercourse, as in most of the other assaults, lasted less than one minute. They each thought he had a small penis.

Their combined description of the suspect was no surprise. WMA, no more than 5 ft. 9 inches and weighing between 150 and 160 lbs. He had a thin to medium build, was possibly in his 30's, but more likely a little younger. His clothing consisted of a dark, bulky coat that went to below the waist and was not a windbreaker. He wore ski gloves and a dark colored, full-faced ski mask. Weapons were a hand gun and a knife. The flashlight was held in his left hand.

Three to four weeks prior to this assaults, someone broke into their garage and stole tools. Over a three or four day period, both girls answered the phone to hear a man with a "funny sounding voice" ask for their mother.

A witness came forward and made a composite of a suspicous person. Without access to the "Holy Grail," I am not sure who was a witness to what. But that witness described a person seen as 18 to early 20's, weighing 150 to 160 lbs., with brown, shoulder-length hair. He wore a maroon or purple windbreaker and Levi's. Mode of transportation for this person was a newspaper carrier-type bike with heavy or balloon tires.

Chapter 50:
Rapist to Murderer

February, 1978
La Alegria Drive
Rancho Cordova

As Patrol officer Fred Mason was getting out of his squad car early one evening, he spotted a young couple walking their dog. A casual exchange of good evenings and the couple continued on their way and Officer Mason went into the house. Although he did not know it, Officer Mason was probably the last person to speak to this couple; they would be dead within minutes of this encounter.

Brian and Katie Magiorre were murdered while out for a leisurely evening stroll with their dog. At the time, the homicide detectives did not release any information about these homicides to anyone.

In 2010 homicide detective Ken Clark joined a group of retired officers who met regularly, continuing to investigate the EAR. Detective Clark brought everyone up to speed on the Magiorre investigation. There were, and still are, a ton of theories and rumors (mostly rumors) about that double homicide. Detective Clark was able to dispel some of those rumors.

It was felt this double homicide was most likely committed by the East Area Rapist. Shoelaces, already formed into a loose loop, had been found at the crime scene.

Brian Maggiore, an Air Force Sergeant, had been stationed in Alaska. While in Alaska, his wife Katie remained behind in Fresno, California. When Brian transferred to Mather AFB, Katie joined him. They were living off base in Rancho Cordova when they were killed.

Katie had been the victim of crank phone calls, and may have been the target of a stalker. The crank phone caller told her he was the one who raped two women in a Regal gas station, and she would be next. Any more information about this possible stalking, or what may have occurred while in Fresno, has not been made public.

As the story unfolded, it appeared Sergeant Brian, a clerk in the 320th Security Police Squadron at nearby Mather AFB, and his wife Katie, were out for an evening walk with their dog.

What transpired next is conjecture based primarily on witness statements. The main witness, a 10-year-old boy, watched from a second story window as the Maggiore's were murdered in their own backyard.

Brian and Katy were apparently out for an evening stroll when their small white dog ran off. Chasing after it they entered a backyard where it is possible they surprised a prowler. The assumed prowler, wearing a ski mask and armed with a handgun, gave chase to Brian and Katie. This is where the ten-year-old witness comes in.

A strong wind had previously knocked down a section of fence in his backyard. As the young witness watched, he saw a man and woman run through that damaged section of fence into his backyard. Immediately behind them was a gun wielding man wearing a ski mask. The man being chased made it as far as the patio before being shot to death by the man with the gun.

Having just taken one life, the man turned his attention to the woman who was running for her life. As she ran, he fired, shot after shot, each one missing her but striking the house. He caught up with her at the gate.

His view blocked by a bush, the young witness heard a single gunshot, then saw a small amount of rising smoke. Apparently Katie's body may have been blocking the gate, leaving the murderer no other option but to climb over, which he did.

As the ski masked killer cleared the fence, a curious next door neighbor was stepping out of his garage. The two came face to face. Probably the only reason this witness was not shot was because the killer was out of ammunition, having just expended it all on Katie.

The ski-masked killer first ran down one block then switched to another direction. He changed directions two or three times before removing his mask.

A few blocks from the murder scene, a woman was doing yard work when she saw a man walking rapidly in her direction. He was staying close to shrubbery near the front of her neighbors as he crossed their yards.

When a car approached, he jumped behind a tree, pressing himself as flat as he could against it. There he remained until the car had passed, then continued on his way.

Shielding his face with his jacket collar, he remarked to the woman as he crossed her yard, "Guess I must be trespassing." He was wearing a WW II-era bomber jacket, with the 320th Bomb Group insignia patch.

A typical procedure of law enforcement, when a major crime occurs, is to cordon off the area as quickly as possible. Usually it is accomplished by strategically positioning squad cars to block all ingress/egress. Patrol officer Patti Butler was assigned to replace another patrol officer who had to leave his position in this grid. As she arrived at her post, sharp-eyed Butler spotted a folded $5.00 bill lying near a curb.

Officer Butler radioed the officer she was replacing and asked if he had noticed anything in that exact spot. This other officer had written down a description of a black-over-orange Fiat Roadster, with license plate number CA 010 CNB that was parked at the spot where she found the money. Both of these officers were on the top of their game that night.

This Fiat matched the description of one seen near an EAR assault a few months earlier. There were other crime scenes where a small sports car was thought to have been involved.

What was done with this information, at the time, is not known, but Detective Ken Clark of the Sacramento Sheriff's Department ran with the information. The car registered to this license was compacted and sent to the smelter in 1995.

Two composites of one, or even two suspects, arose from the investigation of the murder of Brian and Katy. Where they came from, and why two, is as much a mystery as the identity of the suspect we know as EAR. They are included at the end of this book.

Chapter 51:
The "New" Composite

March, 1978

In all professions, information is continously passed through unoffical channels. These channels involve all levels of the profession and always include retired personnel. Most people would recognize this as the grapevine.

It was through the law enforcement grapevine that I learned of another EAR assault that occurred in the city of Sacrameto sometime in early 1978. Not knowing exactly when it occurred, I have elected to include it here.

I have few details about this assault and only know for certain it was in South Sacramento and may have been near what is known as The Pocket area .

 As I pieced it together a young woman, home alone, was paid a surprise visit by her brother. Being from out of town the brother was invited to spend the night.

In view of the EAR's growing casualness about donning a mask before he made entry, it is possible he came face to face with a witness. This could be what happened that gave birth to a composite that was not released at the time. Exactly how that composite came about is not public information, but that it came from this sexual assault is a given.

317

I have not confirmed the above information, but I absolutely believe every bit of what is related here.

There is a list of sexual assaults by the EAR that have been made public. Two assaults mentioned in this manuscript are not on that list; one on Ambassador Drive in Rancho Cordova and this one.

March 18, 1978
Meadow Avenue
Stockton

It was the kind of sound that creates an image of someone kicking sheet metal that startled a lawyer and his girlfriend late one March night. They were certain someone in their backyard had just kicked their air conditioner. It was not the first time there had been prowlers on their property.

Earlier, on New Year's Day, they came home to find that two of their door locks had been damaged. For days they had been receiving phone calls where the caller always asked for someone who did not live at that address. By the second week of January, the phone calls stopped.

Then came the kicking of the air conditioner. Their neighbors were also experiencing hang-up phone calls and were also aware of prowlers.

For three days following the incident with the air conditioner, their life ran its normal course.

Their days were like most days; in the mornings they reported to work then returned home in the evenings and prepared for the next day's course of events. There was, however, a one-day trip, by the lawyer, which was a little outside of his routine. Otherwise all was normal.

Then at 1:05 A.M. on March 18th, their lives took a sudden trip into hell. That was when they awakened to a figure standing in front of them. A bright light shining down from above might have caused some to wonder if they were having a spiritual experience. But the handgun that they could see in the glare of the light dispelled any such thoughts.

Later they would equate that light with the type doctors wore on a head-band during a medical examination. Mostly they made that comparison because it was aimed down at a 90 degree angle from a spot that was just about at the top of the figure's head.

The suspect introduced himself and then began the routine of binding, ransacking, etc. However, once again there were some small variations in this assault.

If you have been paying attention, then you know he applied lotion to himself. But this time he varied his usual method of operation considerably.

This time, he did a little more than just place his penis into her hand. First he sat on her, not just straddling as he usually did. Then placing his entire gonad package into her hands he said, "Make it good." Pulling back, he rubbed his penis along her back. He sexually assaulted her, then picked up her foot and rubbed it over his gonads.

Before he was done, he applied sun tan lotion around the victim's vagina then he sodomized her. The victim said he seemed to enjoy anal sex the most. All of the actual sexual assaults were brief. He was fully erect, never climaxed, and was three inches long, at best.

When he finished with his sexual assault, he could be heard in the kitchen opening the refrigerator door. A short time later they heard him walking on the patio where he could also be heard sobbing. Then he was heard in the garage where it sounded like he was trying to catch his breath.

At the same time that her assaulter was in the garage, she thought she heard someone walking on their patio.

The victim described the assailant as a WMA, 5 ft. 10 inches tall, and 160 lbs. She thought he was maybe 26 years old with a small, round, potbelly. The male victim said he was maybe 6 ft. 1 inch and thin. She said he had an extremely strong grip.

He wore a black cotton button-up shirt and black leather gloves that had a fur lining. The mask was a full-faced ski mask. The suspect was wearing a shoulder holster on the right side of his chest.

The victims thought the suspect's voice had an inflection that might have been a refined Mexican accent. He spoke quickly while exhaling a lot of air.

Afterwards investigators found two empty beer cans in the yard.

It could be argued that the suspect described here was not the same psychopath that had been terrorizing the Sacramento area for the past two years. The MO was almost identical, but not quite. The physical description certainly was not the same. This is one crime scene where a DNA profile is a necessity.

There were two families living in the 1900 block of Meadow Avenue who had some information for the investigating officers. Since the assault occurred in the 3000 block, it was relevant.

One week prior to the assault, a white male adult, 18 to 22 years old, with blond, shoulder length hair, was seen driving an old faded van very slowly while looking into homes in the immediate neighborhood.

Two nights before this assault the daughter of one of these families thought she heard someone in their backyard, but saw no one. Then on January 17th, one night before the assault, a nearby neighbor of the victims saw a WMA, 18-19 years old, 5 ft. 10 inches tall, 150 lbs., with blonde collar-length hair, clean shaven, wearing a white T-shirt and Levi's, get out of a 1972 green Ford Pinto (approximate year) parked in front of his neighbor's house. He removed a gas can from the trunk then set off down the street. No one saw him return.

Yet another neighbor returning home about 11:30 that night probably saw the same man. He was getting out of a small vehicle parked just to the east of their home. He removed something from the trunk of the car. She described him as WMA, 18 to 25, weighing 170 lbs., standing about 5 ft. 10 inches tall. His hair was straight, blonde, and collar-length. A light-colored nylon jacket was all she could describe about his clothing. There wasn't much more she could say about the car except it had a carrier rack on the back.

These same neighbors reported briefly seeing a flashlight in their backyard at about 9:30 the night of the assault.

They lived in the 1900 block of Meadow Avenue, while the victims lived in the 3000 block. It was about 3:30 that same morning they heard someone running down Meadow Ave., then a car leaving. Again they looked, but saw nothing.

It was in that same 1900 block of Meadow Avenue that three men were seen running down the street. They turned north onto Coral where they were soon out of sight. The officer who wrote down this information did not include dates or time, which may be because he had a reason to discount the information or found no connection to the assault. This brought to mind the three men seen running from the scene where the youth was shot, while chasing a prowler.

The brother-in-law of the victim was an attorney. That, in and of itself, means nothing. However later when the EAR moved south, he murdered an attorney and also a brother of another attorney.

But for now the EAR was in Stockton spreading his terror. No one had the foggiest idea whether he would return to Sacramento or not. Everybody was still frantically looking for a connection between Stockton and Sacramento—a task that is not complete.

Chapter 52:
Dog Therapist

March 29, 1978
Ambassador Drive
Rancho Cordova

About 3:20 A.M., someone removed the molding on a side door, then removed a pane of glass. With nothing blocking the way, they reached inside and slid the dead bolt open.

The 32-year-old mother's two children slept through the entire ordeal. The family dog, which was apparently a large dog, did as so many family dogs do—minded its own business. The arriving officers found the dog inside the garage.

This time the suspect only checked on the tightly bound woman twice and was gone in a half hour. She managed to free herself then call for help.

Typically, I am the one to come up with some far out idea to try. This time I was outdone. The investigating detectives wanted to know why the dog did not bark or attack, so they took it to a dog behavioralist. The dog specialist said in all probability the dog was as scared of the psychopath as the people were. But was this work of the East Area Rapist?

April 14, 1978
Piedmont Drive
Sacramento

Like a lot of 15-year-old high school students, Mary occasionally babysat, but only for people she knew well. Taking care of this family's three-year-old was not part of her regular routine, but she was taking advantage of an opportunity for extra money and the opportunity to work on her homework. It was about 9:50 P.M. when the sound of someone kicking in the dead-bolted door startled her.

Even though she was shocked and frightened, her immediate thought when she saw him was, "He's not much taller than I am." Mary stands no more than 5 ft. 6 inches.

The figure charging at her had his head covered with a mask, and he was holding some sort of object in his right hand. That object was later determined to be an ice pick. Sticking to his routine, he told her all he wanted was money and he would leave without hurting her. Those empty promises were followed by the tightly bound hands and feet, and her being blindfolded.

This night would be one of those times the EAR would go home feeling somewhat frustrated. Soon after Mary had been accosted, the telephone began ringing. It rang a few times, quit, then rang again. The suspect ordered Mary to pick it up, say hello then hang the phone back up. As they walked to the phone, he made her hang on to his slick wick.

But the calvary was on its way. The woman, for whom Mary was babysitting, kept trying to reach her. The phone just kept ringing and ringing, each time the lady called to make sure her baby, and Mary, were alright. Becoming quite concerned, since Mary wasn't answering, she telephoned Mary's dad to alert him and ask for assistance.

Just as Mary was being forced into the backyard, her dad could be heard calling out, "Who's there?" Her immediate response was, "Dad." The suspect quietly and wisely disappeared.

Mary had no idea which way he went. As far as she could tell, he might have levitated out of the yard, for he made not a sound as he left.

For up to two months prior, Mary had been receiving phone calls at home where the caller either hung up without speaking or asked, "Let me sell you out." The last strange message was two days before she was assaulted. Two weeks prior to the assault, Mary's sister answered the phone only to hear a male voice say, "I've fucked your sister." She never received any such calls where she babysat.

Mary described her attacker as a white male. Judging from the sound of his voice, she placed his age no younger than 18, but maybe as old as 20 to 35.

His voice was deep and soft, always sounding the same . She did think there was a nervousness to his voice. There was no accent, nor did he appear to disguise his voice other than by talking softly.

Mary was innocent in the world of sex, and other than the terms vagina, penis, and intercourse, she really knew little.

Some sort of explanation was necessary from detective Carol Daly before Mary could describe the suspect's penis as not very erect and quite small.

After the routine medical examination the doctor informed Carol and Mary's parents that her hymen was still intact and no penetration had been accomplished. The EAR did indeed have a frustrating evening. This made twice he had tried to rape a virgin and twice they defeated him.

As in all sexual assaults, the background information of the victim, and sometimes of the family, is equally as important as an examination of the scene. Mary's mother was employed at Sacramento City College as a teacher and her father worked for the State of California in the Department of Water Resources. Mary's last scheduled appointment with a medical doctor had been at Kaiser two or three weeks previous to the assault. She had also been to an orthodontist the Monday before the assault.

Education, medical, and downtown Sacramento; three recurring issues. Eventually, they do tie together.

As had other teenage EAR victims, Mary belonged to the Tioga Ski Club. The club provided buses for the ski trips that would pick the members up at their school, then would return them to the same place at the end of the day. After that, they would find their own way home. Mary usually rode to and from the school with a close friend. Mary also belonged to a swim team from Park Terrace, but did not participate all that often as the team did not practice that much.

The day after the assault, a woman from the town of Rocklin, who had been fishing in the nearby Sacramento River, called to report what she thought was suspicious. The woman said she and her family were fishing in a spot known locally as "Minnow Hole." It was about 10:30 P.M. when she walked up the levee on her way to their car. As she neared the top of the levee, she saw a man jogging by. The jogger looked at her and asked, "Did you catch any fish?" She replied, "No," to which the jogger replied, "Oh my wife is going to be mad."

She did not believe this man had been jogging because he was not dressed for it and he was very much out of breath, as if he had been running hard. She described him as a WMA, 25 years old at most, 5 ft. 8 inches tall with a medium build, mid-neck brown hair and a mustache. He was wearing a light colored shirt that may have been a T-shirt.

Not knowing where "Minnow Hole" is, I have no idea how close it was to the scene of the assault. When I tried to contact this woman, I learned both she and her husband have since passed away.

One other interesting bit of information, volunteered by the public, came from a convalescent hospital on Riverside Boulevard. About a month before this latest assault a man who identified himself as "Jack from the town of Quincy" wandered into the hospital and began a conversation with the nurse at the front desk. He kept telling her he had a sex problem; his father had a girlfriend and he did not. During his ramblings, "Jack" said he had been treated at the Sacramento Medical Center psychiatric ward. In the middle of his personal history lesson, he claimed to be a singer and began to sing the Johnny Cash tune, "I'll Walk the Line." That was when the nurse asked him to leave.

The evening of April 10th, the same nurse was outside checking that all windows were secured when he quietly appeared beside her. Again he began the conversation about his sexual problem. This time the nurse headed him off explaining she was really busy. Jack left and has never returned .

Jack was described as a WMA in his early 20's, 5 ft. 8 to 5 ft. 9 inches tall. His hair was a medium-brown and neatly trimmed above the ears. He wore jeans and tennis shoes. He also wore a medium-blue windbreaker. She described him as looking like a jogger with a thin to medium build.

June 5, 1978
Fuschia Lane
Modesto

Over a period of weeks the phone rang but when answered the caller would hang up with out uttering a word. Then the calls turned obscene. In the last one the male caller said, "I want to cum on your lap." That was three weeks before a couple was awakened in the middle of the night by a sharp rapping sound.

The couple owned and operated a dry cleaning business in Modesto. They were fast asleep when a sharp rapping sound against the bedroom wall brought them to the very edge of sleep. Then the bright light hit them in the eyes and they were beyond that edge. Suddenly the couple was very wide awake.

With one cruel variation, the entire EAR program was followed to the "T". That variation occurred just before he sexually assaulted the woman of the house. Going back to where her husband lay tied and helpless, he said, "I'm going to rape your wife." Apparently taunting a helpless husband was now on his list of torments.

When the suspect was near the victim, she could smell beer but no other odor. She described him as a white male, 6 ft. tall, and in his 20's. There was no estimate made on his weight, but she did say there was no flabbiness on his midsection. His clothing appeared to be one piece and dark colored. Going strictly by feel, she thought his gloves were made of either plastic or rough leather.

Her assailant spoke in a deep, low whisper, but stuttered when it seemed he was angry. Based on his use of language, they considered his level of education to be low. They detected a Mexican accent, however they both tended to feel the accent was fake. Other than that, they did not think he was trying to disguise his voice. When pacing back and forth, the suspect's breathing sounded heavy as if he were sobbing.

Officers contacted the neighbors and located one woman who said she heard a sports car, with a deep exhaust, start up somewhere on Fuschia Lane. Because she was in the back bathroom, she was not able to see the car. The investigators determined this was just about the same time the suspect quit the assault and left.

June 7, 1978
Wake Forest
Davis

Only two days after the assault in Modesto, the EAR switched locations again. This time it was to the small college town of Davis, 15 minutes from downtown Sacramento.

Somewhere around 3:30 A.M., a 22-year-old UCD student was in bed, sound asleep, when she was jerked awake by a hand clamped over her mouth. In the same instant she realized a male voice was whispering through clenched teeth, "Cooperate and you won't be hurt." All the intruder wanted was money and food, then he would leave without doing any harm.

He followed his routine of threatening and promises—not to hurt her if he got money and food. Once she was tied, giving the suspect complete control and his personal safety assured, he introduced his threat routine again. This time they were not so effective. Instead of becoming passive, his intended victim screamed even louder and increased her struggles to escape. Throughout the entire ordeal, she never stopped her efforts to resist.

During the actual rape, when he was trying to move her legs into different positions, she resisted by trying to kick him in the thighs. It was like a monster-bug from a Sci-Fi movie had fastened itself onto her back. She rolled from side to side as violently as she could to rid herself of the repulsive thing.

Her only reward was to be repeatedly slammed in the face with his knuckles while being told to shut up and stop resisting. He told her she would never see her friends again. Once, when she insisted on raising her head, he shoved it back down so hard it broke her nose.

For weapons he had a nail file and a straight edge screw driver. The nail file seemed to be his favored weapon as he kept pushing it into her neck. Once he pushed it into the corner of her eye, leaving her with a small cut.

She noticed, as many of his victims did, that the suspect had a small penis and that it never became fully erect.

A woman janitor for the apartment complex told the victim about a man who had been watching her the previous Tuesday. When the victim was in the swimming pool, a man stood on the third floor balcony watching her. He remained there for some time then was gone only to materialize minutes later near the pool. The second time the janitor saw him, he was walking along looking down and perhaps trying not to be so obvious about looking at the victim.

The following Monday, when the victim stopped to check her apartment mail box, she saw who she thought might be the man the janitor had described to her. As she walked to her apartment, he walked in the same direction but in a perpendicular way.

This man was described as a white male with dark hair brushed back. He also had a mustache. He stood about 6 ft. tall, was light-complected, and was wearing a white shirt and blue jeans.

The description of the actual suspect, given by the victim, was also a white male, about 6 ft. tall, weighing approximately 175 lbs. His hair was light-brown. When he took his gloves off she felt his thumbs and found them to be very rough. Assuming it would be like the rest of the appendage, she concluded his hands were heavily calloused.

He was wearing a dark-blue T-shirt, which was inside-out, and thick, light-brown, corduroy pants. The pants were significant in that they were popular with a small percentage of the population. Being a textiles major, the victim took note they were not brushed corduroy, and they did have a zipper. His mask was a dark-blue or black nylon stocking and once again he wore tennis shoes.

Another astute observation by the victim, and one that opportunity rarely provided, was to take note of the suspect's fingernails. They were very short. She did not comment if they looked chewed or cut, only that they were very short.

June 23, 1978
Grand Prix
Modesto

At 1:30 A.M., the East Area Rapist forced entry into the new home of two Modesto City Hospital employees. There he followed his pattern to the letter. Weapons were again a hand gun and a knife—the knife coming from the victim's kitchen.

They described their assailant as a white male in his early 20's. He spoke only in whispers and with a questionable Mexican accent. Because neither victim was ever standing beside the suspect, they were not at all sure of his height.

They both said he would was not taller than 6 ft. and probably shorter. They described his body build as small—the same word used to describe his male appendage.

They thought he might be wearing a T-shirt and tennis shoes. He carried some sort of bag that had a zipper. When he ransacked the house, they heard it being zipped open and closed.

The next day the police received some very important information. A taxi-cab driver thought he may have driven the suspect to the crime scene the evening before the assault.

On the evening of June 22nd, the cab driver was parked in front of the United Airlines Terminal when he was approached by a man. He did not see this man get off an airplane, but was aware that a United Airlines plane had just landed. When asked his destination the guy replied, "Sylvan and Coffee." When they arrived at a vacant field near that location, the passenger said, "Good enough," and left the cab. When last seen, the man was carrying a zipper-topped, plaid, cloth bag and was walking in the general direction of where the assault would soon occur.

The driver described him as a white male, 30 to 35 years old, 5 ft. 9 inches tall, with a medium build. His hair was light-brown, and he was dressed in dark clothing. If anyone should have made a composite, it was this cab driver.

About half a mile across the field, from where the passenger began walking, was the house where the couple were assaulted. The other houses in that area were recently constructed or were still under construction. It had only been the past April when the couple had moved in.

There are many questions about that cab fare to which I do not have answers. Did he come by plane for the express purpose of the sexual assault? How could he have come to know about his intended victims if he had to travel by plane to get there? How significant was it that most of the other houses near the victims' were still in various stages of construction. In fact, the cab incident opens up a whole litany of questions.

June 24, 1978
Rivendell
Davis

At 3:15 A.M., a 5 ft. 10 inch white male, with a hairy butt, forced his way into a two-story home on Rivendell in Davis. This time he targeted a 32-year-old housewife who was in bed with her husband. Their two small children were asleep in their bedrooms. To some it was the work of the EAR, and to others maybe not.

The two story house was not the only variation from the typical EAR theme. He called the victim by her nickname, a name not written down anywhere in the house. He fondled her breasts, at first gently then very hard. When he pulled her hair away from her face, he was remarkably gentle. This was also the one time that he gently rubbed her back as he moved his penis back and forth in her tightly bound hands. After asking her for money, she heard him sobbing.

In the middle of the attack, one of the young children came out of their bedroom. When the child approached her mother, she was stopped by the suspect and pushed into the bathroom. Closing the bathroom door, he placed a cup and saucer on the door knob with a warning to the child not to knock it off.

This suspect was described as a white male adult with a hairy butt. His build was thin to average, with big thighs. The real kicker came when she described his penis as long, but with a small head. She was sure he was circumcised. His breath was described as sour.

This was not the first time the suspect was described as having heavy thighs. In other instances he was decribed as leaping tall fences in a single bound.

Dressed in dark clothing, he spoke in a mean whisper through clenched teeth, accompanied by a lot of breathing and panting. Besides threatening his victims with a .357 revolver, he had an ice pick.

Not suprisingly, shoe-prints were found around the victim's house and in the neighbors' yards. Using a trained dog, the Davis police trailed the suspect to the private airport at the University of Davis. An assault in Modesto on the June 23rd, the cab passenger from the Modesto air terminal, and now this—it must have been cause for interest among some investigators. There is no record available for what followed.

A woman living close by turned in a jacket she found lying beside her house. It was made of a heavy suede material, waist length and dark blue. The collar and cuffs were knit and had two gold colored stripes. This jacket was identified as a

Golden Bear brand model 300 or 303. Made in California, it was only stocked by three stores: one in Sacramento and two in San Francisco. It was on the market for a year or two before being discontinued due to poor sales.

Sales records for Bluebeards, the Sacramento store that carried that model jacket, had been destroyed in a fire. The store owner and a salesman did not remember ever selling one.

In San Francisco, Hard On Leather and Leather Forever, the other two stores that carried that style of jacket, were unable to help. The San Francisco stores catered to homosexuals and also carried S & M merchandise in their store windows. This information took me right back to the leather hood and the assault on the 15-year-old girl living on Greenleaf Drive. The Davis PD detective did an excellent job of running down all possible leads on that jacket, but in the end he got the same results as I did two years earlier with the leather hood: dead end.

The publicity the media gave this latest assault generated a call from Woodland, a town in Yolo County and only a few short miles from the town of Davis. After watching the news, a woman who lived in Woodlland felt she might have something to report. Three weeks earlier she saw something that she felt might be related to the Davis assault.

It was between 11:30 and 11:45 P.M. when she saw a man 5 ft. 8 to 5 ft. 10 inches tall, weighing, 150 to 165 lbs., walking down the street in front of her home. The all-black jump suit and the ski mask with white stripes above the eyes, and a large, oblong, silver western-style belt buckle caught her attention. As she watched, he disappeared behind the house across the street where she knew a woman lived alone.

The witness, as with virtually all the other witnesses, did not call anybody—not even the lady living in that house. Instead she went to bed. After awhile she thought something strange might be going on, so she got out of bed. Looking out the same window, she saw lights all over that neighbor's house and cops arriving from every direction.

She feared that the man, whom she had seen walking into the backyard of her neighbor's house, might be hiding near her own house, so she chose not to go back to bed. Instead she sat on the floor in the middle of her living room with the lights out.

At 2:00 A.M., this witness heard a vehicle stopping, about where she had seen the suspiciously dressed man. Almost immediately she heard a door slam, giving her the impression somebody was being picked up. As this was going on, she peeked out her window to see an orange colored van. It appeared to have flames painted along the sides where there were two porthole windows. She was not able to see who or how many were in the van. Her son and daughter had also seen this van in the area before.

Two or three months earlier her son had been in their front yard when this same van stopped and the driver offered to fix a large dent in her son's Volkswagen. He described the driver as a WMA, 5 ft. 10 inches to 6 ft., slender with dark, combed back hair, side burns, and no facial hair. He said that the guy spoke with an "Okie" accent. He was wearing a white T-shirt, blue jeans, and cowboy boots. However, the van he saw was cream-yellow, not orange.

The witness's daughter said she too had seen the same van. She was certain she had seen the van in their neighborhood on three occasions, with the most recent being three weeks earlier. Her father was preparing to undergo surgery when she last saw it, which is why she remembered.

July 6, 1978
Amador Avenue
Davis

It was about 2:50 in the morning when the East Area Rapist made his presence known to Carol, a 32-year-old mother of one and a student at Sacramento State College. In spite of the nearly exact replication of the EAR's rigid program, there were a few things of note in this assault.

As said, the suspect kept with his program which included ordering his victim to masturbate him. As Carol complied, she took note that his penis was three to four inches long, close to the diameter of a half dollar and he was circumcised. With as much feeling as grabbing a door knob, he grabbed Carol's breast once. Carol picked up on a strong odor of cigarette smoke.

During the rape he kept moving around, which Carol took to be an effort from him to reach a climax, something he had not always accomplished in this or his other assaults. But this time his failure apparently led to a strong sense of frustration. Laying his head on the pillow next to her, he began sobbing, "I hate you. I hate you. I hate you Bonnie." Carol could not be certain her assailant was saying Bonnie, but that was what it sounded like.

The officers who responded found some of the rooms in the house had been ransacked and others left entirely untouched. Interestingly, tennis shoes with herring-bone style prints were found on the tile surface next to the kitchen sink.

Although her son was the only one residing with her, the victim was not divorced, just estranged from her husband. It was as both her husband and doctor that he provided what aid he could.

Chapter 53:
Security Officer's Badge

October 7, 1978
Belann Court
Concord

At 11:30 P.M., an attractive 26-year-old woman and her husband, a pharmacist at Mt. Diablo Medical Center in Concord, arrived home. As they were pulling up to their house, they noticed a car, not belonging to the neighborhood, parked on nearby Minert Road. They thought it may have been a Volkswagen.

About 2:30 A.M., the same woman and her husband were awakened by a light shining in their eyes. With short clipped sentences, whispered through clenched teeth, the voice behind that light said, "I just want food and money. I'll kill you if you don't do what I say." Interspersed with his BS about only wanting money and food, he told them, "My main man wants gold and silver." To both he sounded as if he were hyper-ventilating.

Without skipping a beat, the suspect continued with his practiced routine. After sexually assaulting this woman, in front of her fireplace, he retreated to a corner. There he sat and cried like a baby.

The description of his clothing was minimal: a ski mask, corduroy pants, and brushed suede gloves. A new description of his body odor was added—musty and cinnamon.

A month prior to this assault, a man and woman had been to the victim's house. What made them of interest is that they claimed to be with the Mormon Church. There is nothing in the report indicating what their alleged purpose was. If on a church mission, then this would probably be the first time ever the Mormon Church sent a male and female duo on a mission. Traditionally, it has always been, and remains, two young men traveling together.

Later, the pharmacist husband of this rape victim underwent a session with a hypnotist in hopes of remembering some details. What he did recall was a white or aqua-green box-shaped van, at about 11:15 P.M., parked near their house the night before the assault. There were no side windows, but there were two windows on the back. He recalled a rear chrome bumper which fit tightly into the body. He saw a white male with dark hair, wearing a white T-shirt and light blue pants, stooping over beside the van.

Information obtained from the residents of that neighborhood made contacting each of them well worth the time and effort. There were the usual reports of prowlers, suspicious cars and people, and phone calls at all times of the day. Only now many of the calls had turned into obscene calls. Another big difference, now the victims were receiving obscene telephone calls after the assaults had occurred.

One piece of probable evidence had everyone excited for a day or two. A neighbor of the Concord victims found a security officer's badge in their backyard. A State of California seal was in the middle of the star shaped badge. The words "Special Officer" were around the leading edge. At the end of this chapter is a picture of that badge.

Like the jacket found in another EAR-related investigation, they followed this one as far back as the manufacturer. Whoever traced that badge did an excellent job.

Hookfast Specialities, a company in Providence Rhode Island, manufactured the badge. They claimed twelve different affiliated companies actually produced that style badge. The best they could do was provide a list of the three thousand salesmen who work for those companies that had the task of selling the badges.

The badge found was a Model B-617 and had a surface described as air-dried enamel. It had to be ordered directly from the company that produced it. This particular badge bore signs of wear consistent with being carried in a wallet.

There was other information that was possibly important. The information came when contacting the neighbors. A woman living very near the victims reported that two nights before the attack they had experienced a prowler. It was about midnight when she and her husband heard someone inside their house. Turning on the light, her husband went downstairs to investigate. Seeing nothing downstairs, he stepped outside. She, still upstairs, heard someone leave the house by way of the dining room door. She ran to the window just in time to see two people running through her garden. They ran to a fence, which they quickly jumped over, disappearing into the neighboring church's parking lot.

The woman witness could only say they were white. One was about 6 ft. tall and dressed in a white T-shirt and Levi's. They were both estimated to be in their 20's.

Sometime, before this assault, yet another prowler was confronted by a neighbor. The neighbor saw someone standing in his backyard. Grabbing a shotgun, he confronted the prowler. Not liking the answer he got as to why the man was in his backyard, he told him, "Get the fuck out of here." The prowler was only too willing to accommodate the request.

He described this prowler as possibly Mexican, standing at 5 ft. 9 inches tall, weighing 175 lbs. The prowler had a light beard and was wearing a Hawaiian style shirt. Before and after this incident, this neighbor found his gate standing open.

The man who chased the prowler suggested the officers talk to a teenage neighbor girl, as he felt she had also seen the prowler. When they located the young woman, she told them about a man matching the description who had accosted her in the park a week or so earlier. She was getting a drink from a public water fountain when he came up from behind and pinned her arms to her sides. At that moment, a man and woman out walking appeared. With the couple so close, the man took off running. Later she saw him driving a 1966 Chevrolet pickup with gray and white paint spots. She saw a chain necklace hanging from the rear-view mirror.

Soon after her encounter, she spoke with another teenage girl she knew who claimed to have been raped by this individual. When the investigators contacted this alleged rape victim, she denied the story. Later, the girl, who had spoken to the police about the rape victim, insisted what she told them was true.

She described him as a white male with a muscular build and clean shaven. He had a very deep voice.

It was around 11:30 P.M., two weeks prior to this assault in Concord, a couple was watching TV when they heard noises just outside their house. Stepping outside to investigate, they saw what they thought was an older black or blue Falcon with a loud exhaust. Two men, running from the area of their house, ran to that car, jumped in then quickly drove away.

Checking the outside of their house, they found all the window screens had holes cut near the window locks. A police report was made.

A teenager reported when she was arrived home after "cruising the drag " about 10:30 P.M., she spotted a faded green fleetside-Chevrolet pickup parked on Minert Road, very near the victim's house. She had seen this pickup before, and it was always at the same location. She never saw anyone near it.

One afternoon on October 1st, a woman, home alone, happened to glance out her window towards the church parking lot behind her house. Sitting in a tree, next to that parking lot, was a white male looking into her yard. She thought nothing of it at the time. The church, which was behind her house and the sexual assault victim's house, was the Most Precious Blood Church. It was into this parking lot that the two prowlers had escaped earlier.

There was one other prowler report that appeared to be significant. Before sunrise, the Saturday before the sexual assault on Belann Court, a man was leaving for work. As he turned his car from the curb, the outer edge of his headlights caught the lower legs of someone running. Just as he focused his attention, the person ducked down behind a large planter in the front yard. The only description he could give was that the runner was wearing brown corduroy pants and tennis shoes. Assuming it was the paper boy, he continued on his way with out investigating it further.

Security officers badge found in the victim's neighborhood.

A normal routine in any major investigation is to determine if other jurisdictions are investigating the same kinds of crimes with the same, or similar, method of operation. In this instance, the Concord investigators contacted the Stockton Police Department. From this contact they learned that some of the Stockton victims and witnesses had undergone hypnosis in an effort to develop more details.

Through the hypnosis sessions, the Stockton investigators learned that an early 60's model, tan or beige Toyota or Datsun had been seen in the area of their victims.

That car had the old style California license plate and two decals. One of the decals stated "Milk Drinkers Make Better Lovers" and the other, "I'd Rather Be Sailing".

Of the license numbers developed from this avenue of investigation, BIK, BTK, or BEK were the only possible combinations. Concord investigators ran the various possibilities of these letters as far as they could. Like the other leads in this investigation, they ended with nothing.

This was the first East Area Rapist assault to occur in Contra Costa County. From this point forward, Sgt. Jim Bevins would spend a great deal of time working closely with detective Larry Crompton and others from jurisdictions outside of Sacramento. He worked closely enough with them that he was eventually able to predict the general area where the EAR would strike. He did predict, within a two-week time frame, when the EAR would strike. He was spot on.

October 13, 1978
Ryan Road
Concord

A San Francisco accountant and her partner, a sheet metal worker, where the next to be targeted. They had only been in their home two months when they were assaulted.

Again, like a broken record, the EAR woke his victims with a bright light which he shined into their eyes. His routine of tying and retying took place, only this time the couple's six-year-old daughter, awakened by her mother's screams, came out of her bedroom to see what was happening.

When she saw the masked pervert standing over her tied up parents, she began screaming. Like most six-year-olds, she ran straight for her mother but was intercepted by the masked man. Following her mother's, instructions she stopped screaming and went into the bathroom. A dresser shoved in front of the door ensured that was where she would remain.

The broken record continued as the suspect claimed all he wanted was food and money, only this time he added something new to his introductory speech. "All WE want is food and money and then WE'LL get the hell out of here." To be sure, since the beginning of this nut's rampage, there had been some hints two people were involved. Personally, I always wondered if there were two people occupying the same space in his head.

The suspect was 5 ft. 10 inches tall, wore a black ski mask, and a long sleeved pullover shirt, without pockets, which was tucked in. He wore black slacks, grayish brushed-suede gloves, and black laceup round-toed shoes.

He spoke in a gruff, muffled whisper. He sounded jumpy, but he knew exactly what he was doing.

For the second time his penis, which was usually described as five inches long and thin—but seldom fully erect, was described as maybe three inches long, fully erect and was thought to be circumcised.

When the suspect was wandering around, ransacking the house, they heard him putting stuff into what sounded like a large plastic bag. There were at least five side-trips from the house into the attached garage. On his last trip into the garage he was heard to whisper, "Here, put this in the car." The garage light was on when the officers arrived.

One neighbor, who lived immediately next door, said they heard a beeping sound, about five minutes apart, three different times. They related it to the noise a car door makes when opened.

As might be expected, there were a number of prowlers and crank phone calls reported to the investigating officers.

One couple said they heard noises behind their house for two nights, and then again the night of this assault. They did not look for what was causing the noise, so the cops who were doing the neighborhood canvass tried to discover the source. They found the couple's screen door had been cut near the latch. One window screen had been pried, and the other was entirely removed. The gate to their yard was open and there were fresh footprints in the dirt near it.

A bicycle was stolen from the backyard of another neighbor the night of the assault. It was recovered three days later in some bushes, next to an apartment complex, on nearby Ryan Road.

October 29, 1978
Montclair Place
San Ramon

A travel agent, working out of Hayward, and her husband, an employee of Marina Heating and Air conditioning, were to be the next victims of this sociopath. The couple was in the process of moving out of their house and into their new home when they were attacked.

It was because of this "in-progress move" that their house was a bit shy of furnishings. There were few drawers to be tossed about, which I would guess frustrated the suspect a bit.

In this assault, the suspect demonstrated a real anger towards women. When the victim asked for a drink of water, he brought her one and then threw it in her face. The one time he ejaculated, he did so on her face then forced her mouth open and ejaculated a little there as well.

After tying up the couple, the suspect began to walk around their room. Even though it was dark the victim was able to see her atttacker's reflection in a mirror. It appeared as though she could see his facial features, but in actuality they could not be seen clearly. It appeared he may have been wearing a nylon stocking over his head.

Right after they thought the suspect had left their house, they heard a car engine start. The motor died, was restarted, then quit again. Then a third try and it was pulling away when suddenly the engine quit yet again. After the fourth start, they heard the car leaving the area. To the victims it sounded like a V-8 engine that was running a little rough.

Clothing was a blue nylon jacket missing one button. His shoes were blue brushed-suede tennis shoes with a white stripe over the toes. He also wore blue socks. His gloves were a loose fitting beige material.

Hoping to assist the victim in recalling details of a suspicious car arrangements were made for a hypnosis session. In the meantime that car had been located, and the driver cleared of any connection with the crime. Other information was to come out of that session however.

First there was a light colored Celica that pulled into their driveway the day of the assault. She was able to recall the license plate number, and the investigators found that it was listed as junked in October, 1977.

In their followup investigation, they spoke with the owner of Castille Auto Parts in Windsor, California. He explained the license plates in question were on a 1973 Chevrolet Vega that arrived on October 14, 1977. The plates would have been taken off the car within six months. Junked cars were left in a semi-secure location that was protected at night by guard dogs. There were only two people allowed to remove those plates, and the owner was one of them.

The suspect's description, given by the victim, is the most detailed one to come out of this investigation. She described him as a white male adult in his early 20's to early 30's, 5 ft. 10 inches to 6 ft., a medium build and larger upper body, with a little extra weight in the stomach. His hair was dark, and especially dark on his moderately hairy, white, but not muscular, legs. He had a double chin and a short neck, but not a neck like a football player. His eyes were close set, and he had a small distinctive nose that did not fit his face. She said his nose was more romanesque and he had small, not full, lips. He had a light olive complexion. There was also a possible mole on the left side of his chin. When walking, he scuffled his feet. She also stated that he was very sure of himself and did not appear to be nervous—he was unafraid.

A 17-year-old-boy, who lived very close to the victims, had something to report to the police. He arrived home about 5:00 A.M. As he was getting out of his car, he saw a man dressed in dark clothing climbing over a fence at 110 Adams Place. The man then started walking down Pine Valley Road.

About 5:30 A.M., a man of similar a description was seen walking on Pine Valley Road. For just a moment he stepped behind some trees where he was lost from sight. Then he stepped back on the road and continued walking.

November 4, 1978.
Havenwood Drive
San Jose

November 4, 1978, between the hours of 3:45 and 4:45 A.M., a woman was sexually assaulted in her home on Havenwood Drive in San Jose.

This investigation was not handled well. Because of that the question of whether or not this attack was the action of the East Area Rapist has never been answered. To be sure, there were some similarities, but then again, many rapes over the years had similarities. What determined this one to be an EAR attack was the whispered words, "All I want is food and money." Also, the attacker on Havenwood Drive had a small man part. The victim thought he might be "oriental" but with no real justification for her speculation.

He used a knife, and the attack occurred in a two-story building. A small boy was asleep in another room, but he did not wake up during the incident.

December 3, 1978
Kersey Lane
San Jose

On December 3rd, a registered nurse employed by Stanford Hospital was assaulted by the EAR.

She and her husband were asleep when awakened by a bright light in their eyes. This time the victim employed her professional demeanor when being forced to hold the suspect's little slick wick.

She took note it was 5 to 6 inches long and circumcised. She also noted he had an erection when he placed it in her hands. This in and of itself was unusual for the suspect, as he seldom seemed able to obtain, much less maintain, an erection. She was menstruating, but that did not slow him down. As he had done a number of times before, he simply removed the tampon, tossing it aside.

After sexually assaulting her, the suspect could be heard in the kitchen pacing back and forth sobbing, "You mother fucker. Motherfucker." Then he resumed his ransacking. A second sexual assault, and he returned to the kitchen where he could be heard whimpering and crying for another three to five minutes. Both times he was heard in the kitchen there were no accompanying sounds of cupboards or drawers being opened, only the sobbing and muttering.

In this assault, the suspect made sure his victim could breathe after he gagged her. In most of the previous assaults, he did not seem to care one way or the other. His concern took away some of her fear of imminent death. When her husband accidentally knocked the dishes off his back, the suspect literally ran to see if he had escaped from the bedroom. This happened twice, and each time he stuck the gun next to her husband's head with renewed threats of death.

As the suspect was preparing to leave, it sounded to the victims like he was retracing his steps, as if making sure he was leaving nothing behind.

They described him as a black man. When asked why, they said that even though he was trying to disguise his voice, it sounded deep—like the voice some black men have. The repeated use of the phrase "motherfucker" helped to influence them as well. Other than that, they put him between 20 and 30 years. He had good diction and vocabulary that was equal to a junior college level. He appeared to be nervous and spoke in a loud, harsh whisper.

The only clothing described was a navy blue nylon jacket.

December 9, 1978
Liberta Court
Danville

It was about 2:00 A.M. when a 32-year-old woman, living alone, was assaulted by a man wielding a dull butter knife. With what she described as a controlled, angry sounding voice, the intruder whispered commands through clenched teeth. The usual binding and ransacking took place, only this time the sex was limited to his masturbating himself and one act of rape. She was not forced to hold his slick wick and could only say it was slick, as he had apparently applied lotion on it.

The description she provided was a white male, 24 to 26 years of age, standing between 5 ft. 9 and 5 ft. 11 inches with a weight between 150 and 160. His hair was brown, and as described in some of the EAR assaults, he seemed to have hairy legs. This time he did not wear gloves which made it possible for the victim to determine that the palms of his hands were rough and calloused. She thought he might be moderately educated as he was articulate. The only clothing description given was a nylon windbreaker.

The woman worked in an office located on Patricia Street in Danville. The house she was assaulted in was not hers and had been on the real estate market for the past two months,

Again dogs were used to follow the path of the suspect. Once out of the victim's yard, the path led to nearby railroad tracks which it followed briefly then veered onto a side road where it ended.

Two dogs were used and each had a similar reaction. Their handlers said that their reactions were not a normal response to a human scent. Although not described in the police reports, both canine officers said there was a difference in their dogs behavior when tracking someone who had a physical or drug problem. By problem, they were referring to a disease or other ailment that might change the chemical balance of the individual. The behavior of these two trained dogs indicated the person they were tracking fit into that pattern. The lotion used by the suspect could not have been the cause of their reactions because tracking dogs live with those substances all the time.

The dogs did more than lead the officers to where the EAR had transportation waiting. They led the officers to what may turn out to be evidence. Right where they lost the scent, a criminologist picked up three pages that were apparently torn from a spiral notebook. There is a real possibility this psychopath simply took the pages from someone else's notebook and left them behind as a false lead.

"Mad is the word. The word that reminds me of 6th grade. I hated that year. I wish I had known what was going to be going on during my 6th grade year, the last and worst year of elementary school. Mad is the word that remains in my head about my dreadful year as a 6th grader. My madness was one that was caused by disappointments that hurt me very much. Dissapointments from my teacher, such as field trips that were planed, then canceled. My 6th grade teacher gave me a lot of dissapointments which made me very mad and made me built a state of hated in my heart, no one ever let me down that hard befor and I never hated anyone as much as I did him. Disapointment"

"Wasn't the only reason that made me mad in my 6th grade class, another was getting in trouble at school especially talking that's what really bugged me was writing sentences, those aweful sentences that my teacher made me write, hours and hours Id sit and write 50-10-150 sentence day and night. I write those dreadful paragraphs which embarrassed me and more important it made me ashamed of myself which in turn, deep down inside made me realize that writing sentence wasn't fair it wasn't fair to make me suffer like that, it wasn't fair to make me sit and wright until my bones ached, until my hand felt every horrid pain it ever had and as I wrote, I got mader and mader until I cried, I cried because I was ashamed I cried because I was discosted, I cried because I was mad, and I cried for myself, kid who kept on having to write those blane (damn?) sentences.

My angryness from sixth grade will scar my memory for life and I will be ashamed for my sixth grade year forever."

me write, hours and hours I'd sit
and write 50-100-150 sentence
day and night I write those dreadful
to Paragraphs which embarrased me and
more important it made me ashamed
of myself which in turn; deepdown
in side made me realize that writing
sentence wasn't fair it wasn't fair
to make me suffer like that, it
just wasn't fair to make me sit and
wright until my bones aked, until
my hand felt every painful pain I
ever had and as I wrote, I got
madder and madder, until I cried,
I cried because I was ashamed
I cried because I was discusted,
I cried because I was mad, and
I cried for myself, but who kept on
having to write those blone
penances. My Angyness from
sixth grade will scar my memory
for life and I will be ashamed
for my sixth grade year forever

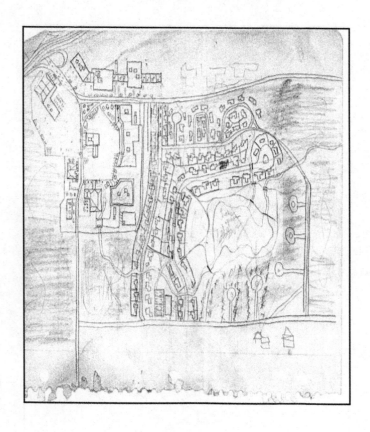

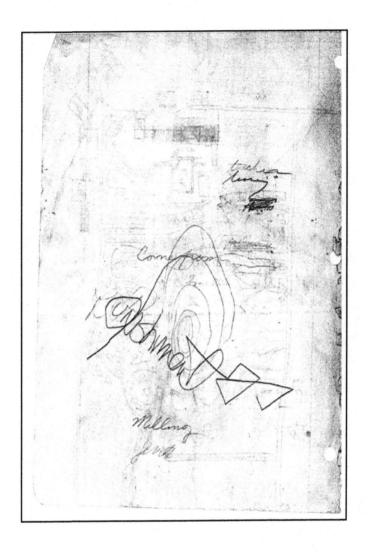

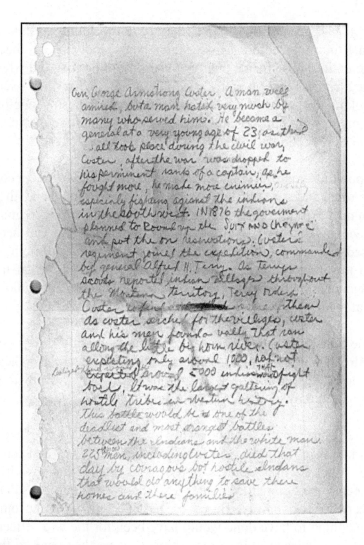

Gen. George Armstrong Custer, A man well admired, but a man hated very much by many who served him. He became a general at a very young age of 23; as this all took place during the civil war, Custer, after the war was dropped to his permenent rank of a captain, as he fought more, he made more enimies, especialy fighting against the indians in the southwest. IN 1876 the government planned to Round up the Suix and Cheyne and put the on reservations. Custers regiment joined the expedition, commanded by general Alfred H. Terry. As Terrys scouts reported indian villages throughout the Montana territory, Terry ordered Custer to find and then as custer searched for the villages, custer and his men found a valley that ran along the little big horn river. Custer expecting only around 1000, happnot expected around 5000 indians would fight back, It was the largest gathering of hostile tribes in western history. This battle would be one of the deadliest and most strangest battles between the indians and the white man. 225 men, including Custer, died that day by couragous but hostile Indians that would do anything to save there homes and there families.

December 18, 1978
San Ramon

A visit by the EAR in San Ramon may have been stopped by an alert family. Having received a heads-up on indications the

EAR had been in their home, they began to follow a routine. Each morning before leaving their home, they would check the entire house inside and out. The first thing they did when they came home was to check it again. What they were looking for were holes in window screens, missing photos, items moved, and possibly a coil of rope under a cushion. A coil of rope hidden in the house was a new one for me.

Upon their return from home, they were shocked to find a coil of rope under a cushion. A little more searching and they found a wedding snapshot had been removed from its regular place and left on a pad of writing paper. That pad had been used the day before and replaced in the drawer with nothing on top of it. This type of odd behavior is exactly what the psychopath, known as EAR, could be expected to do. Actions that made no sense to anyone but himself were his forte.

The San Ramon house backed up to a deep gully near some railroad tracks. It was a perfect setting for the EAR. These people did well to check as thoroughly as they did, for they were certainly on the EAR's planned menu.

After sending the couple away for the night, two officers parked their unmarked car in the adjacent driveway and spent the night in the couple's house. This might have worked except the unmarked car next door was an absolute guaranteed giveaway. Based on past performance, the only wise thing to have done would have been for the two officers to leave their car at least three blocks away, then walk to the house (separately) early in the day.

The rope had been placed under the cushion sometime that same day between 8:00 A.M. and 6:30 P.M. In all probability, the suspect was nearby watching when the officers arrived; that or he checked their car parked next door. He was not about to return to that house.

March 20, 1979
Filmore Lane
Rancho Cordova

There was another home invasion thought by most to have been the work of the EAR, but there were enough differences it could not be certain. This time he chose a duplex where a single mother and her two children had been living for only two months. At the time, she was employed as a secretary on the 2700 block of Cottage Way in Sacramento. She and her children previously lived in Petaluma, a small town close to the California coast. Her ex-husband was a carpenter.

This young mother was jerked awake about 5:00 in the morning by someone holding her shoulders. Her instinctive response was to resist, which was rewarded by four or five whacks on the left cheek with something the intruder held in his right hand.

Here he used the same phrase, "All I want is your fucking money. I won't hurt you if you shut up." She did and he tied her with a nylon tent-cord taken from her garage.

The other distinct similarity between this assault and a typical EAR assault was the extensive ransacking of the house. This time he left the bedroom light on. He even pulled the comforter from over her eyes so she could see his masked face. She felt that was what he wanted her to do, so she stared off into space. He unplugged lamps but did not touch the telephone. There was no use of lotion nor did this suspect sexually assault this woman.

Once he pulled her pajama bottoms down then laid a knife blade against her back telling her that was her last chance to tell him where the money was.

Fearing she was about to be raped she said, "Please don't. I'm telling the truth." Pulling the elastic band of her pajama bottoms taunt, he let it snap back against her backside, threw the covers back over her and said, "Bitch!" and left the bedroom. This was followed by ten minutes of silence after which she got free of her bonds with ease–something not many victims had managed.

As he paced around her bedroom, he could be heard making gasping sounds. Just before he left an alarm clock went off in one of her children's bedrooms. It was right after this alarm clock sounded that he called her a bitch and left .

When describing her assailant, she said he behaved as if on script. He never changed his mind and went through his movements as if everything had been planned out well-ahead.

Her opinion about the assailant and his actions was based on her job which was making commercials for an advertising agency. Speaking through clenched teeth, he enunciated every word as if he were thinking them through before he uttered them. Probably part of the reason for this impression was the fact he spoke very slowly. It was also her professional opinion that the suspect thought out every word before speaking in order to avoid stuttering.

Her assailant stood about 6 ft. and weighed about 180 lbs. She did not think he was fat or over bearing in his physical appearance. His mask was a nylon stocking. His gloves were dark, soft leather. It struck her he tried to make his voice sound huskier than it probably was.

April 4, 1979
Honda Way, Fremont

April 4, 1979, about 12:30 A.M., the EAR assaulted a couple living on Honda Way in Fremont. His intended victim was employed as a secretary in the nearby town of Burlingame and her boyfriend owned rental properties in San Jose.

The assault began with the man standing in the bedroom doorway, shining a light in their eyes, then moving to the sexual assaults and ransacking. There was a difference in the description of the rapist. This time he touched her breasts with ungloved hands. Hands that were not calloused. As usual he failed to achieve much of an erection leaving his penis two to three inches long.

He was described as a white male, 25 to 35 years old, 5 ft. 8 inches to 5 ft. 10 inches tall, 165 to 180 lbs. His legs were white with brown hair. He wore a dark ski mask, a dark nylon parka, dark pants, baggy checkered brown socks, and deck shoes

June 2, 1979
El Divisadero Drive
Walnut Creek

She said later it could have been a sound, or maybe even some kind of sixth sense, that pulled her attention towards the door behind her.

Comfortably seated at the kitchen table, while her young charge for the evening was asleep in another room, the girl was waiting for the child's parents to come home from their evening out. Babysitting was something she did often and for more than one family. Those evenings had always been uneventful, so she had no reason to expect anything different this evening.

Whatever the reason, she turned to see a man, not much taller than herself, wearing a ski mask, holding what looked like a large rectangle object in his hand. On his hip he wore something which she came to believe was a sheath for a long-bladed knife.

Rapidly moving towards her, the masked wonder whispered in a low gravelly voice, "Don't make any sounds. Shut up and be quiet." His commands were probably unnecessary as this young woman had already been shocked into silence.

One hand pushing her head down, the other holding her arm, he both pushed and guided her into a bedroom where he forced her onto a bed. Then the charade began as he told her all he wanted was money. This time instead of shoestrings or twine, he tied her hands with plastic clips which are also known as flexi cuffs or wire clips.

Here the suspect did something the EAR had not done previously. He let his full weight settle on her as he laid on her. "He was heavy," she later said in describing the assault.

There were several attempts by this psychopathic bastard to penetrate her, but all were unsuccessful. Finally, he managed to complete the act of rape on this child. As he succeeded in robbing her of her childhood innocence, he stood up, and with whispered orders to roll over said, "Don't move or I'll kill you." Then he returned to his routine of ransacking the house.

During the rape he kept rubbing what felt like a long knife blade up and down her neck. There was one other trick he pulled in this assault that was different. He bit her on the nipple four times with the last time being hard enough to leave marks and pain lasting for several hours. Prior to this, the EAR rarely touched the breast of his victims, and then it was as though he was handling an inanimate object. But then, who knows what kind of fantasizing went on in this sicko's head.

She gave a description of the suspect as a white male, possibly 5 ft. 6 inches tall, but because of the conditions this was only a guess. The mask hiding his face was white. There was no body fat she could discern.

Not far from the scene of the assault, patrol officers spotted a 1978 Olds Cutlass weaving in and out of traffic. Pulling the driver over on suspicion of drunk driving, they noted he matched the general description of the suspect. An investigator from the assault scene and a canine unit showed up. The dog was first allowed to smell the interior of the car then the driver. When it came to the driver, the dog alerted. Officers then arrested the driver for drunk driving and rape. It was not until later they determined a mistake had been made by allowing the dog to smell the the car interior before turning him towards the driver. After smelling the interior of the car, it was only natural for the dog to alert on the driver. The rape charges were dropped.

Before all the officers left the area, another resident called to report a prowler. With so many squad cars already close by, he was quickly taken into custody

This prowler, born in Sacramento but living in nearby Pleasant Hill, was literally caught with his pants down. He claimed he worked for a janitorial company, and after his shift ended at 7:00 P.M., he set out to search for his lost cat. This "search" lasted until 6:00 A.M.

Inside the prowler's car were several photos of women taken with a zoom lens. One photo showed a woman getting into a car that had just come out of a car wash.

The usual assortment of prowlers and crank phone calls seemed to accompany every East Area Rapist assault surfaced during the neighborhood canvass. Someone reported that their bicycle had been stolen. The bicycle was dumped when the chain jumped the sprocket.

For the past month a woman and her daughter received over ten crank phone calls. Then there were three women sharing a house who had a prowler in their backyard the night before this latest assault. As might be expected, they were also receiving crank phone calls. At the suggestion of one officer they checked for missing photos of themselves. Two photos were missing from a dresser.

Like those women this latest victim had also been on the receiving end of those crank phone calls. These occurred not only at home but where ever she babysat. A month earlier, a night gown disappeared from her bedroom.

She was not the first babysitter assaulted by this suspect who had received those annoying phone calls both at home and where she worked. This time those phone calls were to continue after the assault. These post-assault phone calls even extended to the mother of this young victim. Working for a private doctor in Walnut Creek, the mother answered the phone at work only to hear heavy breathing. The heavy breathing did not intimidate her in the least. Instead she was now on full alert.

The doctor for whom she worked had his office on Ignacio Valley Road in Walnut Creek at a center named Doctors Park. Today their advertising includes a number of doctors who specialize in oriental medicine which may be referring to Traditional Chinese Medicine. Two oriental women had been targeted by the EAR earlier in this series. It is almost certain that no one made the connection between those two women and the Doctors Park, if indeed there had even been one .

In 2011, I made contact at this complex and learned what I expected. Records, of course, had long been thrown away, but I was still able to locate the owner of the building in Canada where he now lives. The results were again zero for investigators and one for pyschopath.

On the alert and ready for battle, this mother was leaving for work just a couple of days after the assault when she spotted a car new to her neighborhood. As she made a bee line to the maroon-colored Ranchero type car, the single occupant, a WMA, drove off before she got close enough for the license number. It was a Ranchero or El Camino that was seen near the house of the victim on Sandbar Circle in May, 1977.

This stalwart mother had reported to police investigators that a few days prior to the assault on her daughter, she had seen the gardener for an Alpha Beta Market near her and her neighbor's house.

The house where the victim was babysitting was located directly across the street from a grade school. Adjacent to the sports field was a vacant house with a "for lease" sign in the front yard.

June 11, 1979
Allegheny Drive
Danville

Whatever drove this rapist known as EAR into action, monotony was certainly no distraction. Maybe for him, there was a sense of security to be gained from repetition. Once again, it was like a broken record when he set out on the night of June 11, 1979, to fulfill some sick fantasy no doubt already played out in his head. That fantasy had been planned and choreographed to the last detail. As always, he was playwright, producer, and director. The actors had already been chosen. They just didn't know it.

Like his other victims, he woke these two with a light shining directly into their eyes. Once he had their attention, he began the job of director by tossing shoestrings at the lady, telling her how to tie her husband's hands behind his back. By now he was getting good at this. While directing her on how to tie her husband's hands, he began his charade–all he wanted was money. His exact words were, "As soon as you give us money, I'll go back to the city." Mixing the singular with plural as he did indicated he was lying. Only after the couple was securely bound did his courage surface and he commenced with threats to kill everyone in the house if he was not obeyed.

The usual routine of placing dishes on the man's back was played out. This time, instead of dishes, he made the Brazilian Tree with perfume bottles placed on her husband's back. Even with the bottles in place, he was still insecure enough to return every two or three minutes to reaffirm the husband was still tied.

About 4:30 A.M., the victims heard a small vehicle they took to be a truck race up the street then stop in front of their house. It sat there for about 45 seconds, then they heard it race away. It sounded like it stopped a short distance down the street where, after a minute to a minute and a half, they heard a car door slam shut then the pickup raced away again.

Based on those sounds the husband, thinking the suspect was gone, started to roll out of bed only to be threatened by the suspect who was standing right next to him. He lay there awhile longer before making another attempt to escape. Sliding the blindfold off, he looked at the clock and saw it was 4:45 A.M. The suspect had been gone for as much as 15 minutes.

As had become routine, a tracking dog was brought in. The dog led the officers through the victims' backyard then through some neighbors' backyards, eventually ending 20 yards south of the intersection of Delta and El Capitan Roads.

All along the trail, footprints were discovered that matched the type and size believed to belong to the EAR.

Later, the investigators discovered the suspect gained entry through the bedroom of the victims' three-year-old child. That was precisely what he had done to gain entry in the assault on Woodpark Way in October, 1976.

The primary victim in this assault earned her keep by performing one of the toughest jobs of all, that of housewife and mother. Her husband was the division manager for a data documents company located in Hayward. The family grocery shopping was done every other week at the Alpha Beta Market on Diablo Road in Danville.

In general, the description of this suspect was like that of the others: a white male adult, standing with a slight slouch and about 5 ft. 5 to 5 ft. 9 inches tall, between 20 and 30 years old who appeared stocky or chunky, as opposed to thin. He may have appeared heavier because of the sweater he was wearing. As described by the victim on Cherrelyn, his hair was soft-bodied and a light-brown color. This time, as opposed to being calloused, his hands were soft and small.

Keeping with his program, he only spoke in a raspy whisper forced through clenched teeth. His voice was described as not a "strong vibrant male voice." His mannerisms were mocking and he also acted like a tough guy. He used the plural "we" a lot and he referred to "going to the city and his van." His victims smelled a feminine-smelling talcum powder on him. There was no similar talcum powder kept in the victims' house.

There was a report of a stolen bicycle, then shortly afterwards a man not known to the neighborhood was seen on a bicycle. A short time later, and not far from where the bicycle was stolen, a sound was heard in some bushes. Suddenly a man on a bicycle burst out into the open and sped out of the area.

There were other reports of prowlers as well. The night before this assault, a man living on the nearby street of El Capitan heard some gravel crunching just outside his window. When he looked out, he saw a 6 ft. 2 inch 210 lb. man, with a heavy build and dark hair. His hair reached the nape of his neck. The suspect was standing on some lava rock, staring at the house across the fence. He was not five feet away and as he watched, the man climbed over his neighbor's fence.

Waiting 10 minutes, the witness went outside and walked around east bound on El Capitan to a midway point between the streets Delta and Allegheny. There he saw the same man riding a 10-speed bike. When the man realized he had the interest of this neighbor, he rode off and was quickly out of sight.

What perhaps was the best lead in this entire investigation was discovered by a woman living on the street northwest of the victim. She reported to the police that when checking on a vacant house the afternoon of the assault, she a found a car wash ticket in the driveway. The ticket had not been there the day before. It was described as 2 x 3/4 by 2 x 3/4 with "Car Wash 6/9/79" printed on it. She found it next to the driveway and close to the garage door.

That car wash ticket brings to mind the man caught with his pants down who had been looking for his "lost cat" for 11 hours. He had been arrested for prowling in nearby Walnut Creek on June 2nd.

June 25, 1979
San Pedro Court
Walnut Creek

Never one afraid to demonstrate just how low he could sink, the EAR assaulted yet another child. This time his victim was a 13-year-old girl living with her father and her 16-year-old sister.

Accustomed to getting up to the alarm at 4:45 A.M., her father awoke before the alarm had a chance to go off. As he lay there relishing the fact he could lie in bed just a little longer, he heard his youngest daughter running down the hall shouting, "I've been raped!"

As he ran to her aid he yelled for his older daughter to wake up and come help. Right in the middle of all this commotion, the daughter who had just been sexually assaulted thought she heard someone in the bathroom.

This particular bathroom was situated between the girls' bedrooms and opened onto the outside. After checking the bathroom they called the police department.

Within minutes, police were on the scene and right behind them, Patrol Officer Judy Robb, of the Contra Costa Search and Rescue. What happened next proves dogs do, in fact, have specific memories.

These (three) dogs had been used to track the EAR in the assault on nearby El Divisadero on June 2. Without going into the victims' house they recognized the scent of the suspect the instant they crossed it in the yard. The trail they followed led to a street near a house where a pool was being built which is where it ended; the same exact same spot it had on June 2.

In this assault, the young victim awoke to find somebody straddling her back and telling her to do what she was told and she would not be hurt. All he wanted was her money. Using this charade long enough to tie and gag her, the suspect set about ransacking her bedroom. What he did not do until later was blindfold her. Her purse was in the room, but apparently he never went through it as her seven dollars was left untouched.

This was probably the only assault where he never entered any of the other rooms of the house to ransack them or the kitchen to eat. He kept telling this girl that he needed money but never asked her where it was.

Again the ritual of lotion followed by all the rest was performed. Only this time he made a statment that mystified most of us. "Let it drop easy" or "Give me a good drop or I'll kill you." No one knew what that phrase meant then and probably not now. Just before he walked out of the bedroom, he re-tied her feet but not tight.

The rapist was in her bedroom for probably no more than 20 minutes. It is possible he was the source of the noise in the bathroom that the victim thought she heard, after she called her dad for help. It may not have been his intention to leave when he did but the whole family coming awake made that decision for him.

What is notable here is the suspect actually seemed to not really be all that into what he was doing. First he only assaulted the girl once. It was just before the sexual assault when he blindfolded her. He never left her room to ransack and he never took any of her money. Only once did he direct any profanity towards her. Even leaving the bonds on her feet loose enough for her to break free was different. If that was the EAR, then his heart was just not in it this time.

This victim and her sister were out of school for the summer. During that afternoon, they were at home when someone called but said nothing when the phone was answered. They were not aware of any prowlers or break-ins into their house or those of their neighbors.

It was about 8:00 P.M. on the evening leading up to the sexual assault that the victim shopped at the Alpha Beta Market. While there, she did not see anyone or experience anything that struck her as suspicious.

This was the third victim in a row to be connected in some way with an Alpha Beta Market.

She said he was a white male. Although she never stood next to him, nor even got that good of a look at him, she felt he was probably about 6 ft. tall. His age she would put at between 25 and 30. There was no weight estimate, but she felt he was broad shouldered and possibly a little chunky around the waist but definitely not fat. In general she thought he was well-built.

Speaking through clenched teeth as he did led her to believe his voice was deep and scratchy. There was no stuttering at any time. However, she thought she noticed a slight Mexican accent but thought he was faking it. That opinion was partially based on the fact he never rolled his "R's when talking. A certain amount of shaking in his voice led the victim to believe the suspect was nervous. He also sounded angry all the time.

The suspect was wearing Adidas type running shorts that had the same configuration as swimming trunks with small slits at the sides. She was positive they were not boxer shorts.

His mask was homemade from a gauze-like material that may have been cheesecloth. She never noticed any gloves. If he did wear gloves, then they must have been the surgical type as they fit very tight and smooth. He also wore a light colored T-shirt.

The afternoon, several hang-up calls were received at the victim's house. Investigators immediately placed a trap on the line. In the end they got the same result as before which was zip.

Investigators on the scene did a good job of on-the-scene-investigating. One of them noted the victim's house was of Eichler type construction which featured a lot of glass at the rear of the residence. They also noticed the house was of a similar design, if not the same design, as the house where the last EAR victim in Walnut Creek lived.

Years later, in an article about the murders in Southern California, the journalist made mention of the exact same floor plan in the houses of two of the victims.

Chapter 54:
Catch and Release

July 5, 1979
Sycamore Hill Court
Danville

A whole separate book could be written about this one attempted assault. It would begin with the suspect hiding exactly as a Colonel from the Green Berets told a group of Sacramento Sheriff's Department officers in 1977, "Look where you would least expect to find someone." In this instance it would have been deep in a heavy growth of ivy, which itself was deep in the shadows. It was after this incident where the EAR was stopped cold by his intended victim, then very nearly caught by the police that he fled North Central California, moving his reign of terror into Southern California.

It was 57 minutes after 5 in the morning when Bill, a light sleeper, awoke to the sound of something rustling. Searching for the source, he pinpointed it as coming from the vanity area. Looking in that direction, what he saw caught him totally by surprise. Reflected in a mirror by a light from downstairs was somebody in the act of slipping a mask over their head.

Bill did not waste any time. Because the media had everyone paranoid about the suspect known as the East Area Rapist, he and his wife had planned what to do should they ever find themselves confronted by this psychopath. Immediately, Bill was up and headed straight for the masked intruder while yelling at his wife to get out of the house. Their plan was to give his wife time to escape. As he was confronting the psychopath, Bill noticed he was holding something in his left hand, but he was not sure what it was. Later investigators found shoestrings the suspect had dropped on the floor. They came from Bill's shoes and the shoestrings were found in front of the closet where the suspect was standing when confronted.

This psychopath, dubbed EAR, had never been in a situation where the odds were even close to even. Having nearly had his butt whipped by one blindfolded and tightly bound victim, he now found himself confronted by someone not only bigger, but much bigger, and not running away, and this time the much bigger man was not tied nor blindfolded. The EAR had just found himself in deep stuff and had no idea what to do about it. It simply did not fit into his imagined world where he was always in control. The possibility for his getting blitzed on the spot was huge.

Bill said when he first jumped in front of the suspect and began yelling, the suspect took two involuntary steps backward. Then he just stood there, blinking widely and slowly while being yelled at. To Bill he seemed to be scared and in disbelief as if thinking, "This isn't supposed to happen." But throughout those few moments, he was passive and controlled. His not being burdened with normal emotions comes as no surprise.

Neighbors were awakened by shouts of "Help!" and "Who the fuck do you think you are?" "Get the fuck out of here now and you can leave." and "What the fuck are you doing here?"

Finding this loud and profane language a bit unusual for the couple living at that address, they did something few others had done. Instead of waiting for the police to contact them, they actually called the cops.

Within minutes the police arrived. Among them were officers J. Robb and H. Drummond of the canine unit. When put to work, their dog, Pita, became excited by the back gate. From there the trail led to the end of the court where Morninghome and Old Orchards streets cross. At the end of the court, Pita became very animated and jumped into a heavy patch of ivy. The ground was damp and the ivy thick which made it difficult for Pita to extricate herself.

The handlers were convinced Pita had come across a very strong pool of scent only moments old. They took Pita back to the starting point and picked up the trail again. This time, after leaving the ivy, it led to a greenbelt area where it was lost.

The reason for starting over was to give the pooled scent trapped in the ivy a chance to spread out. Without doing so they would probably never have been able to track the EAR to the greenbelt area.

Bill gave a pretty good description of the suspect to which his wife—who saw the suspect in the light as he was leaving—added. Later Bill underwent hypnosis and came up with more descriptive details. The drawing that resulted from that session is grouped with others in the chapter on composites.

He described the suspect as a white male about 25 years old, standing between 5 ft. 10 inches and 6 ft. tall, 160 lbs. with a wiry build and square shoulders like a football player. Bill did not think this guy was a football player. Although he had a mask on, Bill could see enough of his face to form an opinion. He said it was a boyish face with lean but not bony features. His nose was not a particularly large nose.

There was more detail about the suspect's eyes to come out of that hypnosis session. They were round, deep set and light-colored. Probably hazel. His eye lashes were full but not feminine. The separation between them was somewhere between medium and wide. His pupils were big, which could be attributed to many different factors. The eyes were also described as being wide open but sleepy looking.

A better description of the jacket worn by the suspect came out of this session as well. It was a windbreaker made of nylon or vinyl. The collar was a regular design with peaked and pointed folds outside and down. Jacket lining appeared to be fleece. It was acknowledged that in the dark, flannel lining could pass for fleece. Fleece lining was normally used in ski-type jackets or for colder temperatures.

The yellow letter seen by Bill on the left breast of this jacket was a 1/4 inch high "C" followed by at least three other letters. "CORN" was settled on as being possible, but only possible. There was also a possibility the letter "C" was actually part of the word Coach. Companies selling these type jackets, and those who put lettering on them, describe the color of the letters as gold opposed to yellow. Those seen by Bill were most likely done by silk screening, a process normally used for groups and not individuals. 'School Block' was the professional term for the style of lettering described.

While investigators did learn a lot about the type of jacket worn by the suspect, it was too common to be identified as coming from a single source. But considering his apparent good physical condition those letters may well have spelled "Coach."

The mask worn by the suspect appeared to be homemade from wool or similar material. It only came to the jaw line, so a beard can almost certainly be ruled out.

Very soon after arriving on the scene, patrol officers spotted a man wiping the dew off the back window of his car parked a short distance from the scene. Since this man matched the general description of the suspect, they brought Bill to him for a street-side line-up. Bill was unable to make an identification, so a saliva sample was obtained and he was released. Later it was learned the sample indicated he was a secretor so he was dropped from the suspect list. In light of what is now known about secretors vs non-secretors, eliminating him as the EAR was an error.

A standard neighborhood canvass was conducted. As expected, some reports of prowlers and hang up phone calls had been made. One woman reported a prowler peeping into her bathroom.

A next door neighbor of Bill and his wife heard a sliding door opening about 3:50 A.M. But, she neither checked for the source nor called the police. When officers checked, they found this person's sliding door unlocked.

Officers also learned there were utility crawl holes under the condos throughout the complex that were available to the suspect, if he so chose. These avenues connect via the floor to the closets. In the case of Bill and his wife, the door to this crawl space was blocked with heavy objects.

A house near the victims' had been on the market with a large number of people stopping by to view it.

This marked the first time the suspect had chosen a condo to attack. The master bedroom was on the third floor, which was also different. Until this one, he had only chosen houses with slab floors. The back of the house contained a large amount of glass, which looked out onto a greenbelt area. There was a pathway from the victims' house to that greenbelt area.

It was after very nearly being arrested that the Visalia Ransacker stopped his series of crimes. Visalia investigators worried they had driven their suspect north—now investigators were concerned they may have driven their suspect to an area where no one had any idea of what to expect.

Composite of suspect confronted by his intended victim in his house in Danville. It was after this incident he fled to southern CA

Chapter 55:
The EAR Moves South

Everything related here about the crimes in Southern California came from police reports and talking with others involved in the investigations.

There have been many stories told about German shepherds connected in some way with these crimes. Other than rumors I know literally nothing of any German shepherd involvement. I do know one dog that suffered an eye injury inflicted by a burglar. That was probably the EAR/ONS who injured it. Contrary to rumors it is my belief the EAR/ONS does not like animals. He would kill one in an instant if it displeased him. Should he be living with one now, it would only be part of his disguise.

October 1, 1979
5425 Queen Anne Lane
Santa Barbara, California

Goleta, a close neighbor to Santa Barbara, is a small, quiet town. There is a one story house with the backyard next to a dry creek. About 2:30 A.M., a man and woman asleep inside that house are jolted awake by violent kicks to the end of their bed. Opening their eyes they are momentarily blinded and confused by a bright light aimed directly at them.

A male voice from behind that bright light whispered, "Don't move mother fuckers or I'll kill you." Repeatedly telling the couple to lie on their stomachs, the suspect said all he wanted was money. "I gotta have money." After tossing some nylon rope and twine to Jennifer, he told her to tie her boyfriends hands and feet. He then tied her hands before re-tying those of her boyfriend. He tied both bonds so tight the circulation blood flow was stopped; not restricted but stopped. Both of his victims felt he tied them in a sadistic manner.

While ransacking their bedroom he repeatedly paused, leaned over them and said: "I'll kill you, you motherfuckers." It was their impression the intruder was not wearing a mask when he was tying their hands. From the back glow of the light, they were also able to pick up on what they took to be dark hair with curly ends just above his collar. He had what looked like a holster strapped to his right side. They gauged his height at about 5 ft. 10 inches.

All the time the intruder kept repeating, "I gotta have money," and all he was after was money. Then he said, he would be gone and no one would be hurt. Once he had them securely tied he could be heard wandering around their house opening and closing drawers and doors.

After a short time, and still complaining about not being able to find any money, he re-entered their bedroom. This time he was wearing a ski mask. Pretending to want the woman to guide him to her purse, he grabbed her by the arm and escorted her first into the kitchen then the living room. Both victims felt he spoke slowly as if he were trying to mask his age by sounding older than he really was.

Half-pushing, half-pulling, he forced Jennifer into the living room where he guided her behind the couch then made her lie on her back. He left her there just for a moment and when he returned. He placed a pair of tennis shorts over her head. Lying there nude, a pair of shorts over her head, she could see the beam of the flashlight as he moved it over her body, rubbing himself at the same time. Just before he quietly walked away he said, "Now I'm going to kill you. Cut your throat."

She knew he had moved away when she heard him rummaging around in their kitchen. That was when he said at least a dozen times, "I'll kill 'em. I'll kill 'em." She next heard him moving down their hallway.

Deciding she was not about to just lie there and let some random psychotic slice her throat, Jennifer got to her feet and started her escape. With feet bound she could only hop to the front door. By the time she reached the front door the bindings on her feet had come off. Frantically trying to get that door open while still blindfolded she bumped into the wall. After what must have seemed an eternity, she managed to get the door open. Now, with it opened, she went for it.

Driven by the real fear of being murdered, she ran screaming for all she was worth. Unable to see and off balance she slammed into the side of the house. Unknown to her, her neighbor heard the impact of her hitting the wall. It was while blindly stumbling by the wall that she was re-captured.

Once back inside, she was forced into the same prone position behind the couch from where she had just escaped. After re-tying her, the assailant left the room again. As soon as she thought he was out of the room Jennifer was back on her feet and back out that front door. Once again she screamed as loudly as she possibly could.

When Jennifer first screamed, two other things happened. First, Henry, hearing the scream and thinking Jennifer had been murdered made a run for it. Still tied, he only managed to get out of the house and into the backyard.

The other thing that happened was their neighbor, an off-duty FBI agent named Los, heard her scream. He was up late reading a book in front of an open window, which just happened to face Jennifer's house. There was no way this agent could not have heard that panicked scream for help. A sound of someone hitting the side of the house just forced him into high gear a few nano-seconds faster. After calling 911 and notifying the sheriff's department, he grabbed his duty weapon and headed out the back door.

It was while agent Los was springing into action that Henry managed his escape into the backyard. Still hog-tied, he couldn't really run anywhere, so hoping for the best, he hopped over to the fence and yelled for his neighbor—any neighbor would do. One neighbor did open their door, looked outside then went back inside and closed the door. Not getting the response he had hoped for Henry hopped over to a citrus tree where he tried to fold into as small a package as he could manage.

Finding that Henry had also escaped, their assailant walked into the backyard where he only glanced around. Not seeing Henry, he returned to the house. When he got back inside he found Jennifer had once again escaped. It was about this time the suspect determined the best to be running away.

Just as Agent Los reached the victim's driveway, somebody on a bicycle sped down that driveway past him. Agent Los only got a fleeting glimpse of the profile of the bicyclist as he sped past. The bicycle rider was not wearing a mask. He was wearing a dark grey and blue Pendelton plaid shirt plus jeans and tennis shoes.

Agent Los noticed the cyclist turned west on Queen Ann Lane. To give chase, he needed his own transportation, so he jumped into his company car. The car failed to start right away, then a few attempts and the engine caught. Making a U-turn, Agent Los headed off in the direction of the bicyclist.

By now the cyclist was long out of sight. As anyone who has ever tried to tail a car will tell you, it only takes precious seconds to lose your target. Your target turns left and you blindly choose to turn right and it is over. But in this case, Los made a correct decision in choosing to turn down San Patricio, for that was where the fleeing cyclist was.

Being about 200 yards ahead of Los, the suspect jumped the bicycle onto the sidewalk. He quickly abandoned both the bicycle and the serrated kitchen knife which he had used to threaten his subject. The suspect was last seen jumping a fence into a backyard.

Agent Los, knowing from the traffic on his police radio that deputies were fast approaching, made what was probably a wise decision. He did not go over the fence behind the fleeing psychotic. To do so might well have put him on top of the fence making himself a perfect target, should the suspect have a gun. A decision young Mr. Roberts doubtlessly wished he had made three years earlier in Sacramento.

Agent Los, accompanied by a sheriff's deputy, returned to the scene where he had heard the screams. What they found was a nude woman running down her driveway screaming hysterically. Jennifer had been totally unaware of the pursuit agent Los had just engaged in on their behalf.

The bicycle abandoned by the suspect was traced to a U.S. parole officer who lived four or five blocks away on Via Bolzano. It had been stolen earlier that evening from the officer's locked garage. The parole officer's garage door was electronically operated and could not be opened from outside without the opener.

Shoe prints, found in the yards of the two residences where the suspect made good his escape, indicated the suspect was wearing a size 8.5 to 9 Adidas running shoe.

The place where Agent Los had seen the suspect jump the fence was very close to where four Glasby brothers lived with their family. Right behind the Glasby home was a dry creek bed which, after a few twists and turns, connected to the dry creek bed behind the victims' home.

Brian and Brett were the Glasby brothers of the most interest to detectives. Detectives learned that one of them had lived in Sacramento for a brief period of time. For some time the police were interested in these brothers, but then in 1984, Brian and Brett were murdered while on a scuba diving trip to Mexico. With the advent of DNA the brothers have since been cleared of any involvement in the EAR / ONS crimes as their DNA did not match that of the suspect.There was never anything beyond speculation that actually connected them to the EAR crimes.

There were two minor differences between this crime and the East Area Rapist's crimes in North-Central California. He was not wearing a mask when he first woke his victims up, and he delayed in blindfolding the female victim. As for placing dishes on the man's back, that may have yet happened had not the woman managed her escape first. In my opinion the EAR was settling into Santa Barbara County. His last two attempts had both ended in failure and near capture. Something he was not going to allow to happen again.

Chapter 56:
Murdered - Dr. Robert Offerman & Dr. Debri Manning

December 30, 1979
767 Avenida Pequena
Goleta & Santa Barbara

Early in January, 1980, I was on duty as watch commander for the Sacramento Sheriff Department, when Sgt. Bevins approached me with a handful of papers. Handing them to me he said, "Dick, would you look at this and tell me what you think?" It was a copy of a double homicide report from the Santa Barbara Sheriff Department. Apparently Sgt. Bevins and Lt. Root were in a dispute (as they often were) over whether or not the one responsible for that double homicide was the East Area Rapist.

It was Lt. Root's opinion that the EAR never lost control of his victims. Root believed because the suspect lost control of the two computer programmers followed by (apparently) Dr. Offerman and Dr. Manning, he was not the East Area Rapist.

After reading that report through once, I read it a second time. The second time I made a list of similarities and dissimilarities. There were 14 similarities with two or four dissimilarities. I agreed with Sgt. Bevins; this was the clearly handiwork of the EAR.

There had been two, more or less, virtual witnesses to this double homicide. They were neighbors of the victims.

It was in the middle of the night when a couple, recently returned from a trip to Mexico, awoke to use the bathroom. Still groggy, the male sat on the edge of the bed trying hard to focus on the clock in front of him. At the same moment the clock came into focus he heard three gun shots, a brief pause then a fourth shot. The time was 3:05 A.M.

Realizing what it was they just heard, the couple headed upstairs where they would have a better view of the surrounding neighborhood. From that vantage point they could see into more than one neighbor's yard. One of those yards was the backyard of 767 Avenida Piquena, Dr. Offerman's home. They did not see any lights on inside the house, but could see the sliding door was standing open with the inside screen door closed.

Another few minutes passed before they looked out a different window and saw a white, boxy car without lights, slowly driving out of the common parking lot. They thought it was similar in size to a Pinto or Honda. Thinking the time might be important, the couple checked the clock and saw it was exactly 3:17 A.M.

It would only be a few hours until this couple learned from detectives of the Santa Barbara County Sheriff's Department the meaning of those gun shots. Of all the neighbors who heard those gun shots that night these were the only two who made a real effort to determine where they came from, and if possible who might be involved.

Inside the condo at 767 Avenida Pequena lay the bodies of Dr. Robert Offerman and his companion Dr. Alexandria

Manning-Kiniry, a clinical psychologist at a pain clinic, she was from Santa Maria. Both had been shot to death.

Deputies Billester and Pia were the first two officers to arrive at the crime scene. Entering the house, they carefully made their way to the ground-floor master bedroom. Seeing two bodies in that room and determining they were dead the officers did as trained. They carefully retraced their exact steps back outside where they awaited the arrival of the homicide investigators.

Those homicide detectives were Ray Spinner and J. Johnston. Using the same path as the two officers before them, these two sleuths ventured inside the master bedroom just far enough to photograph both bodies. Returning outside, all the investigators present conferred over the photographs just taken. These photos showed a nude woman lying face down on a bed with her hands tied behind her back. The second victim, a nude man was in a kneeling position. The quilt, top sheet, and pillow were partially beneath him and on the bed.

Closer examination showed the nude man, now known as Dr. Offerman, had one piece of twine tied around his left wrist. Death had been by one shot to the chest and four to his back. Both of Dr. Manning's hands were tied very tightly behind her back. Death was by one gunshot wound to the back of her head, execution style.

The autopsy found two blue-green flakes on her big toe as well as some loose hairs on her back. Those blue-green flakes were later classified as architectural paint.

Based on what I have gleaned from years of following the EAR crimes, it is my personal opinion that he made entry, then went through the routine of getting his victims tied. Only this time one of them, which happened to be Dr. Offerman, managed to get loose and confront his attacker. The EAR, never being one for confrontation on equal terms, used his gun to save himself from certain defeat.

This double murder was probably not planned, but once done he found it was the ultimate high.

In searching the residence, officers found evidence the suspect had gone through dresser drawers and closets. He had also gone into the refrigerator and eaten some left over Christmas turkey. A turkey bone was found inside the house near the slider door where entry had apparently been gained. The actual turkey carcass was found on the patio. It appeared this freak had taken the time to treat himself to dinner at the expense of his victims. Quite probably AFTER he murdered them!

Bindings used on both victims were short 1/16 diameter strings of nylon and rayon. Besides being found on the victims, other pieces were found in various locations about the victims' house. As with the bindings on Dr. Manning's wrists, these short pieces of twine had been tied together by a series of "fancy" knots to make them long enough to use as a binding.

Investigating Officers were contacted at the scene by a neighbor to be of Dr. Offerman. What follows is quoted from the actual report:

"Detectives were contacted by Mrs. ——- who at the time was in the process of moving into the adjacent condo at 769 Avenida Pequena. She advised that there had been an entry to her residence which had been vacant the night Drs. Offerman and Manning were murdered.

The residence was checked and pry marks were found on the sliding glass patio door on the north side of the residence. Some twine, consistent with that found at the murder scene was found in the master bathroom of the ——— residence. Also in a cabinet under sink in master bedroom. Partial roll of twine with a cardboard holder was found on mantle over the fireplace. This twine was seized by technician Moore of the Sheriff's Department. He also processed the residence for latent fingerprints. Cast of shoe impressions were made."

I understood this new neighbor was employed as an RN.

While contacting the nearby residents and examining the general neighborhood, officers found even more twine that appeared to be the same as that used in the murders. Some was found on the patio of 773 Avenida Pequena. A small piece of it was found on the dirt trail on the east side of the roadway across from nearby 825 North Kellogg. A second piece was discovered on the trail leading into a greenbelt area adjacent to 866 North Kellogg. A piece of similar twine was also found in the backyard of 5470 Queen Anne Lane.

Two shoe impressions were found near the pieces of twine found on the trail. These impressions held a pattern of diagonal lines and then several dots. It was thought these were prints typical of a deck shoe. Keeping these shoe prints company were those of a medium to large dog. As the trail passed Norma Lane, it disappeared into the main creek area. The twine and prints were not found until two days after the crimes.

Analysis of the twine found one real distinction about the pieces found on the mantle next door to the victim on Avenida Quena. It was made of rayon that is most commonly used in tire construction or drive belt cords. This was the only piece of rayon found.

A neighbor of Dr. Offerman's, whose bedroom window is only a few feet from his front door, heard what she took to be his Porsche pull into the parking lot about midnight on the night of the double murder. She heard two men's voices and one woman's voice. She recognized Dr. Offerman but not the other two voices.

As might be expected, investigators discovered a number of prowlers and burglaries that had occurred from as close as next door to a mile away.

Sometime between 4:00 and 8:00 P.M., using a round shank screwdriver, an attempt was made to pry open a door at 5419 Pareso. This house is close to Queen Anne Lane, the home where the couple managed to escape the suspect's control.

Between December 18th and the 29th, and the hours of 5:30 and 8:05 P.M., someone forcibly entered the home at 5422 Hannah Drive. The property taken from there consisted of one wedding band and cash from a safe that had been forced open. Valuable jewelry was left behind.

That same night at 10:15 P.M., a couple returning home from a night at the movies found a surprise waiting for them. As they pulled into their driveway on Windsor Court, they saw someone running out of their living room towards the back of the house. As this couple, a teacher and a registered nurse, entered their house, they could hear the intruder jumping over their fence into the yard of Mountain View School.

No property had been taken, but they did find the suspect had injured their dog's left eye. The left side was also the side where the dog had been struck and killed in Rancho Cordova in 1975. This family lived close to a mile from where Drs. Offerman and Manning would be murdered about four hours later that same evening.

They could only describe the intruder as wearing a fisherman type hat and dark jacket. The cap was probably a rolled-up knit cap or stocking. Shoe impressions matching those found at both 767 and 769 Avenida Pequena were found and casts made. Some matching shoe impressions were also found in the Mountain View School yard near the fence to this couple's property.

The same night about 9:30 P.M., a home at 5470 Queen Anne Lane was broken into. This time some jewelry and two-dollar bills were stolen. One significant class ring from the Merchant Marine, class of 1946, was among the items taken. It bore the initials H.J.H. What exactly this couple did for employment was not stated. But there was a comment he could be contacted at the UCSB Department of Engineering.

A neighbor of the family with the injured dog reported seeing someone on their front porch that same evening. At 6:10

P.M., a woman about 25 years old with shoulder length hair and dressed in dark clothing was standing at the front door. Then at 7:00 P.M. and again 7:30 P.M., a white male about 5 ft. 8 inches was seen standing at the front door.

As might be expected, a bicycle was also reported as stolen from 773 Avenida Pequena.

Officers putting their full efforts into this investigation learned a prowler had been seen in the area a year earlier. What they learned from their investigation was that on two occasions, when the people who lived next door to 5345 Vineyard Road, Santa Barbara, were on vacation, they had had a prowler. Twice between 2:00 A.M. and 2:30 A.M., their neighbor saw a man standing in their backyard. Each time the man left by jumping over the fence. He was described as maybe 6ft., tall and dressed in dark clothing and a cap.

At the time of their deaths, both Dr. Offerman and Dr. Manning were in the process of getting divorced, not from each other. For Dr. Manning that process had just ended that day or was to end the next day. Dr. Manning's now ex-husband was on a skiing trip at Lake Tahoe the night she died. Her "ex" voluntarily underwent a polygraph examination in which no discrepancies were found. He was totally and completely eliminated as a suspect in those murders.

Dr. Offerman's divorce was amicable and in the midst of the division of property phase when he was killed. A real estate sale of November 30, 1979, that he and his soon-to-be-ex were both involved in, was no doubt part of that divorce settlement.

What is known is Dr. Offerman's soon to be ex-wife held an insurance policy with Frederic Sauer Insurance Company, Inc. What kind of policy this was has never been determined. This same company does turn up later with another homicide victim.

Frederick Sauer and Company was registered in Sacramento, which was probably due more to the fact state licenses are issued from there. The insurance company was based out of Stockton. Fred Sauer himself died in 2002. There is no current listing for that company and their license has expired.

Among the women Dr. Offerman was known to date was a manager for a travel agency in Goleta. This is only mentioned because one of the EAR victims had been a travel agent.

Dr. Offerman was partners with a Dr. Mazzetti.They worked out of the Goleta Valley Community Hospital and what they called the Goleta office, 5333 Hollister Avenue, Goleta.

Acquaintances of Dr. Offerman, a Mr. and Mrs. Jay Smith, held a house party in their home at 452 Toltec Way on December 28, 1979. Both Dr. Offerman and Dr. Manning attended. The list of people who attended that gathering included, among other professions, both doctors and lawyers.

Chapter 57:
Murdered - Lyman and Charlene Smith

March 13, 1980
753 High Point Drive
Ventura, California

First the failed attack on the couple at 5425 Queen Anne Court, followed by the double homicide on nearby Avenida Pequena, Santa Barbara police were on the alert. They were becoming aware of an unappreciated kinship with Sacramento; that being they probably had Sacramento's psychopath loose on their turff. But it was not Santa Barbara where the next double homicide was to occur. It was just up the road.

The town of Ventura became the location of another double homicide. The murders probably happened sometime after midnight on March 13, 1980. Lyman Smith and his wife Charlene were home in bed when they were brutally struck dead.

Lyman, a prominent lawyer, was awaiting word of an imminent appointment to a judgeship when he and his wife were senselessly murdered. Three days later at about 2:00 P.M., Lyman's son Gary, anticipating to work at some assigned chore, arrived at his father's house.

It was young Gary who found the couple in bed with the blanket pulled over their heads. Pulling that blanket back shattered his world. The sight that greeted him has probably has never left him.

Lyman Smith was found nude with his hands and feet tied with nylon drapery cord.

Charlene, lying face up, was clad only in a T-shirt. Her hands, wrists crossed, were behind her back and tightly bound, as were her feet. The cords used to bind Charlene were slightly different from those used on Lyman in that they contained copper threads at the cores. Some astute investigators noticed the knots used on her bindings were more ornate than those on Lyman.

Later, Detective Poole of Santa Barbara Sheriff's Department researched the knots used to make the bindings and learned what the Sacramento Sheriff's deputies already knew. It is called a diamond knot, a Chinese decorator knot, or a lanyard knot. Its uses include decor, nautical, and horses. As Det. Poole found out, it takes a lot of practice to make one of those knots. Whoever made these knots has undoubtedly shown off his skills on more than one occasion. No one at the Sacramento Sheriff's Department knew what they were much less how to tie one.

Blood was splattered over the walls as well as over a piece of firewood lying between the two victims. This bloody piece of wood almost certainly came from a stack of firewood just outside the house. Also left behind by their killer was a 28-inch piece of rope on the victim's bed.

There were no indications of a struggle by either Lyman or Charlene. They were probably murdered as they laid there trying to comply with the commands of a psychopathic personality.

Responding investigators described the scene as showing some signs of ransacking with drawers pulled out and the contents spilled about.

When investigators contacted neighbors, they learned the people immediately next door to the Smiths had a great dane that woke them up about 2:00 A.M. on the morning of the homicides. The dog led its owner directly to the gate leading to the Smith's yard, then just stood quietly. This was the only time this dog had ever done that.

Other neighbors had experienced prowler activity over the previous days as well. There were a few neighbors who felt their homes had been entered but nothing taken. One found a small hole near the lock on a bedroom window.

The follow up medical exam showed that Charlene and Lyman had, as in the case of the two previous assaults on couples, been intimate that night. Only in this instance, Charlene had also been raped.

Lyman Smith once lived in Sacramento and attended Bella Vista High School. By coincidence, one of his high school classmates worked for the Sacramento Sheriff's Department and is a friend of mine, as well.

The Smith's and Dr. Offerman's home bore strong similarities. They were very close in size and design. Diamond knots were used at both locations to bind the victims. But the victims in one were bludgeoned to death and in the other shot. In one there was a rape and in the other there wasn't.

I believe there was no rape in the case of Dr. Manning simply because Dr. Offerman resisted and was shot dead. Probably because the suspect enjoyed killing and didn't want witnesses, he shot and killed Dr. Manning. In the case of the Smiths, he fulfilled whatever distorted fantasies were in his head, which included the brutal murders.

An acquaintance of Lyman Smith, Joe Alsip, was arrested for the Smith murders. His arrest was based primarily on a claim by a local clergyman. The clergyman claimed Alsip had confessed those murders to him. Although Alsip denied the accusations, he still reclined in jail for over a year. Finally the clergyman's credibility was heavily impugned and Alsip was released; bankrupt, unemployed, and no prospects—but "free."

Chapter 58:
Murdered - Keith & Patrice Harrington

August 19, 1980
Dana Point
3381 Cockleshell Drive, Niguel Shores

What was the ONS suspect doing between the months of March and August, 1980? That question remains as much a mystery now as does the identity of this psychopath. But on August 19, it became apparent he was in Orange County, California, to kill again.

It was probably after midnight when the recently married couple were making love to each other in their home inside a gated community at Dana Point. As far as they were concerned, they had their whole life ahead of them and the world was their oyster. Keith Harrington, a third year medical student about to begin his medical internship, and his wife Patrice "Patti," a registered nurse, thought they had no real worries. But they were wrong–dead wrong.

Unknown to them, just outside their bedroom window, they were being watched by a truly evil monster. Slithering from house to house, window to window this monster—now known as the Original Night Stalker or ONS–was on the alert for anyone having sex. As mentioned before, that might have been the catalyzing element that pushed him into action.

There was no sign of forced entry into the Harrington home. Apparently they, too, were not aware that the psychopath known as the EAR was now loose in Southern California.

It was Keith's father who found the bodies of his son and daughter-in-law when he arrived to meet them for dinner. When he entered the house, he saw full Alpha Beta Market grocery bags, sitting on the kitchen counter. They had been there for at least two days.

Worried, he checked their bedroom where he found them in bed; a blanket pulled over their heads. Each had been killed by blunt-force trauma to the back of the head. This time the blanket was pulled over their heads before they were bludgeoned to death. Evidently, the EAR had figured out how to prevent splashing blood on the walls.

No weapons were found at the scene. There were bruises about their wrists and ankles, indicating they had been bound tightly. The only materials that might have been used to bind them were three lengths of twine found on the bed. These bits of twine had been removed from the victims after they were murdered.

A motorcross glove, stained with blood, was found several blocks from the crime scene.

The Harrington's house, owned by Keith's father, was built like the Smith's house. Their identical floor plans made it possible to see the ocean in the distance.

Keith, a student at UC Irvine, had one brother who was a psychologist and two who were attorneys. The first victims of this psychopath, loose in Southern California, were medical personnel and their murders were followed by an attorney and his wife. Now, two more medical persons who had relatives in the field of law. Was there a connection? If so, it remains an unknown to the general public.

As a result of this crime, Bruce Harrington, older brother of Keith Harrington, managed to help usher in Proposition 69. Now a law, it mandates that a prisoner WILL donate their DNA to a statewide data base. Up until then, the prison staff would not press the issue if a prisoner refused to cooperate. Since the law passed, it can be taken by force if necessary.

Sometime after this case had seemingly gone cold, investigators contacted Bruce Harrington and told him forensics indicated that the man who raped Patrice had had a vasectomy. Then in 2010, Detective Larry Montgomery checked with the scientist who had handled all of the DNA evidence of the EAR/ONS crime series, and learned there was no such evidence indicating a vasectomy. This was especially relevant, as a person of interest, identified as Waz, had been developed. Allegedly he had had a vasectomy. At least for now Waz is off the radar screen.

The Harringtons were the only victims of the ONS to live in a gated community. With this gated community there were three ways to get in: with a gate code; waved through by a security guard; by climbing the hill then over the wall.

Chapter 59:
Murdered - Manuela Witthuhn

February 6, 1981
Columbus, Irvine

Nearly a full year after the senseless murders of Keith and Patty Harrington, the ONS returned to Irvine, which is also in Orange County, to continue his spree of senseless deaths.

The night before her death, Manuela Witthuhn had visited her husband in the Santa Ana-Tustin Community Hospital where he was a patient (today the Newport Specialty Hospital).

The day after her visit, Manuela was found raped and murdered in a sleeping bag, on her own bed, at 35 Columbus, Irvine. The details of the report are not available, but here is what I do know.

Manuela was a pretty 28-year-old housewife employed as a mortgage broker. When found, she had bruises on both her wrists and ankles indicating she had been tied. However, the ligatures used were missing and presumed to have been taken by the suspect. Death had been by blunt force trauma to the back of her head. Like the bindings, the death weapon was also missing.

Entry into the house was the same as in many residential burglaries, by forcing a sliding door at the rear of the house. In this instance, however, the prying was done from inside. Burnt wooden matches were found both in the house and in the garage. There had also been an EAR attack in Sacramento where the suspect had asked the victim if she had any matches.

Left behind by the suspect was a flat shank screwdriver which matched the pry marks on the slider door. A smudge of brown paint was apparent on the screwdriver shaft. There was extensive research done by detective Montgomery in an effort to identify the paint. In the end, it appeared to be consistent with the Behr paint brand but nothing significant was developed.

Among the items taken by the suspect were a lamp and a crystal curio; both weighed about 9 lbs. The recording tape from the telephone was missing as well. Like the property stolen from the other victims, none of these items has ever been recovered.

Investigators felt strongly this crime was done by someone who knew the victim and their way around the house, which is probably why that recording was taken. It was the collective opinion that the crime of burglary had been (very poorly) staged, but for what reason they were never able to establish.

Because of these differences, the investigators made the tentative determination that someone other than the ONS was responsible for the rape and murder of Manuela. It wasn't until a few years later, when the forensics of DNA was developed, that it was confirmed the ONS was responsible.

Chapter 60:
Murdered - Greg Sanchez and Cheryl Smith-Dominguez

July 27, 1981
449 Toltec Way
Goleta, Santa Barbara

The attack against Manuela Withuhn, a woman home alone, was just a minor variation in the style of this psychopathic personality. Most likely the variation was because of some twist in his sick fantasies, or maybe it was because he knew the victim, or it could be he just saw an opportunity. But it was not to be long before he returned to his standard mode of operation.

Not that far away from where Manuela was killed, Cheryl Domingo, a 35-year-old mother of three was house-sitting for her aunt at 449 Toltec Way in Goleta. Her aunt told her the neighborhood spooked her which was why the aunt refused to stay there. So she put the house on the market and her niece Cheryl took up residence until it sold. On this night, Cheryl and Greg Sanchez, both employed working with computers, were spending the night together. They had worked for the same company at one time.

Sometime on July 26, 1981, a real estate agent was showing that house to a prospective buyer when a second buyer arrived. Not expecting this new arrival, the agent suggested that he just go ahead and look around. What the agent did not realize was that this prospective buyer was not interested in buying anything. Instead he went outside and removed the screen to the bathroom window in preparation for later entry; a characteristic trait of the East Area Rapist.

The next morning, July 27, 1981, real estate agent John Sullivan, escorting some prospective buyers, arrived to show them the house. Peering into the bedroom, Sullivan spotted Sanchez lying partially inside a closet and Cheryl lying on the bed.

Peeking in the door at the same time as Sullivan was the 3-year-old son of the prospective buyers. It has been said that seeing the bloodied head of the dead man, so shocked the child he did not utter another word for a year.

It was determined by the bruises on Cheryl's wrists and ankles that she had been bound, but there was no indication Sanchez had been tied. Only one piece of shipping twine was found, and it was on the floor near the bed. Some unidentified fibers were scattered over Cheryl's body.

Sanchez had been shot in the face but that was not what killed him. Both victims died as a result of blunt force trauma to the back of their heads. No weapon was ever found.

A neighborhood canvass found at least one witness who had seen a WMA, with a dog, jogging away from the area of the crime scene.

Chapter 61:
Murdered - Janelle Cruz

May 4, 1986
13 Encina
Irvine, California

Five years after Manuela was murdered, the suspect struck at 13 Encina Avenue, Irvine, California. This is the last confirmed assault by the suspect known as the EAR/ONS.

On that evening, while Diane and Alan Stein were vacationing in Mexico, Diane's 18-year-old daughter Janelle Cruz, a cashier for Bullwinkle's Pizza, was at home visiting with a young male friend. Not long before her visitor departed, the two of them heard some unusual sounds just outside the house. Investigating no further than the window, they decided there was nothing to worry about, so they continued their visit. A short time later her young friend left. Janelle was now home alone in a house that was posted for sale.

Late in the afternoon of the following day, a real agent wanting to show the house to a prospective buyer, knocked on the door. When no one answered, he assumed the house was empty and walked in. This was how Janelle was discovered—her body lying on the bed, covered with a blanket.

Janelle was first struck on the back of her head then viciously struck in the face. The weapon was thought to be a pipe wrench missing from the backyard. It is probably hanging up in a garage somewhere as part of this evil bastard's collection of 'memorabilia.'

Blood was found in various places in the kitchen, just inside the front door, and on some shutters. As in most of the other crime scenes, tennis shoe prints were in the backyard. The point of entry was not determined, but all doors and windows were locked except for a rear slider.

At the time of her death, the house was listed for sale with Century 21. There was some sort of insurance policy by the Frederic Sauer Insurance Agency, Inc. associated with the house at the time. As mentioned earlier, this was the same company with which the estranged wife of Dr. Offerman had a policy.

There are numerous rumors surrounding the short life of Janelle. As a matter of record many of them dealt with her being molested by various members of the military as well as a stepfather. We dug into some of those rumors, but we were unable to substantiate any of them.

One persistent rumor is that Janelle was expecting a man, now known to others as "kitten man," at her home that evening. The information about this "kitten man" was provided by her high school friend, Greg.

Greg had seen kitten man at the public swimming pool when Janelle pointed him out. Janelle told him she had just met the man and he was going to bring some kittens over to her house the next day to see if she wanted one.

The kitten man, as Greg remembers him, had an olive complexion, dark hair, blue eyes and was good looking. In Greg's eyes definitely a predator . He told Janelle to stay away from him. Greg tried to talk to this man but he seemed to purposely keep his distance, so the two never met.

Greg remembers the kitten man was a friend of a girl from the local Woodbridge High School. Her name was named Amber, but she went by the name Bambi. She had Bambi tattoos, which could have resulted from or been the reason for the nickname. The rumor now is that a few years later Amber (Bambi) was pregnant and living with kitten man on the Marine Corps Air Station, or MCAS, at El Toro.

Janelle's sister, Michelle, said someone told her Amber was living with her mother in the town of Irvine. Neither Amber, nor the kitten man, have been identified, nor have they been proven to exist. We have never spoken to Janelle's friend Greg.

The rumors of sexual molestation focused on two stepfathers and a marine stationed at nearby El Toro. All of these rumors had been discounted by local investigators at the time. The one regarding the neighbor marine was of interest only because of where he lived, and because of a business owned by him and his wife.

The marine lived less than a mile from where Janelle was murdered. Three blocks in the opposite direction lies the house were Manuela Witthuhn was murdered. The business owned by this marine and his wife is the marketing of dental supplies.

We have since learned that Janelle had completed $2,000 worth of dental work shortly before her untimely death. Prior to that, due to emotional stress, she had spent some time in two psychiatric hospitals.

Chapter 62:
The Visalia Ransacker Revisited

An argument can be made for one person being responsible for all these crimes and one with the opposing view. Conversations with current Visalia detectives lead me to believe they are mostly of one mind, and that being the VR and EAR/ONS are not one and the same.

IF the VR, EAR and ONS are the same person, then most likely the ransacker was in the early stages of a psychosis called paraphilia. Voyeurism and sadism are associated with this condition. Sexual sadism, when taken to the extreme, includes murder. If you make the assumption the same person is responsible for all of these crimes, then the path leading from peeping tom to thrill killer is one that even the most obtuse among us can see.

It is believed the Visalia Ransacker began the burglaries in 1974 and they continued to plague Visalia until at least December, 1975, when he shot at Officer McGowan. He typically gained entry, as any burglar would, by prying a door or window open, if an unlocked one was not found.

It is my understanding it was not uncommon for him to set up an impromptu alarm system to alert him if someone came home suddenly. Little tricks like a dish on a door knob, or chair in front of a door, or even a hooked up chain latch served the purpose. Once he placed a bottle of perfume on the doorknob as an alarm.

Another aspect of his MO was to arrange avenues of escape such as ensuring doors or windows were open. But what he did while in those homes is mostly what set him apart from a "normal" burglar.

Officers determined the master bedroom was his usual starting point. Dresser drawers were opened and the contents thoroughly rifled. Women's underclothing was scattered around the room. Once a woman found her panties turned inside out as if someone had tried them on.

But even here, there was a twist. He occasionally stole men's underwear. Responding officers found men's underwear neatly stacked in a line down a hallway. Theft of men's underwear was never associated with the EAR/ONS.

The VR seemed to be especially fond of piggy banks and silver coins. Frequently a single piece of jewelry would be taken, such as one earring, while leaving behind the rest of the set. Sometimes hand guns were taken and any ammunition within reach was stolen.

Taking only one piece of jewelry was not the only sign of erratic behavior. At times money in plain view was untouched or he might leave dresser drawers open with the contents undisturbed. Other times he tore up, moved around, or stole photos of the women who lived in the homes he was ransacking. The use of lotion, while in the homes, was apparent. What he did with that lotion is best left to someone else's imagination.

It was the habit of this suspect, once he removed a window screen, to toss it onto the victim's roof. To take advantage of this habit, the Visalia Police Department began to fly air patrols over the neighborhood watching for those telltale signs.

Footprints found at the scenes measured 11 ¼" to 11 ½" in length. All prints were from tennis shoes. Later into the investigation, officers came across a person of real interest who was wearing tennis shoes that seemed to match in detail those they had casted and photographed. This individual said his dad, who worked as a janitor at a local school, found them in a locker when cleaning it out at the end of the school year.

Typically, the VR struck on Friday, Saturday and Sunday evenings. The nights when the neighborhood high school was involved in a game were his preferred. It was well known he would prowl one area repeatedly, then in a few weeks move into another area and prowl it for several days. Eventually he returned to areas he had previously been active in to repeat his aberrant behavior.

There were times homeowners saw someone thought to have been the VR, and at least once gave chase. The man who chased him said the suspect was very fast and very agile, as he leaped over fences with apparent ease. This observation was backed up by others who saw him fleeing an area.

What the investigators gleaned from all of these reports was the suspect never crossed a street at an intersection. It was always mid-block at a dead run. If a house did not have large lot or a lot of shrubbery, he avoided that house entirely. For whatever reason, they concluded he did not drink alcohol or smoke. The East Area Rapist, on the other hand, appeared to do both.

All of these burglaries were of the annoying variety until September 11, 1975, at about 2:30 A.M. That was when the VR was interrupted, in the act of abducting a young teenage girl from her bedroom, by the girl's father.

A few months prior to this abduction, the intended abuctee's father, Professor Snelling, had stumbled onto a prowler around his house. He told a co-worker the prowler was a white male about 5 ft. 10 inches tall with collar-length hair. Not long after that incident someone broke into two cars at the professor's house, prying open the glove boxes in both. Nothing was taken from the cars. It was then the tenor of the petty crimes changed drastically.

The professor's daughter awoke to the weight of somebody lying prone on top of her. With his left hand on her arm and right hand around her mouth and nose he growled, "You're coming with me. Don't scream or I'll stab you." Being threatened while being pulled from bed only compelled her to scream and struggle all the more. All that got her was a spectator's view down the barrel of a small black revolver that materialized from the would be abductor's left rear pocket. Then the threats changed to, "Don't scream or I'll shoot you."

As the girl and her abductor neared the street, the father of this young girl, Professor Snelling, came to her rescue. She heard her father call out, "Hey, what are you doing? Where are you taking my daughter?" The professor was in the doorway when her abductor let go, pointed the handgun at the professor and fired twice. The first shot struck the professor in the arm, passing through, and into his body. The second one struck him in the right side of his chest turning him around. Either the bullet knocked him back into the house, or realizing he had just been shot twice, the professor retreated inside for safety. It was there he bled out within minutes.

After shooting the professor, the abductor turned and pointed the gun at his intended victim. He paused briefly, then he lowered the gun, shoved her to the ground, and kicked her in the face three times. Other than some bruising, the teenager was physically unhurt.

A number of neighbors heard the shots and screams. All of them looked outside and some towards the professor's house but saw nothing out of the ordinary. One man did hear a four-speed, standard shift, four cylinder sports car leaving the area.

To contradict the sports car was a stolen bicycle. It had been stolen earlier in the evening and was found in the front yard of the house directly behind the professor's house. This bicycle belonged to a 19-year-old woman.

The description of the suspect was white male, 5 ft. 10 inches, with a medium build, on the heavy side. His age was between 25 and 30 years. He had a round face with a square or wide jaw. His eyes were dark and the pupils not seen. The hair on the back of his hands was light colored. As he was not wearing gloves when he grabbed her, the young teenager could tell that his hands were neither soft nor rough. She also said he had very short, stubby fingers. His hair was collar-length. He was wearing a dark colored wind breaker, zipped to the neck, with tight fitting cuffs around the wrists.

Prowling reports continued to come in. Investigating one such report, Special Agent McGowan found a different kind of print. While examining the backyard, he matched a flower pot with a depression beneath a bedroom window. Apparently the suspect had used it to stand on while peeping into the window. This in and of itself means nothing. However, on at least one occasion, the EAR did the exact same thing.

What is not commonly known is that the professor's daughter had seen this suspect once before. She and her boyfriend were sitting in her room talking about the Visalia Ransacker when her boyfriend asked her what she would do if she were to open her window blind and see him standing outside. Her response was to pull open the window shade. Ironically, outside her window was a man looking at her. She yelled. The man fled.

Knowing the VR was a compulsive prowler and would eventually return to the same areas, a welcoming committee of sorts was arranged for him. Finally, on December 10, 1975, Special Agent McGowan was sitting in a garage when he heard someone passing by on the sidewalk. He knew who it was.

Stepping outside Special Agent McGowan found himself looking at the back of a man who was staring into a window. With his flashlight positioned above his left shoulder and gun in his right hand, Agent McGowan ordered the peeping tom to put his hands up. Peeping tom turned, and in a high shrill voice said something to the effect of, "Don't hurt me." At the same time he was squeaking his plea, he was pulling a cap off his head with his right hand and pulling a gun out of his pocket with his left hand.

One shot was fired. The bullet entered the flashlight lens dead center, drilling down the middle of the batteries. The impact knocked Special Agent McGowan down, stunning him briefly—just long enough for the VR to make good his escape by jumping over nearby fences.

Within minutes, large numbers of officers, including a canine unit, were on the scene. The next day evidence was found indicating the suspect had crossed over the freeway where he stood in the shadows watching the search for him. Passing cars would have destroyed any chance of tracking the suspect over the freeway.

When his flashlight was shot, Special Agent McGowan was a few blocks from the Kaweah Delta Hospital. Highway 198 runs parallel to the hospital, which is on the north side, and the crimes in questions were across the highway (south) from the hospital.

Under hypnosis, Special Agent McGowan made a composite of the Visalia Ransacker. During the session, he recalled seeing the same man in Mel's Drive-In. At that time he was wearing a military fatigue jacket with writing on the right side of the chest. The composite to come out of that session does not particularly resemble any of those thought to be the EAR.

It is generally thought, by those who were not involved in that investigation, that December was the last time the VR was to strike in Visalia. However, I have been told by some of the investigators that the Visalia Ransacker activity continued until late May or early June, 1976.

Another oddity of the VR was reported by somebody who chased a prowler they thought to be him. As he ran from the scene he could be overheard talking to someone else. He was saying things like, "We almost got caught that time." That was not the only time a person thought to be the VR was seen talking to an imaginary person.

One evening a young man and his girlfriend were sitting on her front lawn. They were seated near the shrubbery which put them into a somewhat darker area of the yard. At some point the girl went into the house. Expecting her momentary return, her boyfriend remained in the shadows where they had been sitting. While waiting, he saw a man suddenly step out of the shrubbery by the house next door. As he watched, the man dropped to all fours and crawled up to the window where he pressed his face against the glass.

Overcoming his initial fear, the boyfriend started walking towards the peeping tom, asking as he did, "What are you doing? " Startled, peeping tom jumped back saying over and over, "Stay away from me, stay away from me." To the boyfriend his manner of speaking sounded like a special needs person.

By then, boyfriend was mere feet from peeping tom. Suddenly a mean look came over peeping tom's eyes as he jammed his hand into his left coat pocket. At that moment, boyfriend knew without any doubt this guy was reaching for a gun. Boyfriend quickly began to back away. As he did, the peeping tom turned to his left and said, "Ben, we have to get out of here." Peeping tom then took off jumping a nearby fence with ease.

Boyfriend was surprised that the peeping tom was so agile because of his apparent heavy thighs and wide hips.

Chapter 63:
How The EAR Chose His Victims

What kind of employment, if any, made it possible for this psychopath to prowl neighborhoods and travel around California, seemingly at will? Most felt the answer would lead to the identity of the EAR/ONS. The consensus of opinion was to find that answer first identify something common between the assault victims.

Sgt. Henretty was tasked with finding that answer. To that end he collected and studied volumes of details. That was how he learned three victims of the EAR were at the same pizza parlor in the same month. Sgt. Henretty never identified any other connections between the assault victims. He died believing he failed. He did not fail.

While Sgt. Henretty was focusing on one angle, I was focused on another. I was aware specific professions repeatedly turned up in the investigation, but early into the investigation it was nebulous information. Still, I felt there was something there. I had not quite identified the significance of what I was seeing before being transferred.

Now, 38 years, 53 assaults, and 12 homicides later I can look at that nebulous information more closely. What follows is that closer look.

Chapter 64:
Days of the Week

The closer look began with finding what days of the week the assaults occurred. To avoid a lengthy and detailed explanation, it can be said the EAR probably worked a day shift four days a week. If not, then he was in a position to have a lot of free time.

Twice someone thought to be the EAR was seen dressed in a sport coat and slacks, one time sporting a tie. Maybe that bag heard being zipped open then shut was him changing into his work clothes.

Chapter 65:
Medical

The possible associations in the medical profession were the first to catch my attention. By the time the EAR/ONS assaults stopped, nearly 50% of the victims, or a family member, had some contact with the medical profession. Those contacts included everything from hospital employees, patients, pharmacies, to hospital visitors. That was fifty percent, but what about the other fifty percent?

Chapter 66:
Education

Association with the world of academics was another repeat issue. Again, approximately 50% of the assaults involved someone associated with education. Those connections covered students from middle school through universities. They even included administrative positions and two families whose children car pooled together.

This subject of schools came to light again in August, 2011, when Russ Oase encountered two people familiar with the EAR assaults. One of their families had suffered a burglary in Sacramento where the factors clearly indicated the EAR was responsible. The other person mentioned his family had also been victim of a similar burglary while his sister was a student at California State University Sacramento. After leaving CSUS, she returned to Modesto where the harassment continued.

Chapter 67:
Military

Of the thirty-one assaults in the Sacramento area fourteen, possibly fifteen, had some association with the military. With five military installations within minutes of Sacramento, this number comes as no surprise. Outside of Sacramento County, those associations stopped.

When there was an association with the military it involved some level of rank–the lowest being sergeant and the highest lieutenant colonel.

Consider this: IF the East Area Rapist was the one who beat the dog to death in Rancho Cordova, then his rampage started in the fall of 1974. It was the beginning of 1978 when he began to venture beyond Sacramento. That closely constitutes one 4-year enlistment. Only the air force and navy had four year enlistments, and at the end of this theoretical enlistment, there were no more associations with the military.

Chapter 68:
Real Estate

If there is a constant between the EAR and the ONS victims, it is real estate. Virtually, if not literally, every victim of the East Area Rapist lived in or close to a house that had just sold, was currently for sale, for rent or for lease, or near a house under construction.

For Southern California, that number was more like 66%. Two of the nine houses being factored in here belonged to registered nurses whose homes had been burglarized by the ONS. Those two, plus four where the murders occurred, were, or had recently been, on the market.

Chapter 69:
Security Guard

The first known assault by the East Area Rapist was in June, 1976. That was the same year of the Walsh-Healy Act. Walsh-Healy made it legal for federal, state and local municipalities to utilize private security for the protection of public property. Those security companies were/are required to provide their employees with police equipment and 160 hours of specified training.

Every victim or a family member of the EAR/ONS spent time in locations where you would expect to find a security guard. A large number of those victims worked in downtown Sacramento, a location rife with corporate and government buildings, plus two hospitals.

Not enough is known about the Visalia Ransacker victims to determine if any of these associations are applicable. But there was one teaser gleaned from the homicide report of Professor Snelling.

Professor Snelling was an educator. His wife was a registered nurse. All of the Visalia Ransacker's crimes occurred on the south side of Highway 198, and not far from Kaweah Delta Hospital. Both the hospital and the college probably employed security guards.

Conclusion – Clusters

The profession of medicine was coincidental to how the EAR/ONS selected his victims. The same can be said for education and real estate. Types of facilities, widely diverse locations and the variety of business's rule out any one type of employment.

Although there may have been an exception or two, private security was probably not relevant either. Again, distance traveled to distant and diverse locations, makes it unlikely.

Where the EAR/ONS was employed, if employed, may never be known. But, we know how he selected his victims. The answer comes from those whom he assaulted that worked in downtown Sacramento, and there were several of them. It was right in front of us in 1977.

People working in downtown Sacramento have to at least occasionally visit a popular eatery or maybe a park. From that realization it was a nano-jump to those other professions. This psychopath's strategy was to visit public places where he could blend in–places like a hospital, pharmacy, college campus, or supermarket. There, at his leisure, he could select his next victim. He probably followed them home.

He also selected neighborhoods for their attributes and not a specific individual. Those attributes being nearby greenbelt areas and escape routes. The presence of schools, tree, houses for sale and shrubbery were equally as important.

Once a neighborhood was targeted he did what he enjoyed most. He prowled. He might devote weeks or even a year but in the end he would know the neighborhood intimately. There can be little doubt that while prowling he was also selecting alternate victims.

All of this resulted in clusters: a woman was first seen in a cafe then followed home. The prowling around her neighborhood led to another victim. This explains why some women, living in the same neighborhood as an assault victim, were victims of prowlers, crank calls, etc. It is a recurring theme to be found throughout the reports.

Here are just two examples:

Two pharmacy clerks were assaulted. Immediately following them a woman who just had a prescription filled was assaulted.

Assault #21 occurred next to the American River Parkway and the Sacramento Water Treatment Plant. Victim #22's husband, a marine reserve, was a supervisor at that plant. The husband of a later assault victim worked for the California Department of Water Resources.

Epilogue

It was late at night when the man woke up thirsty. Standing by the sink in his unlighted kitchen, he looked out the window and saw something unusual. There, directly across the street was a man standing by his neighbor's front window. As he watched, the man stooped forward and looked through the bottom of his neighbor's window. After a moment he stood up, then walked to the side of the house where he disappeared from view. Another couple of minutes passed and he reappeared where he again stooped over and peeked through the same front window.

It was then the thirsty man's dog began barking. For reasons he does not know, he flipped on the kitchen lights. As soon as those lights came on, the man across the street turned and looked straight at him. Moving rapidly, with a stiff-legged walk, he started down the street. Quickly, he was in a full-out run—stopping only when he reached a sports car that was parked at the end of the block.

The witness described this apparent prowler as wearing a sports coat and slacks. To the witness the man looked like a car salesman.

This information was not reported to the Sacramento Sheriff's Department until years after it actually occurred. What is as important as the information itself is that it was eventually reported. Even more significant is that this is not an isolated instance of information being reported. That so many people are providing information, years after the crime wave seemingly stopped, shows that there is aa strong, popular, ongoing interest in finding this rapist/murderer. It is this persevering, if not growing interest, that will ultimately bring this psychopath out of his dark hole into the light of day. Only then will he be identified and excised.

When this happens, the status of "victim" need no longer exist for those who were made to suffer by him. With his identity known, and his being removed from society, the influence he has exercised over their lives can cease. That determination will naturally be up to them. But this I do know: Where there is an end, there is a beginning, and nothing should keep that beginning from being a good one.

Anecdotal

The Deacon

The Pacific Northwest is well known for its dense pine forests. While the forests are no longer as wide spread as they once were, pockets of them still exist. What has not changed are the frequent light rains that feed those forests. It was right after one of these bouts of inclement weather that Russ again found himself in the state of Washington. Only this time, he was squatting in the middle of one of those remaining stands of dense timber on some rather damp ground.

A hundred yards away Mrs. Russ waited in the relative comfort of their heated car. While her attention was focused in part on their cell phone, and the other for the sound of a gun shot or high-pitched scream, Russ focused his attention on Deacon's house.

They were three days into their second trip to Washington in an effort to collect a DNA sample from a new person of interest. The first trip had been a total strike out.

Russ had no idea what he expected to discover, squatting there among the creepy crawly creatures of the forest. But maybe, just maybe, this guy would step outside and spit or fall down and lacerate an arm. Perhaps a random piece of space-junk would land on him. Russ didn't care what, so long as he got his DNA sample.

This all consuming interest in the NorthWest began early in 2010. It was then Russ decided to take the data compiled about the EAR's possible employment and use it as a basis for starting the investigation all over. Essentially go back to the beginning.

With some trial and error, he came up with an individual who had attended college with one for sure, and possibly five, of the EAR victims. He dubbed this newest person of interest "Deacon." When Russ fit the pieces together, Deacon became a person of much interest.

Fitting the pieces together required Russ to make a number of out-of-state trips. November, 2011, and February, 2012, were two of his trips. What transpired both during, and in-between those dates, came as a real surprise to both of us.

Twice Russ came face-to-face with Deacon. Each time Deacon looked startled, then quickly looked away. The second time he averted his face to avoid being seen.

While this peek into Deacon's past was progressing, some unusual activity began at Russ's home, his mother's home, as well as my home. We were investigating another POI at the same time and cannot know for a fact which investigation, if either, might be connected with the activity.

Suspicious Circumstances

As mentioned, unusual activity occurred when we were simultaneously investigating both "Deacon" and another person of interest who we dubbed "The Specialist."

The face-to-face encounters between Russ and Deacon might be viewed as brackets. The unusual activities took place right after their first encounter and ended with the last encounter.

Within a few short days of their first encounter, on November 11, 2011, Russ and his wife began answering their home phone only to be greeted by silence from the other end. In the words of his wife: "That's new around here."

Returning from an out of town trip to visit "Deacon," Russ found a field stripped filter-tipped cigarette butt among some waffle-stomper type shoe prints near his dog pen. Because it had rained, in his absence, any DNA would have been washed away. As for the footprints, Russ wrote those off as belonging to the person caring for his dogs while.

Lending to the possible significance of this cigarette butt, was the timing. Within that exact time frame, a neighbor of Russ's elderly mother saw a strange man in her backyard. Afterwards, a cigarette butt was found near where that man had been standing.

Russ's mother, Russ, and his wife are all non-smokers. His mother lives an hour's drive from where "Deacon" lives and works.

For several months prior to Deacon becoming a person of interest, Russ had been monitoring an internet message board where the discussion was mostly about the EAR/ONS investigation.

Right along with the board chatter, the suspicious activity around Russ's house continued. In fact it appeared to be entwined with what was going on.

Russ lives in the country with a 300 or so foot driveway connecting a single lane, dead-end road. One morning at the end of his driveway, he discovered two more field stripped filter-tipped cigarette butts. A week or so later, someone poured an unidentified liquid into and onto his mailbox.

Returning from another of his myriad trips out of town, Russ spotted a message posted on the internet message board; one to which he felt he needed to respond. In Russ's response, he made a comment which refered obliquely to the name of Deacon's boat; a message to which only Deacon would have known the meaning. Within two minutes, he received a reply, "Yah. See you in Germany."

Another of those messages suggested someone watch a film clip taken from a documentary about the EAR/ONS investigation. It gave a specific date and time for the clip. Russ watched the film clip which began and ended with him responding to a question.

A couple more weeks passed then one final message which seemed relevant was posted. It ended with a comment about a German shepherd and White Fang. White Fang is the name of the German Shepherd in the book White Fang, with the setting Alaska.

After reading this message, Russ remembered he had a DVD of the movie White Fang in his home office. His office is in a building some distance from his house.

He took a photo of those two stacks of DVDs then scanned it to me. On one stack, the title White Fang is crystal clear. On the second stack, and not noticed until it was scanned, were two fingerprints; both were clearly visible in the dust and very recently placed there.

While Russ was focused on the Deacon I was investigating a whole family. Like Deacon, a number of circumstances turned up that made them of interest. When I learned one of them was on death row for kidnap, rape and murder I thought I might have something. We dubbed them the Specialists.

In the meantime there was unusual activity around my house as there was where Russ lives.

Like Russ, my wife and I live in the country. In fact we are surrounded by a Sierra blue oak forest. The denizens of those forests are among our frequent visitors. Wild Russian boars and deer to name but a few.

Within days of Russ finding that first cigarette butt, I also found a field stripped cigarette butt in the cab of my truck. Since I cleaned the truck the morning before, none of my family smokes, the windows had been rolled up, and no one outside of family drives it, there was but one choice. I had the cigarette butt tested and learned the DNA on it did not match that of the EAR.

This was not the first time unusual activity had occurred on our property. Over the past few years, and possibly even a little before the interest in "Deacon" and "The Specialist" there have been indications of prowlers both outside and inside our house. Among those indications are two that, without a doubt, have taken place inside.

One morning, as I closed the bedroom door, a quarter fell off the top of the door frame. Another time, I was my missing my debit card. I only carry it in an old ID holder, and I only use it at one ATM. I keep it stored in a drawer beneath our bed.

One morning it was gone. The same can be said for some other identification and credit cards. Arguably it could be said those were left behind somewhere. I am certain they were not. The question to be answered is, "Why the quarter on top of our bedroom door? Was it a calling card?"

Prior to these incidents I had worked on a motion sensor light just outside our bedroom, making sure the bulbs were in tight when I finished. That same night I re-checked and discovered both bulbs had been loosened.

The most recent incident was early one mid-August, 2013 morning. While sitting on our front deck enjoying a cup of coffee, my wife and I spotted a prowler.

Keeping in mind we are surrounded by forested land, this individual probably thought no one could see him. The only reason we were able to see him was because several cedar trees had recently been removed.

When we first saw him, he was stooped over, running towards our fence line where he would have been hidden from view. At the same time, a motorcycle could be heard approaching on a half mile long private road. That private road is about 100 feet above where we saw him, and the road is not visible from where we sat. Just below him was a small canal, and below that what remains of the grove of cedar trees.

As long as he kept low, a small rise between him and the road prevented his being seen by anyone in the direction of the private road.

As the motorcycle passed, the prowler quickly turned, stood upright and started in the direction he had come from. Almost as quickly there was a change in the sound of the motorcycle as if it was about to stop. With that change in sound, the prowler instantly turned, stooped over, and rapidly headed back towards our fence line. Just as quickly the sound of the motorcycle changed and moved off into the distance. With the change of sound, the prowler again stood up and started back in the direction he was coming from when we first saw him. That was the last we saw of him.

He was dressed all in blue, was slim (but not a thin build), appeared to have dark hair, and moved like someone definitely less than 70 years old. He was not particularly short, nor particularly tall.

As for hang up calls, we would never know if we did get any. Telemarketers and charity drives have simply taken control of our telephone. There are so many that we no longer bother to answer. Personally, I think all phone bills should be divided equally among each of those callers.

We did collect DNA from both Deacon and The Specialist. Neither matched that of the EAR/ONS. Interestingly enough all suspicious activity stopped as soon as we collected those DNA samples and submitted them for testing.

Carlos

While preparing for retirement in March, 1993, I was contacted by a reporter from *The Sacramento Bee* who had some questions about the East Area Rapist. A woman quickly responded to the article. She insisted the East Area Rapist was actually a team; her ex-husband and his friend. The number of ex-wives making this claim is legion, but still their claims have to be investigated.

At the top of the departmental food chain was a personal friend of Sgt. Bevins. He offered Sgt. Bevins an all expense paid trip to Seattle, Washington to meet with this woman's contact. Retired and with no desire to become involved again, Sgt. Bevins declined. Thinking someone should at least hear her out, he passed the information on to me.

Within two weeks, my wife and I set out for Washington to meet with the then Chief of the U.S. Marshall's Seattle office, for he was this woman's contact. He was not at all happy "they" did not send a "real cop" to pursue the lead. Never mind I possessed considerable knowledge about this investigation and had only been retired two weeks. In his eyes, I was not up to task for I was no longer a real cop. What I did not tell him was "they" had no interest in sending anyone. I was there strictly of my own volition. Sgt. Bevins had only been offered the opportunity for a paid trip to Seattle as a personal favor. The truth is, the trip to Seattle was unnecessary. Arrangements could have been made through the U.S. Marshall to meet with the woman in Sacramento.

Arrangements were made to meet with this woman and the Chief U.S. Marshall in the Federal Court House in downtown Sacrmento. Also present were a local district attorney, the local U.S. Marshall, Sgt. Vaughn, another officer from Visalia, and I.

This meeting resulted in a 30-page report. What is related here is from memory with input from Sgt. Vaughn and Sacramento Sheriff's Department homicide detective, Ken Clark.

The woman coming forth with this information is related in some fashion to the Chief U.S. Marshall. She had been married to a man called Carlos. She described Carlos as about 5 ft. 9 inches tall, weighing between 150 and 160, with light brown hair and a medium complexion. She said that he keeps himself in good physical condition. One of his hobbies, that he never explained, was learning how to speak with different accents. One accent he did not need to learn was Brazilian, as he speaks with a heavy Brazilian accent. He leans more towards use of his left hand, but he is also comfortable with the right one. In her opinion he is ambidextrous.

The necessary question about sex habits was asked. Carlos enjoys normal sex, and if there is any foreplay, he does it to himself. He is not circumcised.

One day she found two complete sets of women's clothing in the trunk of their car. When she asked him how he came by the clothing Carlos insisted he found it. In time, she learned he is a transvestite.

She described different guns and cars of which Carlos had possession, and when he had them. Descriptions of most of the cars had been publicized by the media. However, some car descriptions had not been mentioned. At that time, I knew which cars went with which assault and which caliber gun had been involved. These were not broadcast by the media. That he had similar cars was confirmed by the Chief U.S. Marshall; they were his.

The couple lived together in Visalia from about 1974 until January, 1976. A native Brazilian, he immigrated to Rochester, New York in 1969 and left around 1974 or 1975. He once commented to his wife that he felt bad, "But they made me do it." He was talking about the murder of two young women.

Their Visalia home was close to Kaweah Delta Hospital and adjacent to a drainage ditch; right in the midst of the area where the Visalia Ransacker was then active.

Carlos, a meter reader for a local utility company, was taught short-cuts by colleagues. This meant his duties were finished before the end of his shift. Using the scope that meter-readers carry, he spent that extra time spying on people.

For whatever reason, it was decided they would move to Sacramento. She was to go first and he would follow in a few weeks. She moved in September, 1975. In January, 1976, Carlos joined her.

Their first Sacramento house was again next to a drainage ditch. Carlo's first employer was Lord Byron's Pizza. Later he worked for a chemical company based in Stockton.

Among his duties was delivery of chemicals to Stockton and Modesto. There is no information available on what else he did, or where he may have made deliveries.

Somewhere, Carlos made friends with a man from Diamond Springs, a small community in a neighboring county. The two became close friends. Together they would start walking down the nearby drainage ditch in the evening, and they would not return until late if at all. Neither ever told her where they had been or what they had been doing. Occasionally, she watched them hide what she thought was a piece of jewelry. The hiding place was a small opening in the garage that led into the attic.

Within days of learning about the small hole into the attic, Sacramento Sheriff Detective, Nogender Rye and I, contacted the people living that house. The hole, and the access to it, was exactly as described. Unfortunately we found nothing but insulation.

It was while the East Area Rapist was active that they lived in the Sacramento area. After each EAR assault, Carlos appeared agitated. He would insist the EAR was trying to frame him for the assaults.

On a night, when Carlos was absent, his wife heard someone outside of their house. She was certain it was him trying to prove his claim that he was being framed. For that reason she never mentioned the incident to him.

One day Carlos seemed to be very agitated. For most of that day and into the evening, he seemed fixated on a young girl saying, "She could make more babysitting." From his ramblings, she learned the parents of this young girl were planning on being out of town for two days. While they were away, the girl was going to stay with a girlfriend from school. This girl was to meet her friend after she got off work, then later they were to attend some sort of school function. This may have been when Carlos talked about tapping into private phone lines and listening to conversations.

Either that night or the next, an EAR assault that matched every detail that Carlos had described, occurred on Benny Way. The 16-year-old victim worked at a Kentucky Fried Chicken in Rancho Cordova.

Early the next morning, Carlo's friend from Diamond Springs called to make sure Carlos had gotten home safely. He said the two of them closed a bar down and when they separated Carlos was intoxicated.

Carlos's wife knew this was a lie for Carlos had gotten home at 1:30 A.M. and did not smell of booze. However, he did smell of sex.

She confronted Carlos about the assault and reminded him of how detailed his information was. Carlos became upset, claimed the EAR was framing him, and then he assaulted her.

It was about May, 1977, that Carlos house-sat for a friend in the town of Davis. He was there for about two months before returning to the Sacramento area.

In 1979, Carlos invested in a new 37.5 ft. boat which was classified as a "ship". Trailering it to Southern California, they stopped at just about every port they came across. His wife put them in Orange, Santa Barbara and Ventura counties at the same time the ONS was active. Today, Carlos lives on that boat.

Immediately, after that 1993 meeting in the Federal Court house in Sacramento, Sgt. Vaughn got to work validating her story. He did confirm Carlos and his wife where living in Visalia at the time the Visalia Ransacker was active. But it took only one meeting with Carlos to discount him as being the Visalia Ransacker. His complexion is very dark, and he speaks with a heavy accent.

Sgt. Vaughn also learned of a technique used by criminals in Brazil. It is called a Brazilian tree or necktie. It is an impromptu burglar alarm consisting of objects placed on top of something, such as a door knob or even a person. When movement occurs, the object falls off alerting the criminal.

Long after I retired Sacramento Detective Ken Clark reopened the investigation into Carlos. The first thing he learned was Carlos's family had emigrated from Germany to Brazil. He does have a Brazilian accent, but he is also light skinned with dark blond hair. In summer, the sun not only tans him, but bleaches his hair to a light brown. Sacramento detectives, hearing Carlos speak, describe his voice as high pitched.

Composites

It would be hard to imagine anyone who does not know what a composite is, in relation to a criminal investigation. The investigations into the Visalia Ransacker, the East Area Rapist have produced a number of such composites. Most of the composites do not resemble each other, much less anyone of interest. What follows are a select few of those composites. A close examination will show they could all easily be of the same person.

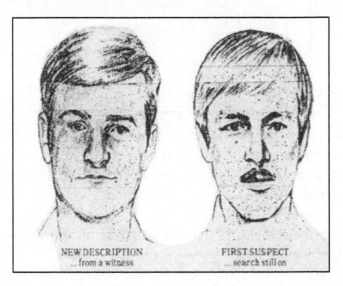

These are the composites to come out of the investigation into the deaths of Brian and Katy Magiorre. There was only one suspect seen. Probably the composite on the right is the correct one.

Richard Shelby

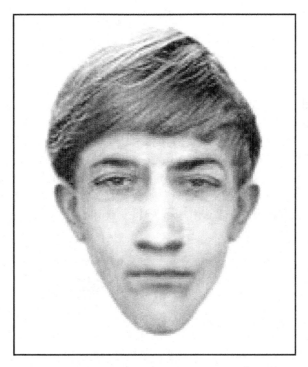

This composite came from a witness on Point Reyes Way, Sacramento. A street in between and parallel to La Rivera Dr., and Toulomne Dr., where three EAR assaults occurred.

The enhancement of the features was accomplished by Robert Neville.

Investigative journalist Michelle McNamara was contacted by a witness to a stalker who said this composite bears a strong resemblence to the man he saw. The only difference being the hair was parted on the opposite side and his jaw was not so elongated. He added the suspect had a rough / reddish complexion with some possible acne scarring. We believe he did see the EAR suspect,

Michelle also located a report by an FBI agent who reported something similar. The agent was jogging in an area where an EAR assault had occurred when he spotted a jogger he had never seen in the area.

This jogger, a white male about 25 years old, was wearing Bermuda shorts and Cochran boots; the kind used by paratroopers. His complexion was rough / reddish with some acne scarring. His hair was short and blondish cut in a fashion similar to military. He had a mustache. He would jog, then walk, then jog. Even sat down once. This person of interest probably has rosacea, an all too common skin disease.

February, 1977 a prowler believed to be the EAR was chased by a teenager. As the teenager started over a fence the prowler was waiting on the other side. Two shots fired at the teenager, one striking him in the abdomen.

The composite to come from an EAR assault that occurred sometime in 1978 in Sacramento.

*Composite drawing of the Visala Ransacker as described
by Special Agent McGowan.*

Appendix 1

EAR/ONS-Related Reports:

Sacramento Sheriff's Department :
All the reports of the East Area Rapist Investigation
Interviews of investigators
Sacramento Police Department:
All the reports of the East Area Rapist
Interview of investigators

Related sexual assault reports from the following
jurisdictions:

Stockton Police
Modesto Police
Davis Police
Concord Police
San Jose Police
Fremont Police
Danville Police
Walnut Creek Police
San Ramon Police
Contra Costa County Sheriff
Visalia Police Department homicide report 65030
Santa Barbara Sheriff of the Original Night Stalker
Goleta Police Department
Orange County Sheriff
Irvine Police Department
Ventura Police Department
2011 Interview of FBI Agent Stan Los
Interview: members of Janelle Cruz's family
California Proposition 69 by Erica Shen

CPSIA information can be obtained at www.ICGtesting.com
Printed in the USA
BVOW08s0934211015

423449BV00002B/63/P